THE
EVERYTHING®
FILMMAKING
BOOK

From script to premiere—a complete guide
to putting your vision on the screen

Barb Karg, Jim Van Over,

and Rick Sutherland

Adams Media

Avon, Massachusetts

For all our touchstones—Ma, Pop, Dale, Chrissy, Glen, Anne, Terry, Kathy, Jimmy, Jason, Ellen and Jim, Jim S., Karla, the Scribe Tribe, the Blonde Bombshell, and especially Jeans. And to all filmmakers who bring their visions to life and in doing so make us laugh, cry, think, and boldly go where we've never gone before.

An Everything® Series Book.
Everything® and everything.com® are registered trademarks of F+W Publications, Inc.

Published by Adams Media, an F+W Publications Company
57 Littlefield Street, Avon, MA 02322 U.S.A.
www.adamsmedia.com

ISBN 10: 1-59869-092-2
ISBN 13: 978-1-59869-092-7

Printed in the United States of America.

J I H G F E D C B A

Library of Congress Cataloging-in-Publication Data
Karg, Barbara.
The everything filmmaking book / by Barb Karg, Jim Van Over, and Rick Sutherland.
p. cm. -- (An everything series book.)
Includes bibliographical references.
ISBN-13: 978-1-59869-092-7
ISBN-10: 1-59869-092-2
1. Motion pictures--Production and direction. 2. Motion pic-
ture authorship. I. Van Over, Jim. II. Sutherland, Rick. III. Title.

PN1995.9.P7K35 2007
791.4302'3--dc22
2006028438

This publication is designed to provide accurate and authoritative information with regard to the subject matter covered. It is sold with the understanding that the publisher is not engaged in rendering legal, accounting, or other professional advice. If legal advice or other expert assistance is required, the services of a competent professional person should be sought.

—From a *Declaration of Principles* jointly adopted by a Committee of the American Bar Association and a Committee of Publishers and Associations

Many of the designations used by manufacturers and sellers to distinguish their products are claimed as trademarks. Where those designations appear in this book and Adams Media was aware of a trademark claim, the designations have been printed with initial capital letters.

*This book is available at quantity discounts for bulk purchases.
For information, please call 1-800-289-0963.*

Contents

Acknowledgments

Many individuals worked hard to bring *The Everything® Filmmaking Book* to fruition. As always we thank our friends and family for their never-ending love and support, and we'd like to thank the fine folks at Adams Media for their encouragement. A heartfelt thanks to editor Lisa Laing, whose quick wit and utter professionalism were greatly revered during the writing process. We'd also like to thank Paula Munier, whom we eternally admire for her exquisite taste in wine, chocolate, and friends, and Rachel Engelson for her tireless work and exceptional humor during the developmental process. Thanks go out as well to Laura Daly, Brett Palana-Shanahan, Andrea Norville, Sue Beale, and copy editor Suzanne Goraj for their hard work and expertise. And a hearty thanks to publisher Gary Krebs for giving us the opportunity to do this book.

A big thanks to Heather Hale for providing a jumping-off point, as well as signposts along the way. And for all her hard work and dedication to *The Everything® Filmmaking Book* we offer our unending praise to Arjean Spaite, without whom this book could never have been done. And thanks, as always, to Buckaroo Banzai, Charlton Heston, John Carpenter, Gandhi, and the entire population of *South Park* for keeping all of us sane on a daily basis.

Top Ten Things
You'll Learn About Filmmaking

1. That filmmaking is one of the largest collaborative commercial and artistic media in history.

2. That anyone can make a movie with just a hand-held video camera and a few friends.

3. The ins and outs of all phases of production from script to screen.

4. What every crew member does, and who you'll need to hire to make your film.

5. How to present yourself and your concept to potential investors and the innovative ways you can find funding for your project.

6. The science and art of sound, lighting, editing, and musical accompaniment that can take your film from dull to dazzling.

7. The amazing innovations in digital technology that allow you to make movies on your home computer, limited only by your own imagination.

8. That having a great script can make or break your film, no matter whether it's no-budget, low-budget, independent, or blockbuster scale.

9. How the major studios got started, and how they operate and strategize the release of their films.

10. The history of Hollywood's illustrious journey down the yellow brick road, and all of the epic filmmakers whose legendary works are beloved today.

Introduction

▶ From the early days of the silent film era to the modern-day digital revolution, motion pictures have captured the hearts and minds of everyone on the planet. Movies offer us an escape from the everyday sights, sounds, and stresses of our existence, allowing us to meet ordinary and extraordinary characters and visit places we could never have dreamed of. Arguably the most innovative and exciting industry in the world, filmmaking has a potential artistic and commercial value that is staggering. Each year, billions of dollars are pumped into the film industry, with everyone from studio executives to directors and production assistants working hard to develop, film, and promote new motion pictures.

If you sat down and counted how many movies you've seen in your lifetime you'd probably be shocked. As a kid you no doubt saw everything from *Snow White* to *Star Wars*, and by adulthood you probably sat through at least two or more films a week, either in the theater or on television. All those marvelous creations, from *film noir* to romance and from westerns to science fiction, have at some point or another provoked an emotional response. Movies make us laugh, cry, scream, ponder, and, on occasion, just shake our heads in bewilderment. That's the beauty of film. The variety is endless and there's something for everyone.

As an aspiring moviemaker, you're no doubt a fan of all things celluloid related. What you might not be aware of is just how complex and difficult it can be to make a film, regardless of whether you're on a shoestring budget or have *Titanic*-sized financing. Filmmaking is all about having a concept, we hope a winning one, that can be nurtured into a work of art that ultimately is universally understood and enjoyed. In order to do that, you need to immerse yourself in the filmmaking process, and not just the technical aspects. While all phases of preproduction, production, and postproduction are crucial, none of it can be accomplished until you've got a polished script in hand and a strategy for pitching your film to potential production companies, studios, or investors. You also need to familiarize yourself with all the Tinseltown players.

The Everything® Filmmaking Book offers up all manner of tips on how you can develop your idea from script to screen, and have a great time doing it. If you're unfamiliar with the process of moviemaking, you'll find this an invaluable resource, as it outlines the basics of how scripts are born, how you construct a production package, and the creative ways you can go about finding financing. You'll also learn about the massive preproduction process, and how filmmakers can better plan and organize their projects to maximum perfection.

Then, of course, there are the truly fun production phases when actual shooting begins, where you finally get the chance to direct or produce a story that you've only envisioned through the written word. The power of seeing your dreams enter reality is overwhelming to any filmmaker, and it's what moviemaking is all about. This is when your unique style and talents can really shine, especially if you've created an atmosphere that encourages freedom and innovation among your cast and crew. If you lead well, they will surely follow, and your film will be a direct reflection of your patience, tenacity, and humanity.

With the right tools and rules you can film anything you can dream up, and do it with a style and panache all your own. It doesn't matter if the entire world or just your grandmother sees it onscreen—the beauty is that you made a movie. Don't let a small budget keep you from realizing your filmmaking potential. Even filmmakers like Steven Spielberg and George Lucas had to start small and work their way through the ranks.

The more you know about Hollywood and the worldwide filmmaking industry, the better off you'll be as a filmmaker. *The Everything® Filmmaking Book* will help guide you on your celluloid journey and hopefully inspire you to pursue your ambitions. The rules of the game are simple: start small and think big.

Chapter 1

When I Grow Up, I Want to Make Movies!

These days, everyone and their mothers can make movies. If you've got a video camera, a tape recorder, a computer, and a few willing friends, you can become a filmmaker. If your sights are set high, you can reach for the stars and work your way up the industry chain one film at a time. In order to do that, however, you need to learn the basics about every phase of filmmaking including its history, and all stages of production from script to screen.

The Origins of Film

Whether you decide to enroll in a film school, or even move to Hollywood to pursue your dream, you need to learn the nuts and bolts of the industry, all its pitfalls and potential, and immerse yourself in its history. By learning about the history of film, you will develop a basic understanding of the fundamental workings of film equipment and a sense of where your project will fit in the constantly evolving industry of film.

Humble Beginnings

The actual filmmaking process has evolved over the decades from the Silent Era to the present-day blockbusters full of special effects. Film continues to capture the hearts and imaginations of audiences the world over and remains one of the few common art forms shared among all manner of people. In 1893 America's first "studio" was built by Thomas Edison in West Orange, New Jersey. The building was called "The Black Maria" because it resembled the era's dark, cramped police patrol wagons known by that name. It was here that Edison filmed his first motion pictures, including *Fred Ott's Sneeze*, a comical version of one of his employees sneezing for the camera.

FACT

At the same time as Edison, French brothers Louis and Auguste Lumiere were working on developing projectors that could show a film to a small audience. Their invention, the Cinematograph, was introduced in Europe in 1895. A year later, Edison released his Projectoscope, and the individual Kinetoscopes were gradually replaced.

Before Edison built the studio, he developed a camera to record and show his movies. In 1888, he filed a plan to patent the *Kinetoscope*, a device that would "do for the eye what the phonograph does for the ear." The Kinetoscope recorded objects in motion and reproduced them. A prototype of the device was debuted for a woman's group in 1891 and patented later that same year. The device was revolutionary, but it didn't allow more than one person to view a film at a time. Viewers had to look through a peephole in the top of the device in order to view the film.

How the West Was Won

The earliest western film, *Cripple Creek Barroom*, was filmed by Edison in 1898. This was followed by the first American narrative film, Edwin Porter's 1903 film *The Great Train Robbery*, and Edison's 1906 *A Race for Millions*. These films originated numerous western clichés such as the damsel in distress, claim jumping, and the shootout at high noon. More importantly, they started a trend that sparked the production of more than 5,400 western silent films, shorts, and documentaries filmed between 1898 and 1930.

Screenwriters Are Born

Early films were called *actuality films*, because they focused on images of everyday life as it occurred. A train rushing by, a vaudeville actor performing, a parade, a sporting event—any event that could be captured on film became a movie. There was no writing done for these films, they were simply slice-of-life imagery. After filmmakers began filming reenactments, such as battle scenes from the Spanish-American War, the idea of portraying fictional stories became popular. As a result, the role of the screenwriter was born and permanently changed the way films were created.

Overview of Filmmaking

Filmmaking, by its very definition, is the art of making a motion picture. As history has shown, the process of bringing a vision to life on screen develops as a direct result of technological advancements in the filmmaking industry. With each passing year, innovative hardware, software, and hands-on equipment becomes available to both industry professionals and the general public. The basic traditional principles of filmmaking still apply, but the processes have vastly improved as a result of digital technology. Filmmaking is an exciting business, the lifeblood of which is the constant battle between creativity and commercial success, and no matter what role you choose, you're sure to have a great time playing it.

Start Small, Think Big

Whether you're already working on a specific idea for a film or have just discovered a general interest in filmmaking, there's a lot to learn. For starters, you need to know what's involved in writing or hiring someone to write a script. Then there's the business of pitching that script and your filmmaking skills in order to secure financing. Once that's accomplished, you need to immerse yourself in the preproduction process by perfecting your budgeting, scheduling, and directorial skills, setting up your production, and hiring cast and crew.

After all that has been accomplished, you'll enter the actual production phase, which includes shooting your film. To do this you need to learn everything about traditional and digital camera equipment, sound recording, lighting, and special and visual effects. When you finally yell "Cut" for the last time, your postproduction phase will begin—that means your film needs to be edited and sound effects and music added to finalize your project.

Low-budget films by some standards can be any film made for less than $500,000 or, depending on whom you talk to, $1,000,000. Many commercially successful movies have been made for less than $250,000, and independent films for less than $50,000.

Casting a Wide Net

Once your film is complete it will enter the marketing and distribution phase. At that point, you'll need to be familiar with all the strategies and concepts involved in making your film a commercial success. Whether your project was made on a small or large scale, it's important to learn the ins and outs of bringing a film to market.

The Script

As any established filmmaker can attest, a successful film begins with a great script. Without it, you're asking for trouble from the word go. Not only will your production be tough to finance, but you'll have a hard time getting a studio, production company, investors, or anyone excited about it in general. Writing a great script is all about doing your homework, and that means researching every aspect of your characters, homing in on your plot, storyline, pace, and all elements of suspense and conflict.

ALERT!

Keep in mind that the same principles apply whether you're hiring a writer or team of writers to bring your vision to life or you're writing your own script. In the first instance, just as much time and energy should be invested in order to feel comfortable pitching and getting people enthusiastic about your script.

It's also important that you feel comfortable with the genre you've selected. If you're a dedicated science fiction fan, you may not get enthused about a historical romance or comedy western. Forcing yourself to write a genre that doesn't interest you will most likely produce unsatisfactory results.

So before you even consider loading your first camera, you need to learn everything there is to know about your film and its characters. Only then will you be able to continue your motion picture endeavor with complete confidence (see Chapter 2).

Airplane! *Meets* **Predator**

It's often said that in Hollywood there's no such thing as an original idea, that everything has been done on one scale or another. In some instances that may be true, given that certain genres tend to rehash the same old story. On any given day, you can find several science fiction films featuring genetic mutants gone horribly wrong or kickboxer flicks where a couple of guys spend the final hour beating the tar out of each other.

Original ideas are still possible if you take the time to research your story and characters, paying special attention to plots or quirks that you can add to give your film a different spin. Quite often, when it comes to *pitching*, which is selling the concept of a production, you'll hear industry professionals describe a film by saying it's "*Indiana Jones* meets *Omen*," or "*The Fisher King* meets *Sleepless in Seattle*," or "*Aliens* meets *Braveheart*." What that refers to is a plot based on previously successful films.

Why Write First?

It will be debated until the end of time, but arguably the most important element of a film (aside from funding) is the script. Logically then, it makes sense that before you do anything you need to write a screenplay, acquire a screenplay, or hire someone to write a screenplay. Without one, or at least a story synopsis or treatment, you'll have nothing to pitch to studios, production companies, or potential investors.

Writing the script first also has a host of benefits that will help your film in the long run. A finished script will enable you to better understand your story and examine its strengths and weaknesses, to ascertain financing and budgetary requirements, and, above all, to have the chance to absorb your characters. The better you know your script, the better off you will be when it comes time to sell your idea.

Preproduction

The preproduction phase of any production is arguably the most important. During this stage you'll need to get all your ducks in a row, and to do so in the most organized fashion possible. This means perfecting your script, securing financing either by private means or through a studio or production company, budgeting and scheduling your film, and hiring crew and cast. And that's just the beginning.

Dream a Little Dream

With little or no budget, you can bring your vision to life in any number of ways. For newcomers, creating sample reels of your film work is one of the first priorities. Without samples, no one will get a feel for your personal style or your seriousness in wanting to become a filmmaker. Having a script perfected and in hand is yet another step toward achieving your dreams.

Show Me the Money!

Funding is paramount for any filmmaker. In order to secure financing from either private investors or a studio or production company, you need to assemble a business plan in the form of a production package. This includes a cover letter, a synopsis of your script, a resume, pertinent back ground information, and a breakdown of your proposed budget. Chapters 7 and 8 discuss how you can go about securing financing, maintaining a budget, and scheduling your production.

Professionalism is the key to any successful financial venture and is especially important in the filmmaking industry, where a company is considering investing millions of dollars in you and your project. Everything you propose in your budget will be meticulously scrutinized. Be sure your estimates are accurate, your proposal shows familiarity with the project, and your sales pitch is perfect.

Assembling Your Crew

Any film that has a production budget, whether it's big or small, will need a crew. However, the funds you have available and the type of film you're making will dictate the size of your crew and cast. Regardless, it's crucial that you understand the responsibilities and specialties of all the professionals who work hard to create motion pictures. Chapters 10 and 11 give you the background you need when it comes time to hire both essential and additional crew members. Whether they're assistants or gaffers or associate producers, you should know what they do and how they do it on a typical production.

Production and Postproduction

The actual production phase of a film is very complex, but it can be made much easier if you've organized everything you possibly can at the preproduction level. If you're directing your film, you'll have your hands full working with your producers, cinematographer, sound and lighting technicians, and all department heads. Ultimately, it's your vision that everyone is striving to bring to life by finding the right locales, using the proper camera and sound techniques, and providing illumination for every scene.

Once the camera stops rolling, your postproduction phase begins. This is an important step in creating and finessing your final product, and it cannot be underestimated. Just as much care should be given to this stage of development as to the other phases of production. Many a film has come to life or dearly departed as a result of incorrect editing, poor sound, or inappropriate music, so take the time to make sure everything about your film sounds and feels right to you.

ALERT!

Learning everything you can about the postproduction process is critical. The more secure you are about the methods used, the more secure you'll be when your film is released for all the world to see. This means paying close attention to film continuity, pace, flow, sound effects, and musical score.

Filmmaking is a craft, and like any artistic or commercial endeavor it requires careful research, innovation, and, ultimately, financing. Many individuals dream about playing a role in the entertainment industry; these days, anyone can take part if he has the patience and tenacity to make his dream a reality. If there's a will, there's a way, and by immersing yourself in the rich history, technology, and artistry of the motion picture industry, you're one step closer to the silver screen.

Chapter 2

The Art of Cinema

The beauty of filmmaking is that there are so many genres from which to choose. Romance, comedy, drama, horror, fantasy, western, suspense, science fiction—any of these popular artistic categories can be realized or mixed and matched to create a silver screen masterpiece. The trick is finding the genre you feel most comfortable filming, and to do that, you need to understand the inner workings of each classic category.

Finding Your Niche

Before embarking on any filmmaking journey, you need a great concept or script. Without it, you're just another *Bio-Dome* in the making, and no budding or experienced filmmaker wants that. Finding the perfect genre that suits your artistic and technical style will not only enhance your passion for your film, but it'll also energize everyone working with you on its production.

By definition, a *genre* denotes a distinctive style or format. In the filmmaking world there are many genres from which to choose, most of which are often mixed to form a different entity like a romantic comedy, sci-fi western, or horror spoof. Each genre has its own dynamics and intricacies that showcase mood, setting, and format. Find the genre you're best suited for, and you'll be comfortable pitching, producing, marketing, and ultimately creating a stunning body of work.

The Drama

Dramas are the broadest genre in the filmmaking world and are often combined with other genres to create a tailored product. In general, dramas tend to be character-driven stories that follow a central theme, be it triumphant or tragic. The goal of any good drama is to create memorable characters with whom your audience can relate in one form or another. You want the audience to see, feel, and experience the world through someone else's eyes.

Dramas are about the trials and tribulations of life, with stories that weave intricate tales of individuals, families, and entire nations. These films can fall into any number of subgenres including social, political, legal, historical or epic, personal, affliction, rebellion, and many others. A few examples of these subgenres are as follows:

- **Social** (*On the Waterfront, The Grapes of Wrath, The Champ, Cool Hand Luke, Guess Who's Coming to Dinner, Inherit the Wind, Traffic, Witness, Lost in Translation*)
- **Political** (*The Year of Living Dangerously, All the President's Men, JFK, Network, Hotel Rwanda, Schindler's List, Nixon, Gandhi*)

- **Legal** (*To Kill a Mockingbird, Mr. Smith Goes to Washington, Twelve Angry Men, Kramer vs. Kramer, A Time to Kill, A Few Good Men*)
- **Historical or Epic** (*Titanic, Last of the Mohicans, Lawrence of Arabia, Dr. Zhivago, Cleopatra, The English Patient, The Godfather, Sense and Sensibility, Dances with Wolves*)
- **Personal** (*Ordinary People, Sophie's Choice, The Piano, The Hours, Marty, The Bridges of Madison County, Million Dollar Baby, Seabiscuit, Ali, The Aviator, Mystic River*)
- **Affliction** (*One Flew over the Cuckoo's Nest, Terms of Endearment, Frances, A Beautiful Mind, My Left Foot, Beaches, Forrest Gump*)
- **Rebellion** (*Cool Hand Luke, Norma Rae, Silkwood, Rebel Without a Cause, Mutiny on the Bounty, The Shawshank Redemption, In the Heat of the Night, Easy Rider, Top Gun*)

Dramas can be extremely emotional and often elicit strong responses from audiences and critics alike. The fact that this genre is character dependent makes the filmmaker and actors a huge factor in a film's success. Throughout the history of film there have been hundreds of dramatic motion pictures, many of which are now legendary masterpieces like *Gone with the Wind, Ben-Hur, Casablanca,* and *Citizen Kane.*

The Romance

Romance is a genre that remains timeless, its films providing many of the most memorable moments in film history. Ask someone who her favorite onscreen couples are and she will likely mention Vivian Leigh and Clark Gable in *Gone with the Wind,* Ingrid Bergman and Humphrey Bogart in *Casablanca,* Julie Christie and Omar Sharif in *Dr. Zhivago,* and Audrey Hepburn and Gregory Peck in *Roman Holiday.* The romance genre can be funny, tragic, ridiculous, ironic, or gut-wrenching, and can span all levels of passion in both the real world and otherworldly environments.

Romance is an easy choice for crossing over almost all genre lines. Romantic comedies in particular haven't lost their appeal over the decades. From *Bringing Up Baby* to *Sleepless in Seattle,* audiences continue to love a happy ending—especially if the road is paved with humor. The same goes for many of the other romantic subgenres, which include:

- **Romantic Comedy** (*It Happened One Night, The Philadelphia Story, Annie Hall, When Harry Met Sally, Roxanne, My Man Godfrey, Ninotchka, Some Like It Hot, Desk Set*)
- **Dark Romance** (*War of the Roses, Body Heat, Anna Karenina, A Place in the Sun, Bram Stoker's Dracula, Rebecca*)
- **Classic Romance** (*African Queen, Sense and Sensibility, Out of Africa, The Way We Were, The Thin Man, Breakfast at Tiffany's, Sabrina, Pillow Talk, The King and I*)
- **Supernatural Romance** (*The Ghost and Mrs. Muir; Ghost; Truly, Madly Deeply; Somewhere in Time; Heaven Can Wait; The Bishop's Wife*)
- **Historical Romance** (*Wuthering Heights, Dr. Zhivago, A Room with a View, Dangerous Liaisons, The Unbearable Lightness of Being, Last of the Mohicans, Pride and Prejudice*)
- **Love under Adversity** (*An Affair to Remember, Moonstruck, Titanic, Pretty Woman, Witness, Coming Home, The Bridges of Madison County, The Crying Game*)
- **Fantasy Romance** (*An American in Paris, Gigi, The Princess Bride, Lady and the Tramp, The French Lieutenant's Woman*)
- **Romance Gone Bad** (*Double Indemnity, Niagara, The Postman Always Rings Twice, Damage, Fatal Attraction, Disclosure, Revenge*)

As are romances in life, romance movies are anything but predictable. More often than not, the key to a successful romance is the strength of a screenplay and the charisma of actors involved in the production. Always remember that if you're going to play the love game, romance in film is part intuition, part execution, but almost entirely chemistry.

The Action Movie

The action genre, like romance, often crosses over into many other genres. The difference, however, is that action hasn't always been a mainstay of the silver screen. Only in the last two decades have action films been transformed into blockbusters, and that's primarily due to the arrival of bigger-than-life tough guys Sylvester Stallone, Mel Gibson, Bruce Willis, Harrison Ford, and Arnold Schwarzenegger. Together, their franchise films such as *Die Hard, Lethal Weapon, First Blood, Terminator,* and *Raiders of the Lost Ark* brought the genre to the forefront and made millions in the process.

That's not to say that action hasn't been around for a good long while—just ask any swashbuckler fan. Legends such as the 1903 film *The Great Train Robbery, Ben-Hur,* and Akira Kurosawa's timeless masterpiece *The Seven Samurai* set the bar for scores of future productions. Rising to the challenge—and indeed setting the bar even higher—was the 007 franchise, which has been entertaining fans since the arrival of Sean Connery's *Dr. No* in 1962. Action films come in a variety of subgenres, including dramatic action, comedic action, capers, thrillers, heists, science fiction, and horror.

Enter the Dragon

James Bond was still going strong in the '70s, but it was an unknown martial artist named Bruce Lee who ultimately captured universal attention and acclaim with his stunning athleticism. The 1973 film *Enter the Dragon* set in motion a new breed of action film that would showcase actors such as Chuck Norris, Jean-Claude Van Damme, Steven Seagal, and Jackie Chan.

Lethal Weapons

Audiences in the 1970s saw yet another new incarnation of action figure that carried bigger and better weapons and a truckload of attitude. *Dirty Harry* made his debut in 1971 as did Gene Hackman's Popeye Doyle in *The French Connection*, and Richard Roundtree in *Shaft*. From there, all manner of action heroes and hoodlums made their way to the big screen from *The Untouchables* to *The Hunt for Red October* to *The Fugitive* and several *Mission Impossibles*.

Chicks with Uzis

The role of women in the action genre has been slow to evolve on the big screen, with only a smattering of films showcasing true female action heroes. While Wonder Woman was waving her golden lasso on the small screen during the 1970s, Carrie Fisher picked up a gun and started shooting Imperial storm troopers in *Star Wars*. By 1979, the public was introduced to Sigourney Weaver's Lt. Ellen Ripley, whose epic showdown with the mother of all aliens began with *Alien* and ended eighteen years later with *Alien Resurrection*. Along the way, director James Cameron gave us a strong female action hero in Linda Hamilton and her role as Sarah Connor in the *Terminator* trilogy.

Thanks to Ripley and Sarah Connor, female action heroes have become a hot commodity. Films including *Nikita*, *Thelma & Louise*, *Speed*, *True Lies*, *The Fifth Element*, *The Matrix*, *Charlie's Angels*, *Lara Croft: Tomb Raider*, *Underworld*, and *Crouching Tiger, Hidden Dragon* have catapulted a host of talented actresses into the action history books.

The Western

The western genre is most definitely a fixture in regard to film history, and its fans are nothing if not devoted to everything from classic to spaghetti to contemporary cowboy tales. Over the years, western films have diminished in popularity, but they're not yet extinct despite the remake of *Wild, Wild West*.

The overriding grumble—the good, the bad, and the ugly, as it were—from those who aren't hardcore western fans is that many films seem to have the same plot: lone cowboy has gun, horse, conflict, shootout, and on occasion grabs the girl before riding off into the sunset. What most folks tend to forget is that westerns are built on history and legend, and the captivating tales woven throughout western films remain timeless to this day. Several western legends have been portrayed on film throughout the genre's history. Buffalo Bill, Billy the Kid, George Armstrong Custer, Wyatt Earp, Wild Bill Hickock, and Jesse James have shot their way through dozens of films.

Man and His Horse

Director John Ford and his favorite actor, John Wayne, will forever be associated with the American western. Although he's considered to be one of the most influential directors in the history of cinema, Ford's westerns were seldom viewed as serious filmmaking by the Hollywood elite. Still, Ford's portrayals of the moral virtue of western communities and families, and the ethical standards of his leading characters, would shape America's view of western history for decades.

FACT

In 1980, Michael Cimino's western *Heaven's Gate* was wildly over budget and universally panned by critics and the press. Bombing at the box office, the fiasco virtually bankrupted United Artists and forever destroyed the studio perception of the director as the all-knowing auteur.

Italian director and producer Sergio Leone revised the traditional good guy/bad guy formula of early cowboy films with *spaghetti westerns* that launched Clint Eastwood into stardom. The hero of *A Fistful of Dollars*, *For a Few Dollars More*, and the huge hit *The Good, the Bad and the Ugly* would no longer be ethically faultless, and shooting first became a commonsense approach to Wild West survival.

Worldwide Appeal

Many major film stars, and actors who would become major stars, are part of western cinematic history. John Wayne, James Stewart, Henry Fonda, Charles Bronson, Yul Brynner, Steve McQueen, and Mel Gibson all played leading roles in successful westerns. Some argue that *Heaven's Gate* pushed the western into its grave, but in 1992 the western roared back to life briefly in a single film, Clint Eastwood's starkly brilliant *Unforgiven*. The genre has remained popular in DVD rentals and on cable television's Western Channel, but it's unlikely that the western will ever resurface with the same widespread acceptance that it enjoyed in the twentieth century.

Science Fiction Films

Science fiction has the distinct advantage and disadvantage of being one of the most elaborate, expensive, and sometimes unintentionally humorous genres in filmmaking history. It has been in existence since 1902, when Georges Méliès made *From the Earth to the Moon* (*Le Voyage dans la lune*), based on the Jules Verne novel. This was followed by Fritz Lang's 1927 masterpiece *Metropolis*. From that time on, science fiction became a motion picture mainstay, and filmmakers have taken all kinds of creative and technological risks with varying degrees of success.

The science fiction genre covers a wide range of subgenres, each with its own challenges, charm, budgetary limitations, and audience appeal. There's also a certain amount of confusion about films that on first glance appear to be sci-fi, but also cross into other genres, like horror or fantasy. The debate still continues over the 1979 film *Alien*, which is alternately classified as a sci-fi or horror film. Regardless, there are a host of categories from which to choose when writing and filming sci-fi:

- **Alien Invasions** (*Earth vs. the Flying Saucers, War of the Worlds, Invasion of the Body Snatchers, Independence Day, The Abyss, Men in Black, Contact*)
- **Disasters** (*The Day the Earth Stood Still, When Worlds Collide, Armageddon, Deep Impact, The Day after Tomorrow*)
- **Viruses Run Amok** (*The Andromeda Strain, The Omega Man, Resident Evil*)
- **Post-Apocalyptic Worlds** (*Soylent Green, Terminator, Mad Max, Road Warrior, Starship Troopers, Blade Runner, The Matrix, Strange Days*)
- **Hero's Journeys** (*Star Wars, Forbidden Planet, Outland, The Fifth Element, Back to the Future, Planet of the Apes*)
- **Outer Space Excursions** (*2001: A Space Odyssey, 2010, The Martian Chronicles, Alien, Red Planet, Solaris, Event Horizon, Star Trek*)
- **Technological Rebellion** (*Westworld, Gattaca, The Stepford Wives, Total Recall*)
- **Genetic Mutants Gone Horribly Wrong** (*It Came from Beneath the Sea, The Deadly Mantis, The Fly, The Island of Dr. Moreau*)

Sci-fi fans are die-hard dreamers who will often watch anything remotely alien, robotic, time disoriented, mind altered, and genetically mutated. Sci-fi films typically require not only a brilliant script but a huge budget, as in the case of *Aliens*, *Independence Day*, *Armageddon*, *Contact*, the *Jurassic Park*, *Matrix*, and *Terminator* trilogies, and the *Star Wars* franchise. If you're writing or considering filming a science fiction masterpiece, your overwhelming concern should be budget. It's easy to get carried away when you're dealing with the high-end special effects and technical wizardry necessary to create a blockbuster hit.

Horror Movies

Things that creep, crawl, stare, scream, bite, howl, vanish, or simply go bump in the night will forever be a fascination to all humankind. The primary success of horror films is the varying levels of fear an audience is willing to absorb. As a result of this enduring love/hate adrenaline rush, the horror genre has survived and most certainly continues to thrive on.

Legendary masters of the horror film include actors Boris Karloff, Lon Chaney Jr., Vincent Price, Christopher Lee, and Peter Cushing and directors Roger Corman, Alfred Hitchcock, Wes Craven, John Carpenter, and George Romero.

Whether the tale told is of *Nosferatu*, *Frankenstein*, or Michael Myers, horror finds its roots in literature and real-life events, ultimately becoming twisted by the creative genius of talented cinematic manipulators. From Mary Shelley's *Frankenstein* to Bram Stoker's *Dracula* and Clive Barker's modern-day *Hellraiser*, the horror genre has kept millions of people on the edge of their seats for decades in terrified anticipation of the unknown. Like many other genres horror is subjective, and the making of a horror film requires a strong study of films past and present. Learning from the true horror masters will only enhance and inspire you to embark on your own twisted supernatural endeavor.

Creative Terror

Horror films are a terrifying mixed bag of creatures, evil entities, demonic forces, menacing ghosts, possessed animals, and all kinds of supernatural phenomena. Vampires, werewolves, witches, zombies, mummies, and poltergeists are just a few of the frighteningly hideous elements that compose the genre. Horror has never suffered from a lack of memorable characters and supremely talented actors, writers, and directors. Filmmakers and their legendary characters like Dracula, Norman Bates, Jason Vorhees, Freddy Krueger, Lestat, and Rosemary and her satanic baby have made screen history. And just as horrifying are big-screen monsters like Godzilla, Jaws, and King Kong.

There's no doubt that horror films are a huge enticement to individuals of all ages regardless of whether they are classic black-and-white films or modern-day scary movies. Recent Hollywood hits like *Scream*, *The Ring*, *The Blair Witch Project*, *The Sixth Sense*, *Identity*, and *The Others* along with endless *Halloween*, *Nightmare on Elm Street*, and *Friday the 13th* sequels prove that horror remains a hot commodity.

Monster Mash

Of all the genres, horror has long been hampered by the B-movie curse. Despite the fact that horror is one of the industry's earliest genres, its reputation runs a razor's edge. Modern-day horror is often criticized for its level of violence and the sheer gore it splatters across the screen, but that certainly wasn't the case when the genre first began in the early 1900s.

Films of the 1930s and '40s were frightening in their simplicity, making excellent use of lighting and technologies available at the time. During the 1950s and '60s horror evolved with the help of Britain's Hammer Film Productions, which showcased Christopher Lee and Peter Cushing in a number of films, and American International Pictures (AIP), which with Roger Corman and Vincent Price's help brought Edgar Allan Poe to life. Then came Alfred Hitchcock with his flock of birds and an eccentric young lad called Norman Bates, and the rest is history.

The Comedy Shop

It should come as no surprise to anyone that humor, which runs the gamut from the traditional to the avant garde, is highly subjective. If there's one single genre that's prime for debate it's arguably the massive comedic genre. What makes one guy laugh doesn't necessarily make the next guy even giggle. How many times has a friend or colleague recommended a comedy that he thought was hysterical? How many times have you watched that comedy and wondered why on earth anyone thought it was funny?

The Birth of Comedic Film

Comedy has made a long and highly successful march down the red carpet, having first showcased itself silently through the brilliance of comedians like Charlie Chaplin and Buster Keaton. By the 1930s audiences were laughing with the Marx Brothers, W. C. Fields, the Three Stooges, and the beguiling Mae West. They were also entranced by Cary Grant paired up with Katharine Hepburn in *Bringing Up Baby*, and Rosalind Russell in *His Girl Friday*. During wartime, comedy films belonged to legends like Bob Hope, Bing Crosby, and such comedic teams as Laurel and Hardy and Abbott and Costello.

By the 1950s and '60s, a new breed of comic genius was enchanting audiences courtesy of Jerry Lewis and *Pink Panther* extraordinaire Peter Sellers, but it wasn't until the early 1970s that comedy took a decidedly opinionated and oddball twist. A combination of dark and slapstick humor was the mainstay, with filmmakers Mel Brooks, Woody Allen, Neil Simon, and the infamous Monty Python gang banging out one hit after another. Popular comedies of the '70s include *Blazing Saddles*, *Young Frankenstein*, *High Anxiety*, *Annie Hall*, *The Sunshine Boys*, *Monty Python and the Holy Grail*, *The Life of Brian*, and *National Lampoon's Animal House*.

Naked Gun *Versus* Annie Hall

By the 1980s, comedies had again taken a turn with the emergence of movies like David and Jerry Zucker and Jim Abrahams' *Airplane!* Arguably one of the funniest movies ever made, *Airplane!*, with its relentlessly goofy fun, is a guilty-pleasure movie that jump-started dozens of similar spoofs like *Top Secret!*, *The Naked Gun*, *Police Squad*, and *Hot Shots!* On the other side of the comedic spectrum, the popularity of *Saturday Night Live* gave rise to a host of permanent comedy superstars like Eddie Murphy, Chevy Chase, Dan Aykroyd, Bill Murray, and Steve Martin. And who could forget a young—and terminally stoned—Sean Penn in *Fast Times at Ridgemont High*?

FACT

Dramatic, romantic, or social comedies of the '80s include *Tootsie*, *Big*, *A Fish Called Wanda*, *Nine to Five*, *Private Benjamin*, *Splash*, *Broadcast News*, *When Harry Met Sally . . .*, *Honey, I Shrunk the Kids*, and *Ghostbusters*.

There has always been a need for good comic actors such as Jack Lemmon, Audrey Hepburn, Tom Hanks, Meg Ryan, Reese Witherspoon, and Jack Black. Since the 1990s there has been a coming of age for unique and highly talented comics including Mike Myers, Jim Carrey, Robin Williams, Ellen DeGeneres, and Adam Sandler who made the jump from standup venues to legitimate acting.

If you're filming a comedy it's important that you feel comfortable with the style of comedy you've selected. Within the genre there are all types of comedic subgenres including romantic, horror, social, and science fiction comedies, slapstick, parodies or spoofs, black comedies, and fish-out-of-water tales.

Some comedies have had the good fortune to become a franchise, as with *National Lampoon*, *Crocodile Dundee*, *Austin Powers*, *Scary Movie*, *Police Academy*, and the *Naked Gun* films, to name a few. Others, like *There's Something about Mary*, have become cult classics. But no matter the comedic genre you choose, the overwhelming factor, aside from budget, is that your script be funny, whether it be ha-ha funny, gross funny, or wet-your-pants funny. The ultimate goal is to tell a good story or spoof and make as many people laugh as possible.

Shoot to Thrill

The thriller genre, which is built primarily on the element of suspense, encompasses a wide range of subgenres. Thrillers often cross into other genres; plot elements include, among other things, technology, action, politics, psychology, forensic and medical sciences, conspiracies, and even romance. Few individuals haven't seen a thriller in one form or another, whether it's an Alfred Hitchcock masterpiece or a film adapted from works by novelists such as Tom Clancy, Michael Crichton, Ian Fleming, Frederick Forsyth, or Robert Ludlum.

QUESTION?

Which films are considered to be to the best thrillers?
In 2001, the American Film Institute (AFI) ranked the ten greatest thrillers as: *Psycho, Jaws, The Exorcist, North by Northwest, The Silence of the Lambs, Alien, The Birds, The French Connection, Rosemary's Baby,* and *Raiders of the Lost Ark.*

No matter their slant, thrillers are meant to keep your adrenaline pumping and your gray cells exploding from start to finish. Alfred Hitchcock was a master of classic suspense thrillers, with films such as *North by Northwest, Psycho, Rear Window, Vertigo, Dial M for Murder, Rebecca,* and *The Birds* eternally keeping audiences enthralled. The sheer volume of classic thrillers is too great to list, as they run the gamut from *The Manchurian Candidate* to *The Sixth Sense* to *Cellular,* but most of them are well worth studying if you intend to keep audiences riveted.

Crime-themed thrillers have been prominent for decades; *Manhunter, The Fugitive, Silence of the Lambs, Marathon Man,* and *Cape Fear,* for example, have pushed viewers' heart rates to their limits. Similar workouts have come from erotic thrillers, led by *Jagged Edge, Basic Instinct, Fatal Attraction,* and *The Big Easy,* and political thrillers, such as *Day of the Jackal* and *In the Line of Fire.*

Thrillers are often standalone films, but on occasion they become franchises, such as with the *Die Hard*, *The Bourne Identity*, and *Patriot Games* installments. These and many other thrillers have become blockbusters, so if you're looking to make your name in this genre, you'd better be prepared for plenty of competition.

The Musical

The musical genre is one that tends to find a very specific audience, as people either love them or cringe at the mere thought of sitting through them. But regardless of one's opinion, there's no denying that musicals are impressively represented in the historical archives of filmmaking. The shift from silent films to "talkies" actually came to fruition with Al Jolson's 1927 musical *The Jazz Singer*, and from that moment on, film would never be the same. In fact, the musical is experiencing a resurgence in popularity due to the success of *Chicago* and the remake of *Moulin Rouge*.

The Unsinkable Musical

To say musicals are difficult to film is an understatement. Movie musicals are very much like their theatrical cousins, only with far more expensive equipment, crew, retakes, and the added pressure or sheer luck of finding big-name actors who might actually be able to carry a tune. There's also the daunting task of following history.

Director and choreographer Busby Berkeley created a sensation starting in the 1930s with musicals that featured hundreds of dancers who, when filmed from above, created precise and intricate patterns.

Dozens of supremely talented dancers and singers have graced the big screen. Gene Kelly, Fred Astaire and Ginger Rogers, Judy Garland and Mickey Rooney, Bing Crosby, Danny Kaye, Donald O'Connor, Debbie Reynolds, Cyd

Charisse, and Barbra Streisand helped build the classic American musical. Their films, ranging from *Singing in the Rain* to *The Wizard of Oz* to *Top Hat* to *Hello Dolly*, are the stuff legends are made of.

The Beat Goes On

Over the years musicals have had huge audience appeal, covering a wide age range and spanning genres. While it seems nearly everyone on the planet has seen *The Sound of Music*, many other musicals have done well by stretching the boundaries of traditional film. For example, *All That Jazz*, *Grease*, *Footloose*, *Little Shop of Horrors*, *The Rocky Horror Picture Show*, and the Muppet movies are still audience favorites. MGM's 1929 film *The Broadway Melody* was the first musical to boast an original score, which included *Give My Regards to Broadway* and *You Were Meant for Me*.

Animated Films

Animation is undeniably one of the most complicated, intricate, and challenging film genres. It's also one of the most popular and historic disciplines of moviemaking. Animated films have enormous mass-market appeal. Few moviegoers have failed to shed a tear over Bambi or Dumbo or been unmoved to cheer for a determined little fish called Nemo, and it's nearly impossible to find someone who hasn't heard of Mickey Mouse.

Disney Studios, among others, brought animation to the world and with each passing year the genre becomes more popular. It was 1937 when *Snow White and the Seven Dwarves* was released by Disney. Over the next seven decades many classics followed, including *Pinocchio*, *Fantasia*, *Cinderella*, *Peter Pan*, *Sleeping Beauty*, *Jungle Book*, *The Aristocats*, *101 Dalmatians*, *The Little Mermaid*, *Beauty and the Beast*, and *The Lion King*.

Oscar-winning Pixar Animation Studios created many innovative films like *Toy Story*, *A Bug's Life*, *Monsters, Inc.*, and *The Incredibles*. In 2004, *Finding Nemo* was awarded an Oscar for Best Animated Feature Film and has grossed over $864 million worldwide. In a union of the classical and the new, in early 2006, Pixar was purchased by the Walt Disney Company.

Fantasy Films

The fantasy genre encompasses films of whimsy and wonder that feature magic, mysticism, daring quests, otherworldly creatures, and bizarre new worlds. But films in this genre aren't easy to classify, as there tends to be a crossover into the science fiction and other realms. *The Wizard of Oz*, for example, is both a musical and a fantasy film. Demi Moore and Patrick Swayze's tear-jerking *Ghost* is a romantic fantasy. As a rule of thumb, it's perhaps best to think of a fantasy film as one whose central theme involves the supernatural, magic, swords and sorcery, or mythical people and places.

Fantasy films can be hard to sell, but if done well they can be lucrative, as is the case with the *Harry Potter* movies, *Indiana Jones* adventures, and the Oscar-winning *Lord of the Rings* trilogy. Over the years, many fantasy films like *Conan the Barbarian*, *The Princess Bride*, *Ladyhawke*, and *Clash of the Titans* have become cult classics. Films in the fantasy genre can be very expensive to create, often requiring elaborate costuming and innovative special and visual effects. Depending on the subgenre, production costs can quickly become overwhelming, especially when one is attempting to create a new world or mythical creatures.

Subgenres of the fantasy realm include:

- **Sword and Sorcery** (*Conan the Barbarian, Excalibur, Dragonslayer, Harry Potter, Dragonheart, King Arthur*)
- **Surrealism** (*The Adventures of Baron Munchausen, Labyrinth, The Fisher King, Big Fish, The Legend of Sleepy Hollow*)
- **High Fantasy** (*The Lord of the Rings* trilogies, *Ladyhawke, Willow, Pirates of the Caribbean: Curse of the Black Pearl, The Chronicles of Narnia: The Lion, the Witch and the Wardrobe*)
- **Adventure Quests** (The *Indiana Jones* trilogies, *The Neverending Story, The Dark Crystal, The Time Machine, Lara Croft: Tomb Raider*)
- **Classic or Romantic Fantasy** (*Lost Horizon, It's a Wonderful Life, The Princess Bride, Heaven Can Wait, Ghost, Edward Scissorhands, Peggy Sue Got Married*)

One of the master technicians of the fantasy realm is Ray Harryhausen, whose mastery of stop motion animation made silver screen history with such films as *Jason and the Argonauts*, *Clash of the Titans*, *One Million Years B.C.*, *The Valley of Gwangi*, *20 Million Miles to Earth*, and the *Sinbad* adventures.

Have Camera, Will Travel: Documentaries

Filmmakers who work in the documentary genre are extremely disciplined, focused, and in some cases daring. Documentaries often contain historical, political, or social elements presented as travelogues or through interviews or news footage. They can also focus on an individual or group of individuals such as the 1988 film *Imagine: John Lennon*, Stephen Hawking's life in *A Brief History of Time*, and *The Endurance: Shackleton's Legendary Antarctic Expedition*, which tells the tale of Ernest Shackleton's doomed expedition in 1914.

FACT

When it comes to political documentaries, filmmaker Michael Moore has garnered plenty of recognition both good and bad. His films, especially *Fahrenheit 9/11*, *Bowling for Columbine*, and *Roger and Me*, have made him one of the more high-profile documentary filmmakers.

Documentaries are typically made with small film crews on a low budget. Part of their charm is the raw footage and emotion that's often at the heart of the film's subject matter. One of the more provocative and highly successful mainstream documentaries is Luc Jacquet's 2005 film *March of the Penguins*. An exquisite look at the life and breeding cycle of the emperor penguin it really hit the mark with audiences, having grossed to date over $122 million worldwide.

Chapter 3

The Write Stuff

Nothing is more important to a film or filmmaker than a great screenplay. A film's concept, story, characters, dialogue, visual concept, and environment all begin with the script. But be warned—the process of writing or acquiring a screenplay is a long journey that is inevitably fraught with potholes. There is much to be learned about the writing and development process; taking the time to do your homework can make the difference between a B movie and a blockbuster.

From Good to Grand

Now that you know about the different kinds of films to choose from, you must take all the steps you can to ensure that your representation of your chosen genre is a good as it can possibly be. The difference between a good movie and a great movie can be a razor's edge, given that films as an entity are highly subjective. A film could suffer from poor special effects or miscast roles. It could also run too long or be difficult to hear. More often than not, however, films that have a bad script suffer more than others.

The Importance of a Great Script

Screenplays are a dime a dozen in the Hollywood realm. Everyone has written, is writing, or wants to write a script. That said, finding the one silver dollar in a bottomless pit of dimes is like winning the lottery. A poor script featuring blasé characters who accomplish nothing in a nondescript environment with no action potential will never hold an audience's attention. Scripts tell a story from beginning to middle to end, with a resolution that is satisfying to the intended audience. A great script will feature deep, well-constructed characters who thrive amid a story's plot and imagery.

ALERT!

It's not uncommon for filmmakers to change the ending of a film after it has been test screened for a select audience. If a small group of filmgoers dislikes a conclusion, you can bet a larger audience will be equally dismayed.

No Pain, No Gain

Writing a screenplay requires an enormous amount of work, patience, and decision-making ability, as well as an endless supply of coffee. Bringing your vision to life takes planning. No one just plunks down in front of the keyboard and cranks out a feature film; if you do come up with a script that way, it's certain to be rewritten a dozen times before it ever sees the light of day.

Before you even begin writing or hiring someone to write, you need to establish several key elements. You first need to secure a concept in your mind and ask the inevitable "what if" questions. What if a genetically altered eggplant starts running amok in Topeka, Kansas? What if a serial killer starts killing the forensic scientists tracking him down? All possible questions and concepts have to be clear in your mind before you can write, much less pitch, your script.

Settling on a concept also goes hand in hand with selecting a genre for your film (see Chapter 2). Is it a western or a mystery or a western mystery? Is it a comedy, a romance, or a romantic comedy? As the filmmaking industry grows, so do the possible combinations of genres. It's important that you select a genre you feel comfortable with, one that you can really sell and realistically produce within the confines of your budget. Once you have that down, you can move on to developing your characters, plot, and the rest of your story.

Script-formatting Software

Back in ancient times, screenplays were typed on a typewriter. With the onset of computer technology, scripts were keyed into a word processing program. Fortunately, anyone can now write a screenplay with the help of screenwriting software that does the formatting for you. The danger of script-formatting software is that even a first draft looks like something that is clean and ready to submit. In fact, it will need several more drafts before it is fit to be sent out to studio prospective buyers, so don't be lulled into a false sense of security.

There are many different programs from which to choose, and they vary in price depending on whether they're a simplified version or a full package. Hollywood Screenwriter, Movie Magic Screenwriter, Scriptwerx, Final Draft, ScriptBuddy, and Screenwriter 2000 are just a few of the programs on the market. As with any software program, your choice will be based on features, price, and other factors—e.g., whether you are simply writing or need a full package that offers additional capabilities such as budgeting and scheduling programs (see Chapter 8).

Compelling Storylines

One of the most crucial aspects of a script is the storyline. The storyline is the thread that holds together the fabric of a screenplay, weaving color and texture in and out of scenes in intricate patterns that come together to tell a story. A compelling storyline keeps audiences glued to their seats. It's a careful mix of tension, action, suspense, and mystery that is meant to keep the audience thinking and their adrenaline pumping. Even in more lighthearted stories, there needs to be a sense of excitement and the unexpected. In order to successfully write that mix, your script needs to have a strong plot and subplots. Alfred Hitchcock was a master of plot and suspense and could keep an audience mesmerized from fade-in to fade-out. As a filmmaker, hooking an audience should be one of your goals, but it takes plenty of skill and artistry and a clever script.

The Plot Thickens

Concocting a plot that is original yet commercial is no easy feat, especially if you're appealing to a wide audience. Scripts that contain too many plot twists tend to confuse people, and scripts that don't have enough plot turns tend to bore people. Scripts that can pull off a big shocker can often prove successful. Kevin Costner's 1987 role in *No Way Out*, for example, is a great example of this. By film's end, no one saw the left hook coming. The same goes for the big reveal in director Neil Jordan's *The Crying Game*, and more recently in M. Night Shyamalan's *The Sixth Sense*. In 1973, audiences were shocked by Charlton Heston's horrifying discovery in the futuristic thriller *Soylent Green*. Suspense built slowly throughout the film until its conclusion, when Heston yelled the now infamous "Soylent Green is *people*!"

Structure in Three Acts

Screenplays, no matter the genre, are held together by a *three-act structure*—a beginning, middle, and end. The divisions are commonly referred to as acts. It's important to note that in the grand scheme of screenwriting, there is a common denominator in that the majority of films have a main character who must face some form of opposition that by the third act is brought to a resolution.

What does "high concept" mean?
High concept is an industry buzzword that's used when a screenplay's concept is strong enough to establish an audience regardless of the actors who are cast in the film. For example, a man and a woman fall in love by e-mail, never realizing that they've met in person and hate each other. This is the high-concept idea behind *You've Got Mail*.

Act one establishes your environment and primary character, or *protagonist*, describing and showing who that character is and what she hopes to achieve. Act two expands your character by focusing on what she's going to do to reach her goal, the forces that provide opposition in the form of an *antagonist*, and the revelation that results after confronting obstacles she must overcome. Act three focuses on resolution of this character's journey—a payoff of all the suspense, drama, conflict, and characterization you've built throughout the first two acts. As one act ends and another begins there is always a moment of drama or action that turns the plot. Those apex moments that signal a shift from one act to another are called *plot points*.

Character Development

Character development is the lifeblood of any story, whether small screen, wide screen, stage, or literary in form. In order to create a character, you need to start with the basics. How old is your character? What does he look like? What are his habits? Is he intelligent or dim? Where did he come from? It's essential that you ask yourself all of these questions before you start writing. Establishing a character's background, approximate physicality, and personality is crucial. When brainstorming a character's traits you'll find the true nature of your character emerging, and can then begin tailoring your character's role as hero, villain, comedian, killer, ingenue, and so on.

Creating Conflict

A story is nothing without some form of *conflict*, be it subtle or grandiose. Every protagonist needs an antagonist. Think of it as the battle between good and evil, two forces in constant opposition that taunt each other until they finally come to blows. Every story needs that pull in a consistent manner in order to keep the plot interesting and entertaining. Conflict can come from a character, force, disability, flaw, misunderstanding, disaster—any number of worldly and otherworldly situations.

FACT

The least amount of dialogue used in a modern-day film was in the 1976 Mel Brooks film *Silent Movie*. Throughout the entire movie, only one word was spoken—ironically, by French mime Marcel Marceau. He uttered the word *non*.

No matter whether you're writing the script or you've hired a writer, it's important that everyone is clear on the protagonist's initial conflict, how it builds throughout the script, and how it's ultimately resolved. In any film that you view, you should be able to recognize the conflict and the steps taken to resolve it.

For example, in the 1987 film *Fatal Attraction*, Dan Gallagher, played by Michael Douglas, has a one-night stand with Glenn Close's character, Alex Forrest. It's a prime setup for conflict because Dan is married. The conflict begins to build as Alex becomes obsessed. She stalks Dan, then squirms her way into Dan's unknowing family. As her paranoid personality grows stronger, she kidnaps Dan's daughter. By the conclusion, the conflict has exploded and she attempts to kill Dan's wife.

The Hero's Journey

One of the more historically successful structural elements is known as "the hero's journey." For as long as people have told stories and throughout motion picture history, audiences have witnessed the triumphs and travails of characters ranging from Charlton Heston's Moses to Katharine Hepburn's Rose Sayer, and from Indiana Jones to Neo of *The Matrix* trilogy. Heroes and heroines are mystical, dramatic, courageous, virtuous, and moral. They always do the right thing, and audiences love them.

When writing a hero's tale it's important to remember that his journey is central to the plot. His impetus and motivation is what keeps the storyline consistent and interesting. You want your audience to feel the range of emotions your hero feels, endure his hardships, and stand up and cheer when he finally achieves his goals.

The hero's journey has been written over and over again and in myriad genres. As far as concepts go, it's nothing original. The twist you give it can be unique, so think outside the box. Heroes come in all shapes and sizes and ages, but if there's a single film that sets the mark for a hero's journey, it is George Lucas's *Star Wars*.

Throughout the *Star Wars* franchise, and especially in the first three movies, Luke Skywalker epitomizes the definition of hero. The screenplay for *Star Wars* is often used as a benchmark for new writers, and for good reason. Skywalker faces every conflict in the book: good versus evil, selfishness versus selflessness, friendship versus romance, war versus peace, and ultimately father versus son. And he must face it all on an interstellar level.

Writing a hero's journey requires careful study of how your character will think, act, react, and treat others, and what he will do to get to journey's end. You want audiences to cheer and not be apathetic about a hero's success.

Subtext and Backstory

A script, whether it's commercial or artistic, must have depth. Revealing what lies just beneath the surface is an aspect of storytelling that should be mastered by both writer and filmmaker. Whether you reveal a character's thoughts and motives directly or indirectly, through action, flashbacks, or subtitles, it's crucial that the audience becomes privy to certain facts about your characters. That means *subtext* and *backstory*.

QUESTION?

Is a character's backstory really necessary?
If you don't know where a protagonist has been, then it's likely you won't be able to convincingly portray where she's going. Backstory helps an audience appreciate a character's journey.

Subtext refers to the underlying content of your story, and it can be used in many ways. It can throw a thin veil over a film's political undercurrent, in or cast a light on a character's true motivations. Many period films such as *Sense and Sensibility* and *Remains of the Day* are seething with sexual repression. The *Batman* mythos makes great use of the murder of Bruce Wayne's parents as having created his vigilante alter ego.

Moment by Moment

Audiences flock to movies for all kinds of reasons, the most obvious being that they want to be whisked away from their daily existence to explore a new world, experience a love affair, laugh hysterically, or feel the thrill of an action-packed adventure. As a filmmaker, and certainly as a writer, one of your greatest hopes is that after an audience's temporary vacation from life, they will remember certain special moments.

These moments could be a look, some action, or a bit of dialogue. Key moments, whether poignant, humorous, terrifying, or ironic, can make a film memorable rather than forgettable. Sometimes it's the payoff for a long harrowing experience—for example, when Roy Scheider aims his rifle at the great white killing machine in *Jaws*, or when William Hurt discovers a yearbook picture in *Body Heat*.

Many of what are considered to be classic films contain such moments and are written in such a way as to become legendary. Humphrey Bogart in *Casablanca* cooing "Here's looking at you, kid" and Tom Cruise telling Renee Zellweger "You complete me" in *Jerry McGuire* are examples. Another would be Hannibal Lecter taunting neophyte FBI agent Clarice Starling, saying, "Tell me Clarice, have the lambs stopped screaming?" in *The Silence of the Lambs*. Those are moments frozen in time that leave an audience feeling satisfied at film's end.

Creating Memorable Characters

When you think of memorable motion picture characters, who immediately springs to mind? Is it Scarlett O'Hara dressed in her finest drapery? A bullet-riddled, sunglasses-wearing killing machine called a Terminator? The airy, breezy, glamorous Holly Golightly? Or a fun-loving spastic bunny named Roger Rabbit?

In the history of filmmaking there have been dozens of unforgettable characters who have fallen in love, beaten the odds, won wars, chased dreams, and hit balls out of the park. Why are they memorable? Because they were written that way. It doesn't matter whether they were intentionally meant to be quirky or heartwarming, or whether circumstances surrounding them made them more memorable—all of these characters were born in a script.

Place and Time

One thing to consider when writing and filming memorable characters is that some characters become more popular because of the situations they find themselves in. For example, the character of John McClane played by Bruce Willis in the 1988 film *Die Hard* became an unforgettable action hero by performing spectacular feats of daring, courtesy of his ingenuity and an armory. He unexpectedly found himself in a hostile terrorist situation where his wife was a hostage. His situation helped create his character. Had he just been a regular cop on his beat, he might not have become a cult hero.

Characters who are bigger than life don't need a situation to elevate their charisma. They're interesting no matter what. James Bond is a good example of a character who is sensational to begin with. You'd be happy just watching him pull off a boring caper, or simply breathing. What gives the Bond films a double whammy is that an already charismatic character is thrust into outrageous circumstances. This creates a film with even more bang for the buck. Big-budget productions can afford the bang, but that's not to say it can't be done on a smaller scale.

The Rosebud Factor

Memorable characters come in all shapes and sizes, and they don't have to be human. Many an animal, alien, dream lover or nightmare, and inanimate object has shown up its human counterpart to become memorable in its own right. For example, it took a character of incredible magnitude to upstage an adorable seven-year-old Drew Barrymore, but Steven Spielberg's alien in his 1982 film *E.T. the Extra-Terrestrial* did just that. E.T. has gained cultural immortality, and he wasn't even human—he was a puppet.

Animals have equal impact in terms of characterization and can be written in such a way that they pull at the heartstrings. Few moviegoers are able to remain stoic while watching *Old Yeller, Sounder, Babe, Lassie, Black Beauty, Finding Nemo, Dumbo, Bambi*, or *National Velvet*. All of those wonderful animals had a story arc that showed not only their animal instincts but their humanity.

FACT

Beloved heroes aren't the only characters that make an impact on audiences. Evil critters can also leave a lasting impression, as is the case with Cujo, Jaws, v, the tyrannosaurus rex and velociraptors of *Jurassic Park*, and all of the possessed creatures in *The Birds*.

Unsavory characters can also make their mark. Freddy Krueger, Jason Vorhees, and Michael Myers have been taunting and haunting audiences since the arrival of John Carpenter's *Halloween* in 1978. All three of those maniacs are a writer and filmmaker's dream and worst nightmare. Not only do you have to keep a certain part of their character consistent, but you have to constantly elevate their methods and madness with each sequel.

Objects don't often leave a lasting impression, but in the case of Stanley Kubrick's 1968 masterpiece *2001: A Space Odyssey* (and its sequel *2010*), no one can forget the frightening monotone voice of the computer called Hal. Arguably one of the best films ever made is Orson Welles's *Citizen Kane*, but as grand as the Charles Foster Kane character is, it's his childhood obsession—a sled named Rosebud—that has become synonymous with the film.

Films rarely make an inanimate object a lead character, but that was not the case with the 2000 film *Cast Away* starring Tom Hanks as a modern-day Robinson Crusoe. As fate would have it, Hanks's character spends most of his conversational hours with a volleyball affectionately called Wilson.

The Value of a Villain

Writing a villain or having a villainous element in a script is crucial to illuminating your hero. Without a dark side, you'll be very limited in conflict and ultimately give yourself nothing interesting to write or film. Even Disney films in all their perky musicality have villains. Think of evil Dalmatian-hater Cruella De Vil or *The Little Mermaid's* sea witch Ursula.

Audiences love to hate villains, in all their sick, twisted, and sometimes humorous capacity. Villains are typically selfish, wicked, and power hungry. Captain Ahab, Lex Luthor, the Joker, Dr. No, Nurse Ratched, Colonel Kurtz, the Wicked Witch of the West, and Darth Vader have all left an indelible mark in film history books. And they were successful because their characters were written to include various levels of motivation, desperation, and backstory.

Villainy can also be written in the form of internal strife—say, if your protagonist is his own worst enemy on an emotional, physical, or psychological level. Russell Crowe's character John Nash in *A Beautiful Mind*, Tim Robbins in *Jacob's Ladder*, Robert De Niro in *Taxi Driver*, and Norman Bates in *Psycho* are good examples. Scarlett O'Hara's best characteristic was her ambition, but that was also her worst, often self-defeating trait.

Adversity can stand in for a human villain as well. In the landmark film *Kramer vs. Kramer*, the antagonist takes three forms. The antagonist might be Dustin Hoffman's wife, the court system, or Hoffman's own fears about being a father. The important thing to remember when writing a villain is that he must prove to be a worthy counterpart to your hero. Luke Skywalker was nothing without Darth Vader. Moses needed Pharaoh to achieve his goals. Butch Cassidy and the Sundance Kid needed an entire Super Posse to halt their journey.

Go Ahead, Make My Day

Certain actors will forever be associated with legendary lines their characters said. Many of those famous quotes have become part of everyday vernacular. These quotes run the gamut from hilarious to horrific, but they have one thing in common—they are all highly effective in context. Many writers attempt to write dialogue with impact, but if you don't have all the bases covered on your character's traits, mannerisms, and actions—and most importantly, if you don't truly understand your character—even a bright shiny statement will turn to lead.

One of the most important things to remember when writing a screenplay is that your dialogue must be in keeping with your characters. Marlon Brando yelling for Stella in *A Streetcar Named Desire* was in line with the character of Stanley Kowalski. So was Rocky yelling for Adrian. Charlton Heston's frustration was clearly apparent and understandable when he yelled "Get your stinking paws off me, you damned dirty ape!" in *Planet of the Apes*. And Anthony Hopkins as Dr. Hannibal Lecter was never more frightening than when he said "A census taker once tried to test me. I ate his liver with some fava beans and a nice Chianti" in *The Silence of the Lambs*.

Finding Indiana

It's often said in the filmmaking industry that there's no such thing as an original idea, that everything's been done before in one form or another. That may be true, but it doesn't mean that you can't write or film original characters who are marketable. Every creature on planet Earth and beyond has a different look, method, and manner. Assuming you've done your homework and have command of your characters, you should be able to add those distinctive details that will make your character unique.

For example, what made Indiana Jones so special? The iconic action hero has been written and reinvented hundreds of times, but Indiana had a certain aloof confidence, quirky humor, McGyveresque qualities, and a fear of snakes. All those things together catapulted Indiana to movie legend status.

Always keep your audience in mind when you develop your concept. You want everyone to find something appealing in both your protagonist and antagonist, even if it's just some tiny quirk that sets them apart from the rest.

It would be unwise to attempt to write an exact replica of a Terminator or Freddy Krueger or Spider-Man. Instead, create characters that are as genuine, three-dimensional, and interesting as possible, and let the audience decide who will become a legendary figure. Aim well when writing and filming your characters and you could hit the target.

To Write or Not to Write

If you're a filmmaker who has a concept and an entire film emblazoned in neon lights within your brain but you can't write, then you need to find someone who can. If writers are a dime a dozen, than this should be a piece of cake. Or is it? With so many writers to choose from who have experience ranging from amateur to pro, it's crucial to find someone who can clearly envision your concept.

O Writer, Where Art Thou?

Word of mouth is one way to find a writer, especially in Hollywood where everything is about "so-and-so." So-and-so wrote that script so maybe she can write this one. So-and-so couldn't finish his last script so he's not a good choice. If you're a filmmaker with a huge budget, then chances are you'll have no trouble finding a number of reputable writers. If you're an amateur just getting started, you may have to take your chances on a first-timer.

There are plenty of resources that you can refer to when searching for a writer. Online there are dozens of professional writers' Web sites, such as the Writers Guild of America (WGA), and professional screenwriters' sites.

Dealing with Adaptations

If you do want to try writing your own script without starting from scratch, you may want to write an adaptation. *Adaptations* are screenplays that are written from an existing piece of literature, including books and short stories. Before you ever consider writing or filming a script based on a novel, you must ascertain whether the film rights to that book are available. If they're available, the rights must be optioned. Films like the *Lord of the Rings* trilogy, *Out of Africa*, *The Color Purple*, *Patriot Games*, *The Shining*, *The Princess Bride*, *The Hunt for Red October*, and *Jurassic Park* are all examples of adaptations.

E ALERT!

These days, writing an adaptation is difficult for a first-time writer or filmmaker. Studios and production companies are quick to snap up promising works even before they're published, hence before they've had a chance to hit the bestseller list.

Short stories are also adapted to screenplay format. *The Shawshank Redemption* was based on a short story, "Rita Hayworth and the Shawshank Redemption," written by Stephen King. It was then adapted and directed by Frank Darabont, and was nominated for Best Picture in 1994.

Writing an adaptation script does have its plus side in terms of security and marketability. After all, a publisher did invest in the book, and if it sold well then a film should have a head start. Of course, if it's a bizarre bit of literature that only a handful of people read, a screenplay adaptation may have limited appeal unless you can find a producer or financial backer who loved the book.

Registering Your Masterpiece

Once you've finished penning your *pièce de résistance*, you definitely want to get it registered. This can easily be done online at the Writers Guild of America, West, or the Writers Guild of America, East (*www.writersguild .org* and *www.wga.org*). While registering your work doesn't constitute an official copyright, it does establish the date on which the script was completed, which may prove significant if someone writes something very similar to your work after that date.

Scripts on Spec

The term "scripts on spec," or "speculation," is common lingo in the film industry. In general, it can be defined in one of two ways: It can be an original screenplay that you wrote that no one has paid for, or it can be a script that you wrote for an existing sitcom or drama that, again, you were not paid for. Spec scripts are a writer's calling card, a sample script that you can show an agent, producer, or reader (see Chapter 7).

Breaking In with a Spec Screenplay

Your spec script is your calling card. Once you have your spec script written to perfection, it's time to present it to the world. But whom do you send it to? Do you just start bulk-mailing it out to everyone and their grandmother? Before you start wasting valuable paper and postage, you need to stop and take a few calm breaths. Unless you're an established writer or hired specifically for a job, you'll never send an entire script to someone. Tinseltown folks are busy and they couldn't possibly read everything that crosses their desks.

Going Out with a Spec Script

The best way to get started is by doing your homework. Purchase a copy of an agent directory or production company directory and target your market (Chapter 17). Then get on the phone and start calling the offices on your list to ascertain whether each person or company would first like a query letter, outline, synopsis, or treatment. Whatever you do, take careful notes of whom you spoke with, what they said, and when you spoke to them.

When studying various directories and trade newspapers, pay close attention to the types of films that agents or production companies have been associated with or produced. If they've been involved in a film you like or a genre that suits your script, then pursue them. Many actors have also started their own production companies, so if that actor is ideal for your work you could query them (see Chapter 6).

Synopses

Very few industry professionals will ever bother to open your script without having first read your script *synopsis*. The synopsis is your script in a nutshell, and is an essential tool for selling your story. There's no way to describe the perfect synopsis, but there are a few rules. The industry standard length for the synopsis is one page or less. Shorter is better if it will get the job done, and your job is to tell your story concisely. The synopsis should be written as if you were telling your story directly to the reader. One of the most important goals of a good synopsis is writing it so that your reader can easily and accurately describe the story when he pitches your script to someone else.

What is a one-sheet?
One-sheets are a single sheet of paper on which you have given a log-line (your story in a single sentence), and short summary of your script. Officially, no one can ask you for it without incurring obligation to pay you, but you can give it to agents and production companies voluntarily as an introductory pitch.

You'll want to identify the genre of your script in two words, like romantic comedy or action adventure. Keep your focus on the main character, and stay with the basic facts of the story. There shouldn't be a paragraph, or even a single sentence, that raises unanswered questions. Keep your writing simple and uncomplicated. You'll want a twelve-year-old to be able to read the synopsis and know exactly what the story is about.

Treatments

A *treatment* is a multipage narrative of your script written in present-tense story format rather than scene by scene. One advantage to writing a treatment is that it can bring your story and characters into clearer focus. Narrowing your scope gives you the chance to spot flaws and inconsistencies in plot and characterization. You'll need both the treatment and synopsis for your production package (see Chapter 7) when you pitch your film.

A treatment differs from an *outline* in that it is longer and contains more narrative. Where an outline can range from five to fifteen pages, a treatment can run fifteen to thirty. Treatments and outlines are typically written prior to pitching sessions.

Pitching a Winner

So you've got all your ducks in a row and you're ready to get started. How do you distinguish yourself from all the other aspiring filmmakers out there? How do you get someone fired up about your script? Most importantly, how do you sell your story and yourself as a filmmaker?

The most important factor when entering this phase of promotion is that you're completely comfortable with your story and are prepared to satisfactorily answer any questions a potential agent, producer, or director may ask. When you're ready to roll, it's time to pitch your script.

Simply put, *pitching* is an attempt to sell your script and film to a producer or investor who could potentially agree to make your film (see Chapter 7). A typical pitch session can last around five to fifteen minutes, during which you want to describe the plot, characters, conflict, and any special elements that could help sell your film. During a pitch session, you describe your story in such a way as to highlight the artistic or commercial potential. This is a sales pitch, and as with any other sales pitch, you need to show enthusiasm and knowledge while at the same time presenting yourself in a professional manner. With a bit of luck, you'll generate enough interest to incite future meetings and negotiations.

Chapter 4

The Right Write Stuff

One of the most common Hollywood mainstays is the constant process of reshooting and rewriting—the obsessive need to tweak things. Even if you shoot the best short film you can and write the best script possible, even if everyone loves it and a studio has given you serious money for it—it will still likely never seem "quite right" to you. Developing a project is all about quality versus compromise.

What Is Project Development?

Put simply, project development means sanding off the rough edges, polishing the chrome, and getting all the details perfect before beginning preproduction. But project development is never simple. There are hundreds of things that can go wrong from script to screen, and the best thing you can do is be prepared and extremely flexible.

Development Hell

Seems obvious, doesn't it? It's only a matter of getting everyone from the agent's assistant to the studio president to agree that your project is ready to go in front of the camera. The problem is that there are a million little problems. While it's true that "development hell" is not part of official movie industry terminology, it is a common enough experience to get its own nickname.

It would be naive to think that everything related to the production process runs smoothly. It doesn't. Once a studio or production company agrees to produce your film, they immediately begin expressing their opinions. Then you have the typical problems that any industry newcomer will inevitably face. For example, executives leave and new ones come in, bringing their ideas and opinions with them. Actors or directors will want script or production changes made to suit their personal style. Once those changes are made, the actor gets a better offer and leaves the project. Then a new actor is found who has suggestions of his own. You get the picture.

Though usually associated with a "corrupt Hollywood system," these types of difficulties are not limited to big-budget studio pictures. Everything can be going along smoothly for your small, independent medical drama, until the abandoned hospital you had negotiated to use for very little money is sold to a developer who's tearing it down next week.

Keeping Focused

Another typical development problem can occur after your film is complete. Let's say you've filmed a romance and are showing it to an audience at a *test screening*, which is typically held at a studio lot or local theater. After viewing the film, *focus group* feedback shows that the audience had difficulty accepting the love story or found the ending to be depressing. As a result of that feedback, portions of your film will have to be rewritten and reshot. The problem is compounded by the fact that by now your lead actress is in Romania filming her next picture, for which she has shaved her head.

Focus groups have a considerable amount of pull. A good illustration is the test screening of director Peter Weir's 1998 film *The Truman Show*, starring Jim Carrey. It's said that Carrey accepted the role of Truman because it would give him a chance to break away from his "screwball comedy" roles. But early audience tests indicated a high level of disappointment at not seeing the silliness they'd come to expect from Carrey's pictures. As a result of the audience's input, a few new scenes were shot and edited in, depicting Truman as a bit more irreverent than originally intended.

Development Sell

If you're the filmmaker on a studio project and you want to stay the filmmaker on that project, you have to continually sell yourself to the studio. Not in a demeaning, obsequious way, but like the positive, creative team player that you are. If you disagree with their decisions, express your concerns in terms they'll accept—namely, story viability, shooting schedules, audience response, and profits. Maintain professionalism whatever the circumstances. In the end, you'll be given a "green light" not only to produce your work but to continue developing future projects.

The Art of Flexibility

No filmmaker is Midas. None of us can transform things into gold with a simple touch. No matter what you've filmed, it's unlikely that your idea for a movie or your current project is as pure and perfect as you think it is. Flexibility is the key. You must stay true to the original intent of your film, but also be open to making alterations to fit the necessities of production. Filmmaking is a collaborative medium. Usually requiring from ten to 500 people to complete a project, it may be the most collaborative of any art form.

E ALERT!

If you're working for someone else and you ignore their advice, you may simply be fired and a new person put in your place. Regardless, the changes will be made one way or another, so it's often better to stay with the project and find an artistic balance with the "powers that be."

The most gifted filmmakers know that surrounding themselves with talented people will make them look even more brilliant. If the people around you have ideas, consider their suggestions carefully. They might be useful, or they might not, but to dismiss criticism outright is to ignore a chance to make your film better. Consider it a creative challenge to be met and embraced.

To Read or Not to Read

There's a very old Hollywood joke that asks, "Why don't studio executives read scripts themselves?" The answer is: "Because their lips get tired." Across the industry, studios and production companies receive thousands of script submissions annually. For various reasons, most of them will be something a studio can't use, and it would be a waste of resources for a highly paid studio executive to spend her time reading every submission. Instead studios hire story analysts or script readers for the initial "weeding out" process.

Script Readers

The position of story analyst can be as varied as the budget of the company employing them. Larger studios will hire union members, per their obligation as a guild signatory. A union story analyst can receive $25 to $40 per hour as a full-time employee. Some production companies and agencies hire freelance readers, sometimes for as little as $10 an hour but usually at around $50 per script. It's not unusual for an executive's assistant or unpaid intern to provide the services of a story analyst as a favor to the company, and as a way to demonstrate a knowledge of production and development requirements.

After reading the script, the story analyst writes up a thorough summary and critique, called *coverage*. If the coverage is positive, the script moves up the development ladder with the coverage attached for everyone else to read. It's widely suspected that most script readers are unemployed screenwriters taking out their frustrations on the scripts they're hired to read. The truth is, script readers want to impress their bosses just as much as anyone else would. They want to find that one great script. As a writer or filmmaker, be assured that these individuals can be your allies, carrying your banner through the halls, trumpeting your brilliance and insisting (as far as they can) that the studio make your film. Some people consider script readers to be a screenwriter's worst enemy, but you're better off making them your best friend.

ESSENTIAL

When submitting your script for consideration, it's an industry standard that you fasten it with two or three brass brads. When fastening brads, fold the flat points outward, then doubled-back under themselves. This will prevent brads from snagging on the reader's clothes, other papers, car upholstery, or anything that might put the reader in a bad mood while reading your script.

The Upshot of Coverage

The coverage of any material done by a script reader is a summary of material a production company is considering buying. The material itself can be a script, a treatment, a manuscript, a short story, a comic book, a magazine article—just about anything. The 1986 blockbuster action film *Top Gun* was inspired by an article about the United States Navy's flight training school, written by Ehud Yonay for *California Magazine*. Different production companies require different styles for their coverage, but most of them include the following:

- Title of the submission
- Name of the author or authors

- Length of the material (in pages)
- Genre
- Locations (usually in very general terms—e.g., Los Angeles freeway or Arizona desert)
- Budget (low, medium, high)
- Time period in which the story takes place
- Date when the reading was done
- Logline (a one-sentence synopsis of the material)
- Summary (one or two sentences summarizing the reader's reaction to the material)
- Recommendation (typically the script is classified with a "pass," "consider," or "recommend" followed by a checklist of attributes such as premise, structure, and dialogue)
- Synopsis (a full breakdown of the major elements of the story, usually several paragraphs long)
- Comments (the reader's impressions and recommendations about the material, specifically in regard to strengths and weaknesses)
- Conclusion (usually a short paragraph specifying the reasons for the reader's recommendation)

If the script reader recommends the material, it's passed up to her boss, along with the coverage. That person then reviews the material and the coverage before deciding if it should be recommended further. Depending on the size of the production company, the coverage could follow the material through several levels before ultimately being accepted or rejected.

FACT

If a script reader likes a concept but isn't impressed with the actual writing, she can recommend the script, but not its writer. The reverse also holds true. The reader may like a particular writer's style, but not the material itself. In either of those situations, script coverage can be passed on for further consideration.

If the material is given a "pass" at any point, both the material and the coverage are kept on file and tracked. Sometimes old scripts are rescued from files years later by a development executive looking for hidden treasure. Unfortunately, the opposite also occurs. Bad coverage can haunt a script for months or years as it makes its way around town, and it's nearly impossible to get past it once a few companies keep track of the same poor results. Oftentimes, the only clue a writer has of this scenario is continual rejection by production companies. If you find yourself in that situation, it may be best to put that script away and try a new one.

Tracking Boards

A benefit and curse of the Internet age is the online tracking of everything from spec scripts to up-and-coming stars and filmmakers. A highly exclusive club of studio heads, executives, assistants, agents, and readers pays for access to invitation-only chat boards where everything and everyone is thoroughly discussed. These folks network and gossip, and share information as well as some of their workload. And as often as the system might be abused for blackballing, it's just as likely to help get your script or film into the right hands.

For example, the script reader for one company might have enjoyed reading your romantic comedy, but knows that his company is only producing horror movies. But his friend on a message board works for someone who specializes in romance films, so he slips her a good word and perhaps the coverage he's done. The next thing you know, you're getting a call to set up a meeting. There's no doubt that this system is somewhat inefficient and perhaps a bit unfair, but it is one of the realities of the modern movie industry.

Option Deals

If a studio or production company (or even a private party) decides your idea is worth developing, they might offer to option your story. An option is a comparatively small amount of money given to a writer in exchange for exclusive rights to your script for a specified length of time. Rather like a lease on a car with an option to buy, it indicates that a producer has faith in your material, but either doesn't have the kind of funding required to purchase your script outright or is unsure of her ability to get a green light to begin development.

> Option deals can be beneficial for all concerned parties. Producers with limited funds can get access to new material, while providing a way into the business for fledgling writers and filmmakers. As a filmmaker, you can pursue an option deal if you have the rights to your work.

In essence, a producer is paying for permission to shop your script to studios or other production entities. If someone agrees to produce it, the producer pays you the full amount agreed upon to purchase your script. If no one wants it before the specified time limit, the rights revert back to you, and you keep the option money.

An example of this is screenwriter Richard Hatem, who read the book *The Mothman Prophecies* by John A. Keel, and decided it would make a good film. Not being part of any deep-pocket production entity, Hatem contacted Keel personally and before long had optioned the rights for very little money, based on a newfound friendship and respect for the source material. When actor Richard Gere showed an interest in the screenplay Hatem had written, the film was ultimately set up at Lakeshore Entertainment and released by Screen Gems in 2002.

Step Deals

A step deal is when a producer and writer agree to develop a project together but do so in "steps." For example, if a development executive likes your pitch but is unfamiliar with your work as a whole, she may ask that you work out a step deal. After agreeing upon specific milestones and compensation, she'll ask you to write a treatment. Once the treatment is complete, you'll be paid for that step and the producer will decide if she wants to hire you for the first draft, or let you go and bring in another writer. The same will happen if you're asked to write the first draft, second draft, revisions, or whatever the designated steps might be.

A timetable may also be built into a step deal. If you turn in the treatment but then don't hear from the executive for a specified length of time (either to move forward or you are told she is going on without you), the rights may revert to you, and you'll be free to take the treatment elsewhere.

If-Come Deals

It's very rare that a company will ask for your completed script or spec script without paying in advance for the right to set it up. According to the Writers Guild of America, the union that governs film and television writers, this is called an if-come deal and can only be used in the case of television motion pictures. The Guild rule states that money need not be paid to the writer only as long as the production company is actively seeking licensee interest or other financing. The specifics of the contract must be negotiated in advance so that if the producer sets up the project, the writer's deal will already be in place and he will be attached to the project.

Since the producer's "active efforts" are the key, no specific time limit is involved. If those efforts cease at any time, the producer has no further rights and has to let the material revert back to the writer, or renegotiate a new contract. One interesting thing to note about the if-come deal is that, as long as it's in place, no development work can be done on the material. The producer can't ask the writer for changes or additional drafts or work of any kind. The production company can only seek financing and generate interest while the if-come deal is in effect.

Package Deals

Packaging is the stage at which other elements are added to the project. Elements include a director, actors, and other potential attachments. This may occur late in the development stage, after everyone is happy with the script or film concept and feels it will serve to attract the appropriate people. It might also happen fairly early on. If your agent also represents Julia Roberts, for example, he may get her interested in playing your lead so he can shop both the script and her out as a package, greatly increasing your chances of a sale.

The challenge of packaging is the compromise that often comes with it. The role your agent wants Julia Roberts to play might be written for a man. Or perhaps your story is set in Chicago, but the famous director your agent represents lives in Vermont and won't film anywhere but New England.

When it comes to development, the bottom line is this: no matter how good your script is to start with, it will undergo changes throughout the process for reasons that may have nothing to do with the material. Successful filmmakers learn to use the system to make their movies better.

Chapter 5

Breaking Into the Business

Getting your foot in the door of any industry can be tough, but it's especially difficult in the motion picture industry. Given the power, prestige, and visibility the industry carries, it's easy to see why "hitting it big" requires lottery-style luck. There are, however, many ways you can get a film produced if you're willing to work hard, do research, network, and, most importantly, tap into your ingenuity. The Hollywood machine runs on an engine of innovation.

Legend Has It . . .

There's a Hollywood legend that says Steven Spielberg got his big break when he slipped away from a tour at Universal Studios, found an abandoned office (or janitor's closet, depending on who's telling the story), and set up shop. After frequently seeing him come and go dressed in his bar mitzvah suit and tie, the security guards began simply waving him through. Somehow, Spielberg utilized this precarious position to make a short film that caught the attention of Universal's television division. He was then hired to direct a few television episodes, and the rest is Hollywood history.

True or not, the Spielberg legend emphasizes the need for perseverance and ingenuity. As a struggling screenwriter once said, "If you can't walk through the door, break in through the window," meaning that if the most obvious avenue to your goal is blocked, try another way. That's precisely what the now legendary director did. For most aspiring filmmakers, however, breaking into the film industry usually requires the traditional journey of working your way up through the ranks.

E ALERT!

Independent filmmakers have the advantage of visibility, especially at film festivals. Steven Soderbergh's 1989 indie film *sex, lies and videotape* helped launch his career with its festival success. By the year 2000, he was nominated for an Academy Award as director of both *Erin Brockovich* and *Traffic*. He eventually won Best Director for *Traffic*.

Producer A. C. Lyles is the classic tale of starting at the bottom and rising to the top. Lyles began working for Paramount Pictures in 1928, delivering mail to the likes of Cecil B. DeMille. Today he still has an office there, as well as a studio building named after him, a star on Hollywood's "Walk of Fame," the George Washington Award (presented to him by President Ronald Reagan), and a very nice vintage Thunderbird.

Making Your Mark

While Universal Studios has tightened their security these days, there are still plenty of ways to get started in the movie industry. The important thing is that you not wait for the "big break" to find you, but make a plan, step up, and get started. Without a plan, you'll inevitably end up frustrated. Always remember that Hollywood is a commodities market. Making your film and yourself as professional and bankable as possible is the key to opening all the necessary doors.

Starting on the Ground Floor

Every major studio has several entry-level positions open annually. If your goal is to get an inside look at the business, find out what jobs are available and what might be a good fit for you. Keep your eye on the newspapers, trades, and online postings for job opportunities such as mail clerk, tour guide, production assistant, or *page*.

At most modern studios, the job of page can change from day to day. Sometimes a page might fill in as a temporary receptionist, or be used as a tour guide or delivery person. If a studio has any shows with a live audience, such as situation comedies, talk shows, or panel shows, several pages are needed as ticket takers and ushers, among other things. In that circumstance, the best part is that you get to watch the show and learn the inner workings of a set. If you can move from job to job, and stay friendly with everyone in the process, you're sure to catch someone's attention and be offered a more permanent position.

Offering Assistance

The position of *production assistant*, or PA, is a low-level position usually assigned to one specific person or department. But this doesn't mean you're stuck in one place doing one thing. Working as a PA in a production office means taking calls from studio personnel at every level or delivering schedules and script pages to other departments, a shooting stage, dressing rooms, and sometimes to actors' homes.

A PA job is low on the totem pole, but it has many advantages. Many PAs move up quickly, especially if they show enthusiasm and capability. One of the more famous Hollywood truisms is that "the job of a production assistant is to get another job." If you can get in as a PA, your chances of advancement will increase substantially.

A *set PA* works on a *soundstage* or location, in the middle of the action. Set PAs are individuals who can think on their feet, juggle dozens of responsibilities, and keep smiling no matter what their endeavor. They do everything from running for coffee to notifying actors when they're needed on-set. The PA for the art department, the writing team, makeup, wardrobe, set construction, or visual effects has tremendous opportunity to learn what's required for those specialties.

The one thing that is required for *any* entry-level job is the desire to do the job. This may sound obvious, but if the boss gets a sense that you're only there to move up to something better, and you're letting the phone ring in the interim, you won't have the job for long. If you're going to be a PA, make friends, ask questions, and learn your way around—but be sure to do the job you're hired to do.

The Running Start

Once you've made it past the industry's entry level, climbed the long ladder, learned the ropes, paid your dues, and gotten your movie made, what do you do next? Where do you go from here? When you get to this stage, the goal is to get your movie seen. But bear in mind that a movie is not like a portrait—it can't be displayed on a wall waiting for people to walk by. It has to be shown somewhere. One of the best ways to go about accomplishing this task is submitting your film to a film festival or showing it on the Internet.

Gaining Exposure

There are countless film festivals where you can submit your film for consideration, usually for a nominal fee. Not only do gatherings provide exposure, but many of the studios, production companies, distributors, and agencies pay close attention to the films that make it even as far as the semi-finals. There is little doubt that if your film is a finalist, you won't have to call them—they'll call you.

Another way to expose your film to the masses is by researching and targeting certain cities that would be interested in your work. Many cities have film clubs whose goal is to present work by new filmmakers. Some filmmakers rent theaters or screening rooms, even for just one showing, and invite friends, colleagues, and industry professionals to this "showcase" of their work.

FACT

The Internet is also a great place to strut your cinematic creations. Sites such as YouTube (*www.youtube.com*) and GoogleVideo (*http://video.google.com*) allow anyone to post film clips free of charge. You can also post film clips or trailers on your personal Web site.

Editing several of your best clips together into a short *resume reel* is a must. This can be made up of shots from your completed film, from a movie still in progress, or any combination that shows off your best work. Sooner or later someone will ask to "see your reel," so be sure you have something to show them. And while it's still called a "reel" from its historical roots, most people would expect it to be a DVD or Web site, or at the very least a VHS video.

Do You Have to Live in Los Angeles?

One of the first questions an aspiring filmmaker will ask is whether it's absolutely necessary to live in Los Angeles. Obviously, if you want to start out in an entry-level position at a movie studio, you need to live wherever that studio is, but these days that could mean Los Angeles, New York, Austin, London, Vancouver, or Toronto. Nearly every major city in the world has fully operating production facilities.

If your desire is to be a director or screenwriter, note that those jobs can be done by people living anywhere in the world. They travel as needed, and let their work speak for itself. So before you starting packing up the dog and the blender and heading for the City of Angels, take some time to decide what it is you ultimately want to do and where you can best accomplish your goals.

Dealing with Production Companies

Once your film or screenplay is finished, it's time to do research. Scour the Hollywood Creative Directory and the industry trade papers like *Daily Variety* and *Hollywood Reporter*. This will give you leads as to who might be in the market for your film, or at the very least, the genre of your film. Once you've chosen your target producer, run a Web search on her, finding all the information you can about her past films and any current projects she has in the pipeline.

Once you've familiarized yourself with a producer's work, give her office a call. Begin by simply giving your name, and why you're calling. "This is Alan Smithee, and I read in this morning's *Hollywood Reporter* that you're looking for a comedy featuring a serial killer."

By introducing yourself in this manner, you've already established yourself as having done your homework. When the producer confirms that she is indeed looking for that type of feature film, in this case a comedy serial-killer script, give her a very short description of the film you directed. If you're lucky, the producer will be intrigued and can't help but ask you to send it right away. Well, that's what you hope will happen. The important thing to remember in this example is that you can make a direct call without an agent or manager of any kind. All it takes is some preparation, research, and confidence.

Making Professional Contacts Personal

It's a common misconception that networking means shaking hands and exchanging business cards. The truth of the matter is that those filmmakers who are most successful have learned that personal relationships are more valuable than professional ones, and the line between the two can be completely invisible.

QUESTION?

What's the most important factor when it comes to networking?
The most important element of successful networking is not showering a potential contact with insincere flattery. You should be genuinely interested in what others have to say, while at the same time still being yourself. A big part of selling your film is selling yourself as the creative force behind that film.

As in any profession, in filmmaking, when given a choice, people work with people they like. Networking is simply building a network of friends and relationships that can help you attain your goals, but this doesn't mean every person in your social circle has to be someone who can hire you. For example, your buddy who works for the phone directory may know the best place to rent equipment, or the woman who runs a camera for the local PBS station might like the chance to do something more personally creative. You may even have the invaluable resource of a friend who is simply encouraging and supportive.

Charitable Organizations

Many film industry professionals are involved with charitable groups. Some of it may be work-related, like the organization that is pushing for a more responsible depiction of smoking, drug use, and sexual activity in films. Others may focus on community outreach, such as providing the opportunity for handicapped children to go horseback riding. Many others participate in political issues, donate to food banks, or volunteer as mentors.

No matter the cause, this is an excellent way to meet people from all walks of life, and from every facet of moviemaking, while also making a contribution to society. If a big time producer remembers you as the one who jogged alongside her for breast cancer relief, she's more likely to ask you to help her by being a volunteer for her upcoming fundraiser. In that type of situation, you can demonstrate your skills as someone who can be depended on, who is helpful, and can carry yourself well in stressful situations.

Again, the most important element of charity work is your sincerity. Don't pick a charity you don't believe in just because Rob Reiner will be at the next table.

Up the Long Ladder

It's well known that many individuals in the filmmaking industry caught a break by knowing or being related to someone in the business. It's also known that many powerful people in Hollywood started out in less glamorous jobs. That said, it's crucial that you don't underestimate the value of a potential relationship just because someone is "only" a receptionist. If you get that person on the phone, be as polite and courteous as if you were talking with the actual head of the studio.

When speaking to a receptionist or assistant, remember his or her name, and be sure to use it when thanking them before ending the call. If you're rude or disrespectful, that person may just forget to deliver your messages. The reverse is also true. Many executives have the wisdom to ask their reception staff or assistants for an opinion on a current project or prospective employee. This will serve you even better as the assistant you've been communicating with moves up the long ladder, becomes a story editor, then vice president of development, and ultimately forms his own production company. If you've been friends since that first phone call, it won't be forgotten.

Pay It Forward

The premise behind the phrase "pay it forward" is simple: Do something for someone, not because he asked or even because you expect something in return, but because you felt it needed to be done. Here is a true story, by way of example.

A young woman was working as a lower-level assistant for a talent agency when her boss asked her to clear out the old scripts from a filing cabinet. While moving most of them from the cabinet to the trash, one title caught her attention, so she put it aside to read later. It turned out the script sparked her interest and she took it upon herself to call a friend who was an entry-level worker at a production company. She told him about the script and they agreed it was the type of thing his company was looking for. They spoke to their respective bosses, who set up the deal (much to the surprise of the writer, who had evidently given up hope on that script long ago), and it was ultimately made as one of the first original films produced by HBO.

What this shows is how Hollywood can operate. The woman at the agency had nothing to gain except the fun of getting the film started. She received no increase in pay or a finder's fee, but her boss started giving her more attention and respect, even asking for her input on other projects. As a result, she moved up the ladder until she was in a position to be courted as a development executive by another company.

Bootstrapping

In the film world, as in life, it's impossible to pull yourself up by your own bootstraps. Someone else, however, can grab those same bootstraps and lift you up, and the more people you have lifting, the easier and smoother your journey will be. Once you're up, you can then help lift them. Make professional deposits, gain interest, and when your account is full, help others do the same. This principle is one of the most common ways for people to move up the Hollywood employment ladder.

A great example of bootstrapping is the team of Sam Raimi, Robert Tapert, and actor Bruce Campbell. While in their twenties, this trio of friends decided to make a movie. All they really had to work with as sets were the woods behind their house, and a dungeon-like basement. Their first $1,000 (donated by one of their parents) was spent entirely on fake blood. Then they wrangled all their friends and family to be either monsters or victims, and they made what has become the cult horror classic *The Evil Dead*.

Today, the three of them have (together and separately) produced, directed, and/or appeared in some of the most successful films and television shows of the last three decades, including the *Spider-Man* films, *The Hudsucker Proxy, The Quick and the Dead, A Simple Plan, Darkman, Bubba Ho-tep*, and television series *Xena: Warrior Princess, Hercules: The Legendary Journeys*, and *The Adventures of Brisco County Jr.* Raimi, Tapert, and Campbell continue to work together, often hiring the same production crew members from project to project, and ensuring each other's continued success.

In 1968, when asked to direct a film version of the Broadway musical *Finian's Rainbow*, Francis Ford Coppola called upon his friend at the University of Southern California film school, George Lucas, to help with his production. A year later, Coppola and Lucas formed the independent film company American Zoetrope, and began producing each other's films.

As a new filmmaker, you need to remember that everyone was a newcomer at one time or another. Everyone needs some help moving into the film business, then moving up. As best you can, stay on good terms with your crew, and keep in touch with them, because one day you'll need them again, and they'll need you.

The Art of the Deal

Deals are made every day in every kind of business. You may be buying a house or negotiating a corporate takeover. Some deals are flexible and some are firm. In Hollywood, it's a little of both.

There are several things to keep in mind when deciding how to go about wheeling and dealing. In situations involving union agreements, there are very strict guidelines about minimum compensation. But these are only minimums. Most production personnel are *below-the-line*, meaning their payroll is included in a fixed budget, but stars, directors, producers, and writers are considered *above-the-line*, which means the sky's the limit (see Chapter 8).

Making deals is all about the art of compromise tempered by the never-ending quest for getting your money's worth. Basic rules of business protocol apply when discussing a deal, but rules are often bent. There's an industry adage: "In Hollywood there are no rules, and they are strictly enforced." So do your homework and get to know who you're dealing with and who they've dealt with before, and ascertain how they are going to deal with you.

All about Agents

Agent is a word that elicits a response from every filmmaking professional, whether production assistant, caterer, or director. As the primary representative of entertainment professionals, agents are everywhere. They're dealmakers and licensed professionals who, for a specified percentage, will work out details so you can concentrate on making your film.

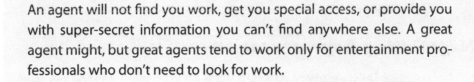

ALERT!

An agent will not find you work, get you special access, or provide you with super-secret information you can't find anywhere else. A great agent might, but great agents tend to work only for entertainment professionals who don't need to look for work.

One of the top five questions at any seminar on filmmaking is always "How do I get an agent?" The fact is that agents don't take just anyone, and it's virtually impossible to get an agent until you have a track record and, ideally, have someone willing to buy your work. This, of course, is a double-edged sword. How can you sell your work without an agent?

Until your film is done or you have a producer who wants to see it, you don't need an agent, but you *will* need an agent at some point. Agents are experts in knowing all the union guidelines and ways to get you more than the minimums. They know what isn't enough, and they know when to stop just short of too much. When you're busy making a film, contracts are the last thing you want to read, so it's best at that stage to have an agent do the paperwork.

So, How Do I Get an Agent?

If you have a successful showing at a film festival or contest, agents will be handing you their cards. If you don't have an agent, and you've cold-called a production company and the producer asks you to send over your reel or script, it's easier to get an agent's attention. You've done the hard part. All the agent has to do is send the film, and collect his percentage if a deal comes to fruition. Even if the agent is concerned about taking you on, he still might agree to represent you for this one deal in what is known as a *hip pocket* agreement.

If you live in Los Angeles or New York, the first place to start your agent search would be the phone book, under "Talent Agency." If you don't live in a city with a thriving film industry, you'd be better off looking for an agent who does. An agent in Los Angeles is more likely to understand the movie business and represent your interests even when you're not in town. Besides the phone book, both the Association of Talent Agents and the Writers Guild of America provide online lists of agents, along with their contact information.

Negotiating Representation

Before your agent can negotiate for you, you have to negotiate with him. An agent's fee is based on a percentage of whatever deal he can negotiate for you, but more importantly, you want an agent who'll understand your goals as a filmmaker. If you prefer to make smaller films that offer a larger measure of autonomy, the agent needs to be willing to pursue that goal. If your ultimate aim is to produce and direct huge blockbusters, your agent should be able to help plan a strategy to get you there.

If at all possible, you should shop for an agent like an athlete shops for a university. You want one who understands the talents and skills you bring to the table, and who will nurture those talents to their full potential. Large agencies like Creative Artists Agency (CAA), Shapiro-Lichtman, or William Morris wield tremendous power. Their stable of A-list talent allows them to package deals in such a way that any studio executive would be hard-pressed to them turn down. The downside to a large agency is that newcomers can get overlooked and shuffled around in favor of the agency's more profitable clients.

Even if a current deal doesn't happen, you want to maintain a positive relationship with an agent, producer, or studio. Inevitably, there will be other jobs in the future that you are well suited for, and a healthy communicative relationship will only help you in the long run.

The hunt for representation can be frustrating. Very rarely can you find an agent with a single phone call. If an agency is huge, your chances of getting through are even tougher. When first starting out, it might benefit you to consider a smaller *boutique* agency. With only a few agents and a smaller roster of clients, boutique agencies can be more focused on your films and your career.

Gun Shy or Gung Ho?

The metaphor of the talent agent as gunslinger is not entirely inaccurate, but you don't always want a mindless enforcer in your corner. Some negotiations take subtlety and finesse. Others require determination and the boldness to turn away from a fight if it means moving to a better position. Hollywood is a small company town and your agent must have the ability to negotiate and understand everything that happens in that town.

Polishing the Brass

While an agent takes a set percentage of the deals she brokers, a manager's fee is much more negotiable. It's usually higher than that of an agent, but a manager is more focused on you. While an agent is negotiating a single deal, a manager is looking five deals down the road. If you have both a manager and agent, communication between the two is paramount.

For example, your agent may have given your name to a producer who specializes in violent action films. That producer wants the fresh perspective of an unknown filmmaker looking to break into the business. Your manager, on the other hand, has been having conversations with a family-oriented cable channel about a series of television movies. The work is lower profile and less money per picture, but it would be two years of regular work plus guaranteed residuals. Not only can you not do both projects, but the separate producers would probably forbid it for publicity reasons.

The bottom line is that both your agent and manager need to be able to sit down with you, without their egos in the way, and work out what is best for your career and your sensibilities as a filmmaker. Getting into a situation where your representation is arguing among themselves will not only cause you extreme stress, it'll keep you from producing your films.

Entertainment Attorneys

When it comes to representation, entertainment attorneys are yet another option. Again, let's say you've called a producer and described your film, and he wants you to send it over. If you don't have an agent and don't think you'll have the time to find one, you should ask if he'd mind if you forwarded it through your lawyer instead. Using an attorney has one big advantage over an agent—you're paying her so she'll usually do what you say. If you ask her to send out a film reel or script she'll be happy to do it—for a fee. The benefit of this is that a producer will receive your film in an official envelope with official letterhead, which in turn gives him confidence in knowing he's dealing with a professional.

FACT

Every town has an attorney, or a hundred. For this first step, the attorney doesn't have to be familiar with entertainment law, film industry contracts, or movie jargon. In this scenario, a producer wants to be sure there is a paper trail to a third party so as to avoid misunderstandings down the road. Your lawyer is that third party.

If you have a friend who's a lawyer, you can often get them to submit your material for free. All that would be required is a polite cover letter, which you could type for them on their letterhead. There's no actual legal wrangling to be done, and many people just enjoy feeling like they helped you get your big break in the movies.

Chapter 6

The Players

In the entertainment industry, the players are many, and their levels of power vary. Studio executives, actors, directors, independent producers, agents, and screenwriters all have a part in getting movies made. A-list, or big name, talent can command a certain movie, screenplay, or salary, but only a select few filmmakers, actors, and directors have the power to green-light a movie just with their name. Ultimately, money is the deciding factor, and those who can consistently bring in the most money are those who wield the most power in Hollywood.

Knowing the Ropes

Before you even begin playing the Hollywood game, you need to familiarize yourself with its players and history. As a filmmaker, you're no doubt already a fan of motion pictures, but keep in mind that the agencies, production companies, networks, and studios you'll ultimately be pitching your film or script to know everything there is to know about the industry. Taking the time to study film, its participants, and all its current and historical aspects will only enhance your professionalism when it comes to creating, expanding, and ultimately selling yourself and your concept.

A movie *studio* is the physical place where a movie is filmed. Throughout Hollywood's Golden Era, however, the term "studio" also applied to production companies, because most of the production companies actually owned their own studios. From around 1925 to 1960, when the major studios were producing and distributing their own films, they had a "stable" of actors and directors under contract to them. They traded those actors and directors from studio to studio for particular films. Many even owned their own theaters throughout the United States in which they exclusively played their movies. Because of consistently good weather and natural sunlight, Southern California was the perfect place to make movies. These studios eventually settled there, and Hollywood was born.

The Studios

The five major studios in the Golden Era were Metro-Goldwyn-Mayer, Warner Bros., 20th Century Fox, RKO, and Paramount Pictures. They were known in the entertainment business as "The Big Five," or "The Studios." Their practices and management were known as the studio system, and they held most of the power in Hollywood. That is, until 1948, when a Supreme Court ruling against Paramount declared the studio system a monopoly, which was against the law. That decision effectively ended the Golden Era of Hollywood.

Metro-Goldwyn-Mayer

Formed in 1924 as a combination of Metro Pictures Corporation, Goldwyn Pictures Corporation, and Louis B. Mayer Pictures, MGM became the predominant and most distinguished of the movie studios. With a hugely talented roster of stars, including Clark Gable, Jimmy Stewart, Judy Garland, Fred Astaire, Ginger Rogers, Gene Kelly, and Greta Garbo, the studio produced glamorous and popular feature films that were profitable even during the Great Depression. These films included *Gone with the Wind*, *Singing in the Rain*, *The Wizard of Oz*, and *Top Hat*.

FACT

Leo the Lion, who roars at the beginning of all MGM films, has been portrayed over the years by five different lions. The original lion, Slats, was trained to growl rather than roar. He toured with MGM promoters for two years, and survived two serious accidents while on tour.

With television becoming more and more popular in the late 1950s, the studio began losing money. MGM was sold several times, and went through many changes over the next several decades. Purchased by Sony in 2004, the studio has returned to producing its own films, and a new era has begun for MGM and its mascot, Leo the Lion.

Warner Bros.

Founded in 1918 by four brothers, Harry, Jack, Albert, and Sam Warner, Warner Bros. studio began its rise to prominence with a series of movies starring a German shepherd named Rin Tin Tin. One of the Warner's biggest accomplishments was producing *The Jazz Singer* in 1927 starring Al Jolson. With that film, the era of "talkies" began, and motion pictures would never be the same.

In the early 1930s Warner Bros. produced many gangster movies starring such actors as James Cagney and Edward G. Robinson. Later it moved to dramas and adaptations of bestsellers, starring A-list actors Bette Davis, Joan Crawford, Humphrey Bogart, and Errol Flynn. It also purchased an animation studio in the mid-forties, and not long after, Bugs Bunny became a renowned Warner Bros. star. More recently, the studio has produced films for television, and cinematic blockbusters such as the *Harry Potter* films.

20th Century Fox

The studio came about as the result of a 1935 merger between Fox Film Corporation and Twentieth Century Pictures. With the merger, the studio signed Henry Fonda, Tyrone Power, Betty Grable, and then-seven-year-old Shirley Temple. Known for its musicals and other light entertainment, Fox became the third most profitable studio by the end of World War II.

By the 1960s, Fox was in trouble. A lavish and seriously over-budget *Cleopatra*, starring Elizabeth Taylor, coupled with the death of Marilyn Monroe, who was just beginning filming on *Something's Got to Give*, nearly shut down the studio. A series of cheap but popular movies brought Fox back from the brink, and it continues today with successful movies such as the *Star Wars* trilogies and *X-Men*.

RKO

Radio-Keith-Orpheum Pictures, known as RKO, was formed in 1928. One of the most important studios during the Golden Era, RKO introduced the world to films such as *King Kong*, *Little Women*, *Citizen Kane*, *Tarzan*, and *It's a Wonderful Life*. In 1948, a controlling interest in the studio was purchased by mogul and aviator Howard Hughes. As it turned out, Hughes' management style was not a good match for a motion picture studio, and the studio began to flounder. As a result, Hughes bought out all the other stockholders, and by 1954, RKO was the only studio with a single stockholder. A year after purchasing all of RKO's stock, Howard Hughes sold the company to General Tire and Rubber Company. By 1959, however, all of the remaining pictures had been released and the studio ceased production and distribution and was ultimately absorbed by Paramount Pictures.

Paramount Pictures

Paramount Pictures became the first successful feature film distribution company when it opened its doors in 1914. Thirteen years later, Paramount built its Hollywood studios, and today it is the only studio left in Hollywood proper that still occupies the same space it did in 1927. Douglas Fairbanks, Rudolph Valentino, Mary Pickford, and Gloria Swanson were just a few of Paramount's early movie stars. In 1928, the studio received the very first Best Picture Oscar for its film *Wings*, and has since produced more than 3,000 films. Among its classics are *White Christmas*, *The Ten Commandments*, *Dr. Jekyll and Mr. Hyde*, *Beau Geste*, *Psycho*, *The War of the Worlds*, *Rosemary's Baby*, and *Love Story*. More recent films include the *Star Trek* films, *Ghost*, *Forrest Gump*, *Braveheart*, and *The First Wives Club*.

Brave New World

During the Golden Era of Hollywood, there were several major studios, including Columbia Pictures Corporation and United Artists, that didn't follow all the rules of the studio system. While they were certainly part of the major studios of the time, Columbia, for example, didn't own any of its own theaters. United Artists eventually became more of a financier and distributor of movies, having no studio or contracted actors and directors. In fact, it was United Artists' style of production, fueled by the Supreme Court decision that affirmed studios as monopolies, that began moving Hollywood on the road to how films are made today.

Columbia Pictures Corporation

Columbia Pictures was created in 1924, and began by producing low-budget westerns and serials. Gradually, it began producing bigger budget films, and after hiring director Frank Capra in the late 1920s, the studio achieved major success. Rita Hayworth, Glenn Ford, William Holden, and Judy Holliday were among the many stars under contract to Columbia, whose films include *It Happened One Night*, *Lost Horizon*, *Mr. Smith Goes to Washington*, and *You Can't Take It with You*.

During the 1960s, Columbia went through a rough period, and by the 1970s the studio was nearly bankrupt. After being purchased by Coca-Cola Corporation in 1982, Columbia bounced back with a decade of films including *Ghostbusters*, *Tootsie*, *Gandhi*, *The Big Chill*, *Stand by Me*, and *The Last Emperor*. In 1989, Sony bought the studio and it was renamed Sony Pictures Entertainment.

United Artists

Known as "the company built by the stars," United Artists, or UA, was begun in 1919 by Charlie Chaplin, Douglas Fairbanks, Mary Pickford, and D. W. Griffith. The stars believed that by forming their own company they could better control their destinies, but they weren't prepared for the cost and time demands of producing and starring in their own films. By 1924, they brought in help, including Norma Talmadge, Buster Keaton, and several independent producers. Still the company floundered, and by the 1940s the studio was neither producing nor distributing films.

In 1952, two lawyers-turned-producers bought the studio rights from Pickford and Chaplin, and in doing so, created the first major studio without a studio. To keep costs down they hired independent producers and leased studio space. For their efforts, they soon produced two major hits, *The African Queen* and *Moulin Rouge*. While other studios declined projects, UA was on an uphill climb, producing the *James Bond* series, the *Pink Panther* series, and several spaghetti westerns directed by Sergio Leone and starring Clint Eastwood.

In the 1970s and 1980s, under the ownership of the Transamerica Corporation, UA produced the highly profitable *Rocky*, but also the legendary flop *Heaven's Gate*, which almost sunk the studio. Sold several more times throughout the 1990s and early 2000s, UA released a few films, but since its purchase by Sony in 2005, the studio has become a specialty line of MGM. No recent UA movies have been released.

Executive Power

As you might expect, the power of any given Hollywood executive is constantly in flux. One minute an individual may be riding high on the acclaim of last weekend's box office smash, the next minute he's scrambling for a table at IHOP. The key to power in the film industry is ultimately success, and as in most businesses, success is defined by money.

Studio Executives

At the top of the Hollywood power structure are the corporate billionaire moguls who run entire media empires. Rupert Murdoch founded News Corporation, which owns 20th Century Fox. Sumner Redstone controls Viacom, which owns CBS and Paramount. Simplifying things a bit, on the next rung down on the filmmaking corporate ladder are the top studio executives. These high-powered individuals have vast resources of production facilities, a global network of powerful relationships, marketing and distribution deals at their fingertips, and billions of dollars available to them. They can start or stop a major motion picture with a simple phone call.

FACT

A studio executive can typically make between $70,000 and $400,000 per year, and that doesn't include the bottomless expense account that is considered necessary for wooing and impressing the "right people."

Despite their power, studio executives are answerable to stockholders, and in that regard the pressure is enormous. Today's hit doesn't guarantee tomorrow's blockbuster, and this fact alone is a large part of the reason that names on executive office doors change quickly.

Earning Their Keep

Besides attending and often presiding over meetings regarding day-to-day projects, a large part of a studio executive's job requires her to attend screenings and premieres. While this may sound like an enviable task, imagine that you've just put in a fifteen-hour day, then have to put on a suit and uncomfortable shoes to go see a movie you either know by heart or don't care to see in the first place. Execs are expected to watch, or at least be conversant with, every film that is currently playing in theaters.

And an exec's job doesn't end there. When most folks arrive home on Friday nights they look forward to relaxing or spending time with their family. Studio executives, however, usually have to read reams of coverage and stacks of scripts that have to be reported on come Monday morning. Worse than high school, it's like having ten term papers due at the end of each weekend.

A-List Talent

When Mary Pickford, Douglas Fairbanks, Charlie Chaplin, and D. W. Griffith formed United Artists in 1919, it was a groundbreaking attempt to enable the "creative" people in the filmmaking process to have more control over the films themselves. When then-head of Metro Pictures, Richard A. Rowland, heard about the forming of UA, he said, "The inmates are taking over the asylum."

The perceived insanity of the formation of UA mattered little in the long run. The bold move marked the beginning of the end of the studio system, and set the stage for the current business model, where actors and directors have very powerful sway over their pictures.

A-List Directors

Steven Spielberg. His list of successes, both as a director and producer, has earned him a reputation that evokes respect from his peers, delight from audiences, and downright glee among investors. But few other directors can get a film started with such ease. Even highly successful names like Woody Allen, Oliver Stone, Spike Lee, or Lawrence Kasdan often have to have a major star in hand before getting the go-ahead.

A-list director (or writer/director) production companies include:

- Ed Zwick, The Bedford Falls Company
- Garry Marshall, Henderson Productions, Inc.

- Ivan Reitman, The Montecito Picture Company
- James Cameron, Lightstorm Entertainment
- Penny Marshall, Parkway Productions
- Peter and Bobby Farrelly, Conundrum Entertainment
- Robert Zemeckis, ImageMovers
- Spike Lee, Forty Acres and a Mule Filmworks, Inc.
- Steven Spielberg, DreamWorks SKG

A-list actor/director-driven production companies include:

- Ben Stiller, Red Hour Films
- George Clooney and Steven Soderbergh, Section Eight Productions
- Kevin Costner, Tig Productions, Inc.
- Rob Reiner, Castle Rock
- Ron Howard, Imagine

A-List Actors

Some say it's talent. Some say good looks. Some chalk it up to charisma. But the fact is, an actor who brings the most people into a theater is the one who also makes it easiest to get a movie made. For this reason, action stars are always at the top of the list. Not only does an action film translate better worldwide (compared to a romance or comedy), but it also reins in the target demographic of American males between the ages of eighteen and twenty-five.

FACT

When it comes to A-list actresses, Julia Roberts has long reigned as the only actress who could green-light a project. Groups of solid actresses seem to have more success, as is the case with *The Hours, Steel Magnolias,* and *The Divine Secrets of the Ya-Ya Sisterhood.*

An example of this is the film adaptation of the comic book *Judge Dredd*, which was originally optioned by producer Charles Lippincott with the intention of budgeting $10 to $15 million on the film—the largest amount his small company had ever spent at the time. They were having difficulty raising that much money until Sylvester Stallone agreed to play the title role. Not only did the production budget jump to $90 million almost overnight, but investors were suddenly fighting for the opportunity to give money to Lippincott and his company.

In 1994, Harrison Ford was presented with an award from the National Association of Theater Owners, naming him "Star of the Century." This was in recognition of what theater owners consider most important, namely appearing in the most films that brought in the most people. To date, Ford has generated enormous film revenue. All of his films in total have a domestic box office gross of over $3 billion, and over $5 billion worldwide.

Passion for Production

Following in the footsteps of the original "united artists," many actors have their own production companies. Usually they have a *first look deal* in place, which means a major studio covers them for things like office space, expenses, and staffing in exchange for first right of refusal to material they acquire for production. Often the projects are straight production deals, and don't necessarily involve the actor being in front of the camera.

A few A-list actors with production companies include:

- Charlize Theron, Denver and Delilah Films
- Drew Barrymore, Flower Films
- Hugh Jackman, Seed Productions
- Jennifer Love Hewitt, Love Spell Entertainment
- Julia Roberts, Red Om Films, Inc.
- Matt Damon and Ben Affleck, LivePlanet
- Mel Gibson, Icon Productions
- Morgan Freeman, Revelations Entertainment
- Pierce Brosnan, Irish DreamTime
- Reese Witherspoon, Type A Films
- Sandra Bullock, Fortis Films
- Tom Cruise, C/W Productions
- Tom Hanks, Playtone Company

By fully funding his 2004 film *The Passion of the Christ*, Mel Gibson and his company Icon Productions took all the risk, and reaped substantial rewards as a result of the film's enormous box office success. By the summer of 2006 the film had grossed over $370 million domestically and over $600 million worldwide. Although production companies are sometimes derided as "vanity" companies, given by studios to assuage an actor's ego, many actors have used these companies to their own advantage, often becoming genuine power players.

Power Agents

As you work your way down the power ladder, you'll find A-list agents. Unlike actors and directors, this level of Hollywood hierarchy is marked by companies more than individuals, but there are notable exceptions.

The top ten agencies are (in alphabetical order):

1. Agency for Performing Arts (APA)
2. Creative Artists Agency (CAA)
3. Endeavor Talent Agency
4. The Firm
5. Gersh Agency
6. Innovative Artists Talent & Literary Agency
7. International Creative Management (ICM)
8. Paradigm Talent & Literary Agency
9. United Talent Agency (UTA)
10. William Morris Agency (WMA)

In 1950, talent agent Lew Wasserman was representing actor Jimmy Stewart. In an unprecedented move, he negotiated Stewart a guaranteed percentage of the returns of his 1950 movies *Harvey* and *Winchester '73* in addition to his actor's regular fee.

Thirty years later, Michael Ovitz turned Creative Artist Agency (CAA) into Hollywood's thousand-pound gorilla by repeatedly securing *first-dollar gross deals* for many of CAA's clients. This meant the talent received a percentage of the total box office dollars, rather than a cut of *net profits*, which were often promised but never materialized due to unscrupulous accounting practices.

Independent A-List Producers

While some independent producers have found regular homes with major studios, most still remain free agents, shopping their projects to the highest bidder.

Independent A-list producers include:

- Dan Jinks and Bruce Cohen, The Jinks/Cohen Company
- Jerry Bruckheimer, Jerry Bruckheimer Films
- Michael Bay, Bay Films
- Kathleen Kennedy and Frank Marshall, Kennedy/Marshall Company
- Mike Medavoy, Phoenix Pictures
- Peter Guber, Mandalay Entertainment
- Richard Zanuck, The Zanuck Company
- Scott Rudin, Scott Rudin Productions

Some of these individuals worked their way up from production assistant or the mail room, others joined the film business with their M.B.A. freshly in hand, and a lucky few were born into Hollywood aristocracy. Whatever their background, all have proven themselves by repeated success at the box office.

A-List Screenwriters

In 1994, writer Frank Darabont told *Premiere* magazine: "If you're going to succeed, you've got to be like one of those punch-drunk fighters in the old Warner Brothers boxing pictures. Too stupid to fall down, you just keep slugging and stay on your feet." In their quest for more control over a film, several of those fighters have formed production companies in order to secure a larger amount of control over their scripts, as well as to produce projects written by others. These writers include:

- Frank Darabont (*The Shawshank Redemption, The Green Mile*), Darkwood Productions
- Scott Frank (*Minority Report, Flight of the Phoenix*), Arroyo Films
- Paul Haggis (*Crash, Casino Royale*), Blackfriars Bridge
- Ted Elliott and Terry Rossio (*Pirates of the Caribbean* trilogy, *Shrek*), Scheherazade Productions
- Ed Solomon (*Men in Black, Levity*), Infinite Monkeys

Unlike his cousin the playwright, a screenwriter has very little direct power in the Hollywood scheme of things. Even highly successful writers such as William Goldman (*The Princess Bride, Misery*), Shane Black (*Lethal Weapon, The Long Kiss Goodnight*), and Robert Towne (*The Firm, Mission Impossible*), whose fees can cross into the millions for a simple script revision, don't have the clout to get a film started on their name alone.

Chapter 7

Money Talks

When it comes to filmmaking, all the creative genius in the world is useless without funding. Even if you can assemble a crew and cast with enough faith in your film to work for free, there are fixed production costs that must be addressed long before you start shooting. Even low-budget feature films require a significant amount of money to make, and whether it's a major studio, network, private investor, or your mother—somebody has to pay the bills.

Law and Order

Understanding how films are made is crucial to the creative process, but knowledge of how funding and budgets work is crucial to getting those movies made. For aspiring filmmakers, one of the key factors in attracting potential investors is creating trust and confidence. The best way to do that is by having and displaying a firm grasp of financial issues, including the legal aspects. Whether you're making your film with the financial aid of your next of kin and a few close friends, or you've drummed up the support of a major corporation and a few wealthy entrepreneurs, you'll need legal counsel to be certain that your interests are protected.

Laws vary significantly from state to state, so you want to be certain that you're staying within the legal boundaries of your location before you approach potential financiers. Many attorneys specialize in entertainment law, and can easily establish your legal obligations. Professional advice will also be crucial to forming the business of your production once you've obtained financing.

Pitching Your Product

Filmmakers in general are driven by passionately creative personalities. To succeed in moviemaking, that artistic mindset requires a balance of financial savvy and a strong element of salesmanship. Establishing a solid grasp of financial issues and money-handling skills can go a long way toward putting together a credible business package that will lay the groundwork for getting your film production under way. Like any trained and eager salesperson, you need to practice selling yourself and your film. Developing a good pitch takes almost as much work as developing a good script, and may require just as many rewrites.

The Pitch in Perspective

The term *pitch* is an abbreviation of *sales pitch*. This may be an obvious statement, but be warned—it's easy to become disconnected from the sales aspect. We've all been subjected to sales pitches, at car lots and electronics superstores and furniture showrooms. At some point or another, we've all had someone try to sell us something that we may not really need, or even want.

ALERT!

Practicing a pitch on potential investors can be disastrous, and because most people are either too polite or, more likely, too busy to tell you exactly what you're doing wrong, you may never have the slightest idea why you're not making any headway.

Salespeople who are pushy, needy, misinformed, badly dressed, overeager, or just plain annoying have probably had a pretty hard time selling you anything. Prospective buyers enduring a bad pitch simply turn off, make polite excuses, and move on. Bear this in mind when you work on pitching your film, and you'll avoid making the same mistakes.

Polishing Your Pitch

Selling a film production concept is really no different than selling any premium product, whether it's a fine European motorcar or a vacation home on the coast. Pitching a high-end product requires a high-end sales attitude. Coming across with a pitch that sounds even remotely misinformed or careless will completely kill your chances of attracting serious business partners or investors.

The best thing you can do is find a trusted advisor to help you fine-tune your pitch. You'll want someone who is interested in you and your film, objective enough to ask probing questions, and able to offer intelligent criticism to help sand down the rough edges and polish your pitching skills. With careful practice and thoughtful revisions, you won't waste those golden opportunities when you're actually pitching your film to potential investors or partners.

Developing a Business Plan and Packaging the Pitch

When you get into the hunt for prospective investors, you'll need a complete production package that describes your film production in detail. This package is essentially a written business plan that will include everything you'll need to make a comprehensive presentation.

Prior to meeting with potential investors, you'll want to prepare a production package for each individual. Every package should consist of several basic elements, each of which serves a specific purpose. In general, a production package is bound and includes a cover letter, script synopsis, budget breakdown, and resumes and background information, along with a film reel.

Sometimes the business plan is referred to as a *prospectus*, but be wary of using that term. Laws vary from state to state, and calling a business plan or presentation a prospectus can have very specific legal ramifications. Discuss your plan with a legal advisor before referring to it as a prospectus.

QUESTION?

How should I bind my package presentation?
Clear plastic report covers work well for binding production packages because they're professional, lay flat, and best of all, they're relatively inexpensive. With clear plastic covers, your title page will show through, giving your package professional flair.

As with any important business endeavor, make sure you've got all the information you need before making any presentations, and be sure to proofread every single word. Little mistakes can damage your credibility, so check every aspect and then double-check it. Be especially careful with your cover letter, as that's the first thing potential investors will read. The cover letter should be written directly to the recipient of your package. If you do enough homework about your potential investors, you can tailor the cover letter specifically to their investment expectations.

Script Synopsis

The heart of the production package is the *script synopsis*. The standard synopsis is usually less than one page and conveys the basic idea of the story so that virtually anyone can understand it. It's essential that the synopsis accurately describes your concept so that investors can easily discuss the idea with other interested parties. Your synopsis should be carefully critiqued by trusted advisors before you present your package to potential investors.

Whatever you do, don't include the entire script in your production package. Instead make a notation that the working script is available upon request. Although the script is an obvious necessity for making a film, it's too cumbersome and distracting for a smooth production pitch. Potential investors may not understand the intent and layout of a working script, and inexperienced script readers may find the format confusing. In the early stages of investigating a film production, experienced investors may not want to read the script at all. The synopsis should tell them everything they need to know about your story.

By this stage, you've taken the necessary steps to protect your script by copyrighting or Guild registration, but don't insult potential investors by making an issue out of this during your pitch. If your idea is brilliant enough to steal, potential investors will certainly assume that you're smart enough to protect yourself.

Budget or Bust

Your ability to knowledgeably discuss finances and budgeting will make or break your sales pitch. Once potential investors become intrigued with the script synopsis and concept of your production, they're going to scrutinize your budget. In your package you need to include a budget *top sheet*. This is an estimate of the final budget and should accurately represent what your budget will be.

Creating an accurate budget top sheet is where careful planning, experience, and education come into play. You can't pretend that you can make a $50,000 movie with a budget of $25,000. You want your investors to trust that you can film your production according to your budget. If you can't do that—or, worse, if you don't even know that you can't do it—be prepared to suffer some serious professional repercussions.

To the uninitiated, a budget schedule can look like a laundry list of film-related terminology stacked against rows of arbitrary figures. In reality, the budget is a financial blueprint of your film that details every projected expenditure for each department of the production. The specifics of budgeting are discussed throughout this chapter.

ESSENTIAL

Understanding every aspect of your budget is essential to your search for financing. Potential investors understand the language of money, and you'll need to become fluent in financial discussions if you're going to secure funding.

Experience counts for a lot in developing a detailed budget, so it can be helpful to seek out the advice of a production manager. Your budget should represent an accurate projection of production expenses. As with most creative endeavors, it's always a good idea to estimate for a higher budget than you may need. Estimating too low will raise serious concerns with your investors.

Resumes and Background

Your production package should include the resumes and backgrounds of all the major players you have involved in your production to date. Effective resumes should read just like your film synopsis—short, to the point, and no more than one page each. Make sure each resume contains only professional and significant scholastic information. No one cares if you were the captain of your basketball team or how many merit badges your cinematographer accumulated when he was a Boy Scout. Investors need to understand why every person on your team is qualified to make your film.

Reel Samples

Given that you're seeking financing for a film, there's one additional element you can include in your production package, and that's a sample *film reel*. This sample is usually in the form of a videocassette or DVD, and can be submitted if it's relevant to the project (it should showcase your best samples or short films). If, for example, the project you're pitching is a comedy and you have samples of a slapstick comedy you've filmed, you can submit that. You wouldn't want to include that reel if you're pitching a horror film.

The Impact of Image Packages

A professional necessity for establishing and maintaining your production credibility is your image package. Sometimes also referred to as an identity package, this is the basic stock-in-trade of any aspiring business and includes letterheads, business cards, and envelopes. Don't make the mistake of overlooking the impact of a good image package. The style and quality of your business cards and letterheads will showcase your production and professionalism, so don't skimp on these vital items.

Going in Style

Advertising and marketing agencies are staffed with graphic artists who will customize designs that enhance any professional business image. If you need to convey a very classy and highly professional appearance, hiring an agency can be worth the cost. Image-conscious investors can respond favorably to the presentation and feel of first-class letterheads and business cards.

Bear in mind that if you're seeking a significant portion of your financing from more frugal investors, including friends and relatives, a high-end image package may be seen as an unnecessary extravagance.

If you take this high road, however, you'll need to weigh the pros and cons very carefully. The price of professional design and printing is a substantial investment, often costing thousands of dollars that might be better spent on other aspects of your production. Those costs may be outweighed by the potential of attracting the financial support of well-heeled investors.

Cost-Effective Image Packages

It's entirely possible to produce a professional-looking image package without killing your business budget. For instance, if you've got a computer and printer and you're handy with graphics programs (and a pair of scissors), you can design and print your own materials.

The drawbacks to this approach are that doing it yourself can be time-consuming, and you still have to buy letterhead stock, card stock, and envelopes. The serious downside to designing and printing your own material is that you'll need significant graphics experience to produce professional-looking work. So be cautious with the do-it-yourself approach. If you're determined to do it anyway, at least give yourself an edge by investing in top-quality watermarked paper and matching card stock.

Bartering Your Image

Hiring a high-profile design agency to create your image package can be pricey, but with a little footwork you can find talented graphic artists who'll jump at the opportunity to work with you. Creative people tend to run in the same circles. As a filmmaker, chances are you're only a few queries away from hooking up with a freelance designer, graphic arts student, or art aficionado who designs as a sideline.

QUESTION?

What could I offer a designer in exchange for help?
This is one of those golden circumstances where offering to trade screen acknowledgments for a few hours of design work can be beneficial to you and the designer. As an additional enticement, you can even offer to give them a mention in your production package.

Graphic artists can help you upload designs to an Internet printing facility, or load designs onto a CD that you can take to your local print shop. If your graphic designer is also a Web site designer, she'll be happy to work out a combination deal for image package and Web design.

Online Commerce

An increasingly popular way to save money on a quality image package is to order materials on the Internet. E-commerce companies such as Vistaprint.com offer low pricing and a wide range of four color design options on business cards and letterheads. You can also order preprinted return address stickers at the same time for use on any size envelope. For under a few hundred dollars, you can set yourself up with a supply of professionally printed stationery and business cards that will help you create an effective and credible image.

Ways to Make Your Pitch

You have a few options when it comes to choosing how to make your pitch. Developing a Web site for your production can instantly put your production package into the hands of anyone with an Internet connection. As with your image package, you don't have to spend a fortune creating an attractive, easy-to-navigate Web site. But avoid using the one-layout-fits-all pages that are available on free blog sites. Freebies are fine, but a cheap, generic appearance isn't conducive to projecting a professional image.

Many Internet service providers such as EarthLink offer Web space with their member packages and include templates for customizing a Web site. You can upload graphics, arrange the site layout, and add links that will quickly take users to pages on the site. A simple, well-designed Web site is an excellent way to promote yourself and your project. By keeping the site simple, uncluttered, and easy to read, you'll keep your potential investors or producers focused on what you have to say about the project you're pitching.

A poorly designed and difficult to navigate Web site can be disastrous to your professional image. Using harsh colors or reversed type set onto dark backgrounds is a visual turnoff, as are overly complicated graphics that load slowly. Always test your site on several different browsers to make sure it loads well on each and is easy on the eyes.

Remember that a Web site is an accompaniment. Don't rely too heavily on the site to pitch your production. For one thing, you'll have no idea who is viewing your site or for how long. Invisible counters can show the number of hits your Web site is receiving and can give you a rough idea of the traffic you're receiving, but they won't tell you if the viewer has logged onto your site for ten minutes or ten seconds. Counters also won't tell you if your site is being perused by a potential investor or a casual Internet surfer.

The Hands-On Approach

Nothing beats working with potential investors face to face. If you direct a financier to your Web site to gather information about your production, you can put yourself and that individual in an awkward position. Will he call you if he likes what he sees? What if you don't hear from him? Will you call him in a few days to ask if he's had a chance to peruse your site? If he hasn't, what do you say next? If at all possible, you're much better off trying to arrange a meeting in person. If a meeting isn't possible or practical, send a copy of your production package so that you'll have a solid reason to make a follow-up call.

Word of Mouth

One tried-and-true method of networking is word of mouth, and when you're searching for financing this is especially helpful. For starters, make sure that everyone you know (including your mother) is aware that you've got a brilliant new film in the works and you're actively looking for financing.

There are a number of ways you can work your project into conversations without sounding needy or pushy, but one sure-fire way to turn people off is to carry on about yourself. Use sound judgment and instinct when promoting your project, and you'll never bend anyone's ear.

A proper approach to this is to speak in glowing terms about everyone else who is involved in the project with you. For example, mentioning your cinematographer's latest artistic accomplishments makes you artistic by association. Discussing the screenplay you've optioned for your production that was penned by a bright new writer suggests that you're bright enough to have optioned it. The trick is not to get carried away. If you insist that your brilliant new screenplay was written specifically with Tom Cruise and Salma Hayek in mind, you'll blow your credibility to pieces.

The Money Chase

In this section, you'll read about some of the obvious and subtle approaches to raising capital. There are no guarantees that all of these suggestions will be successful, but they will encourage you to begin thinking outside the money box. The most obvious potential investors to approach for your film production are in your immediate circle, including family members, friends, and acquaintances who are interested in your ambitions and may be willing to invest with you. If you're concerned that the folks close to you are going to feel exploited, you'll need to work on your diplomatic skills and your own self-perception. As long as you believe in yourself and that your film has artistic and, hopefully, financial value, you can effectively convey your ambitions without creating any awkward situations in your personal relationships. Always be honest, realistic, and forthcoming about every aspect of your production.

Working the Circuit

As a potential filmmaker, you would be wise to mingle in circles that are focused on filmmaking—or circles that attract people with money who are interested in investing—so you can effectively spread the word about your project to prospective investors. The more people you talk to, the better your chances are of making the right connections. Don't think of this as just a game, think of it as a percentage game. For example, let's say that five out of every hundred people who know about your production may be interested in pursuing it as an investment opportunity. From there, you can extrapolate those numbers into infinity. For every two hundred people who know about you, you'll get ten interested people; for every three hundred, you'll get fifteen, and so on. You have to play these percentages when you spread the word about your film production. The more people who know about it, the more likely it is that you'll get responses from truly interested investors.

ALERT!

One example of playing percentages is the ridiculous spam e-mail that clutters your inbox. Why do they keep coming? Because the people who send them know that a percentage of those e-mails will elicit responses. Under no circumstances, however, should you spam anyone when searching for investors.

The Frustration Factor

It can be easy to become frustrated when you're searching for investors. In fact, it's likely that you *will* become frustrated from time to time. The more you accept the reality of the frustration factor, the simpler it'll be for you to move ahead and keep working at finding financing. If you get discouraged, give yourself pep talks. Keep reminding yourself that every movie you've ever seen was made with financing. Better yet, make a list of the really bad movies you've seen, and keep reminding yourself that every single one of them had financial backing. You plan on making a film that's a hundred times better than the worst films on your list, so if other people can find the money to make all those crummy movies, you can certainly figure out how to find financing for yours.

Making Yourself Available

Sharing your talents, abilities, and enthusiasm with other filmmakers is always good business. If someone in a bind needs a fill-in boom operator for a couple of days, offer to pitch in and pick up the pole. If you can make yourself known as a reliable go-to person for helping to fix disasters or solve technical problems on other productions, you'll build a solid reputation for reliability and become the type of filmmaker whom other filmmakers will happily support—this can work to your advantage when it comes time to raise funds.

Rubbing Elbows

Attending screenings and film festivals can put you near people who have the influence and financial pull to get your film off the ground. Try to attend every party you're invited to, make plenty of friends, and strike up acquaintances everywhere you go. The more exposure you get in those environments, the more exposure your project will receive. If you've got free time on your weekends, make a point of visiting high-profile night spots. Don't waste your time in dives or local bars unless you know for certain that potential investors are also hanging out in them. Learn to nurse drinks for hours, and often switch to bottled water or club soda. Relaxed investors can be chatty and amiable.

Health Clubbing

High-end health clubs have member rosters loaded with well-heeled potential investors, so start visiting a club when you've got a few spare hours. If you express some interest in joining, more often than not you'll be offered a complimentary pass for the day. Spend some time around the weight machines and strike up conversations. If you're a handball or racquetball player, challenge a member to a game or two. You'll sometimes even be invited back as a guest, which will give you another chance at making new acquaintances. And don't forget those business cards!

If tennis or golf is more your style, even fairly upscale clubs will have no problem with you hanging out in the lounge or restaurant as long you dress the part. Some clubs, however, won't be so accommodating to nonmembers, so be prepared to search for clubs that'll allow you to mingle without joining. A low-key, very soft sell is the best attitude to take when approaching people in these environments so whatever you do, don't make a nuisance of yourself.

Playing the Ponies

Is there a horse track nearby where you live? If so, spend a couple of bucks to get in and cruise the stables. You're not looking for bettors or gambling addicts—you want to meet the horse *owners*. There are businesspeople with money to burn playing around with buying and training race horses, and those are the folks you want to get acquainted with. Horse racing is an expensive hobby, and racing horses is inherently high risk. These elements give race horse owners the attributes you're seeking in an investor.

You can be chatty and amiable when networking, but remember that you're there on business. Make sure you're thinking clearly and on top of your game. Always bring plenty of business cards and hand them out at every opportunity.

Polo fields are also magnets for type-A risk-takers with expendable incomes. Most people who regularly play polo have the funds to support strings of ponies. By surfing the Internet, you can learn enough about the game to carry on a reasonably intelligent conversation, so check out the polo barns in your area and make a few friends.

Riding academies and dressage barns are also playgrounds for folks with expensive hobbies. Check in with a few of them and get schedules of horse shows and jumping and dressage competitions. Doing some more Internet homework to become reasonably knowledgeable about these sports will help you start conversations. Horse people are passionate when it comes to talking about their horses, and they love an interested listener. Mention that you have a horse-oriented scene or two in your film that might be perfect for their beloved $30,000 Dutch Warmblood show horse, and you'll be talking films and horses all day long.

Biker Bucks

Another group of well-heeled riding enthusiasts are Harley-Davidson fans. The days of the Harley as strictly a bad boy bike are going away quickly. Most Harley riders today are saddled up on a motorcycle that can cost as much as a luxury automobile. It's a thrill and status symbol for many of these bikers, who tend to associate with other Harley riders. Show up on a Yamaha or a Honda, they'll treat you like you've got leprosy. If you have a Harley, or access to one, you'll be golden to this group. If you hook up with one of Harley-Davidson's sponsored Hog Riders clubs, you'll be hanging out with businesspeople, doctors, lawyers, builders, chiropractors, and entrepreneurs who have something in common—they're well-to-do and they enjoy a little risk. It can be the perfect hunting ground for potential investors.

The Sky's the Limit

With ingenuity and a lot of footwork, you can expose yourself to potential investors in an unlimited number of ways. If you get discouraged easily and find that tracking down financing is too daunting a task, then producing your own films probably isn't your best career choice. It takes time, determination, and unwavering faith in yourself. If you're willing to work hard and make sacrifices, however, there's no good reason you can't make your production happen.

The Myth of Credit Card Financing

Stories abound in filmmaking lore about independent moviemakers producing films—that ultimately made huge profits—by financing the project entirely with guts, determination, and credit cards. The concept sounds pretty simple. You apply for a credit card, and a few weeks after it's approved, your mailbox is overflowing with credit card offers from every banking institution on the planet. You apply for a dozen more cards, including a few for your dog, and when you add up all the credit limits, you find that you've been miraculously approved for $50,000 dollars worth of credit. Plenty to finance a low-budget film, eh?

Don't Quit Your Day Job

Unless you have a steady job that provides enough expendable income to make regular credit card payments, you can be in deep financial trouble within the first few months of racking up charges. Card companies expect minimum payments every month, and those payments can get out of hand in a hurry.

Don't be lulled into complacency by low introductory interest rates, either. Miss a payment deadline by a single day, those low rates are out the window and penalties start to mount. No matter how tempting it may be, credit cards are a dangerous way to finance your film.

Your Production Package as a Business

Once you've got solid financial interest in your production package, you'll need to collaborate with your financiers to create a business entity for your production. You may want to form a partnership, a limited partnership, a limited liability company, or a corporation. These decisions will largely be driven by your investors' wishes. While your investors are obviously willing to take a financial risk with you, very few will be interested in acquiring legal liability in the process.

ALERT!

It is imperative that you seek legal advice before committing to any decisions about what type of business entity to form. Professional counsel should be considered a sound business investment for protecting you and your film production.

There are many ways to go about forming business entities. All businesses have specific taxation, liability, and legal responsibilities and ramifications. Discussing these issues with legal counsel saves misunderstandings, miscalculations, and countless headaches during the course of film production.

Partnerships

In a general partnership, two people agree to do business together with equal decision-making authority and equal financial and tax liability. In a limited partnership, one partner is responsible for making decisions, and is also responsible for legal and tax liabilities. The limited partner is generally risking only his financial investment in the business.

Corporations

A corporation is recognized as a distinctly separate business entity from any of the individuals involved in the business. Tax and legal liabilities are the direct responsibility of the business. Corporations are strictly regulated and, depending on your location, can be expensive to create.

Limited Liability Companies

Limited liability companies (LLCs) are generally easier to set up than corporations, while providing many of the same personal tax and legal liability protections. With an LLC, you have a number of options available for directing funds. Many fledgling film production companies are set up as limited liability companies. A good place to start is on the Internet where there are numerous Web sites designed to help you set up a small business. For specific situations, it may be necessary to consult an attorney.

Chapter 8

Scheduling and Budgeting

Scheduling and budgeting a production go hand in hand, with one element always having an impact on the other. By breaking down your script and shooting schedule, you'll be able to determine the financial resources required to shoot each scene. If funding for those scenes isn't available, you'll need to prioritize and adjust each scene to make the shooting schedule fit your budget. Some scenes may require scaling down; some may need to be eliminated. Either way, adjusting scenes saves cash that can be used to emphasize the important scenes of your film.

Breaking Down the Script

Occasionally, production managers are hired during preproduction for the sole purpose of scheduling and budgeting. For producers and directors who have limited familiarity with the details of budgeting and scheduling, this can be a wise course of action. Thorough scheduling is essential to an efficient film production, and breaking the script down into practical production requirements is your first priority.

Breaking down a script means separating it into its component elements such as casting, sets, schedules, and so on. This involves several steps, and is essential to organizing all of your script's elements into a logical production order. A screenplay is broken down by formatting the script, lining it, and then creating *breakdown sheets*. These sheets are used to create *production strip boards* that can be arranged and rearranged to create a shooting schedule. These practices are generally recognized in the film industry as the most efficient process for simplifying and visualizing the production order of a shooting schedule.

Script Formatting

In order to properly break down a script, it's important that the script be written in *standard screenplay format*. This is an industry-wide format that experienced professionals universally recognize and understand and that results in approximately one minute of screen time per page. The screenplay format is set in double-spaced twelve-point Courier typeface with margins set at one and one-half inches on the left and right. Although each script page may amount to more or less screen time depending on the dialogue and action, the average of the total pages should be close to one minute apiece.

ALERT!

When lining the script, be cautious about using colored highlighters directly over the text. Yellow highlighting often fades over time, and darker highlight colors can make the copy difficult to read and impossible to legibly fax or photocopy. Underlining text will eliminate the problem.

Lining the Script

Lining the script is the process of color-coding essential elements of the screenplay using colored pencils, felt pens, crayons, or highlighters. The same color should consistently represent a single category of the screenplay. These categories can include the following:

- Sets/locations
- Cast
- Extras
- Wardrobe
- Makeup and hair
- Special effects
- Stunts
- Props
- Vehicles
- Animals
- Sound effects
- Special equipment

Breakdown Sheets

Breakdown sheets are individual pages that have a header space for filling in the scene number, script page, set or location, whether it is a daytime or nighttime shoot, whether it is an exterior or interior shot, and a scene synopsis for every scene of your film. These sheets provide all of the necessary production requirements for every scene.

Breakdown sheets contain all of the production elements shown in separately drawn boxes. The color-coded text in the lined script provides a quick visual reference for entering the necessary information into each box.

Production Strip Boards

Traditionally, the production strip board is an oversized panel that uses vertical slots for holding individual strips of production information taken from corresponding breakdown sheets. These strips essentially become a jigsaw puzzle of production data that can be arranged into practical production sequences. Each of the production strips should contain the following information:

- Scene number
- Scene name
- Breakdown sheet number
- Location
- Day/night
- Interior/exterior
- Characters
- Extras
- Vehicles
- Special equipment
- Production notes

By grouping elements such as locations, required cast, or day or night shooting, the strip board creates a simplified visual blueprint of the production requirements of each scene. This is an essential tool for producing an efficient shooting schedule. By their very nature, strip boards are designed to be flexible and easily rearranged, and are usually adjusted on a daily basis to accommodate the inevitable ups and downs of production.

Breaking Down the Shooting Schedule

The key to scheduling is reducing each scene in the script down to its essential production requirements. Every scene that has a specific location should be shot while the cast, crew, and equipment are assembled at that location. It doesn't matter if you're at the bottom of the Grand Canyon or the highest level of a parking garage at the local library. Creating strip boards is essential to determine the number of scenes in the script, where they will be shot, and how long it should take to shoot them.

FACT

When it comes to creating the daily shooting schedule, what matters most isn't the page count, it's the camera setups. Most of your crew's production time will be spent moving cameras and lighting equipment.

The art of scheduling is staying several steps ahead of potential problems, and accurately estimating the number of shoot days. As a filmmaker, you should be able to estimate the number of shoot days that your production requires. For executives, cast, and crew members who have signed on at a predetermined fee for the length of the production, the specific number of days may not be a major concern. But for every cast and crew member who is hired on an hourly or daily basis, shoot days are critical to determining your budget. The cost of equipment rentals, such as cameras, lighting gear, and special props, will also dictate the number of days you can afford to film. When it comes to shoot days, the fewer days it takes to wrap up the shooting schedule, the more money you'll have to spread over your entire production.

Creating the Budget

The estimated number of days in a shooting schedule and all of the individuals and equipment that will be needed for those days provides much of the information needed for creating a film's budget. The rest of the information involves compiling the requirements of every other aspect of the production, including preproduction, production, and postproduction costs.

Budget Top Sheet

The *budget top sheet* is a summary of all the detailed budget categories, and as the title implies, is the first (or top) sheet of a production budget. The top sheet provides a quick reference to the budget and serves as an overview of the total production costs. Budget top sheets also show potential investors the financial requirements of a production.

In your budget information, every single item that has a price needs to be itemized and accounted for. All of this information is crucial if you hope to stay on track throughout the course of filming.

Above-the-Line Costs

Top sheets have two primary divisions, *above-the-line costs* and *below-the-line costs*. Above-the-line costs are usually flat fees that are negotiated before production begins and won't alter during the course of the production. These can include the cost of the script (with all of the necessary rights to the script) and the salaries of the producer, director, and entire cast.

Below-the-Line Costs

Below-the-line costs cover virtually every other item a production will require. Crew costs, set production and decorating, equipment rentals, location fees, props, office space, and telephone and fax lines are examples of below-the-line costs.

Despite the inherently tedious nature of budgeting, understanding every aspect of your budget is the only way to ensure that finances for the production are going to be spent in the most appropriate and effective manner. Major studios devote entire departments to budgeting, and many unit production managers have made successful careers out of preparing efficient budgets for independent productions.

When your budget is carefully itemized, the total amount will tell you if the production can be made with the funds you have available. If the budget is equal to or less than those funds, the schedule can be tightened and production can go into high gear.

If available funds are less than the budget calls for, it's time to make crucial production decisions. There are only two basic choices in this case: Find more money for the production or adjust the screenplay so that costs are lowered to match available funding.

Budget and Script Synchronization

In budgeting and scheduling situations where the production requirements outweigh the budget, more often than not the screenplay will need adjusting. This is where a director will take a lead role in conforming the screenplay to the budget, given that it's ultimately his responsibility for telling the story with the means available. Lowering costs in the preproduction stage doesn't have to mean lowering expectations or quality. Many of the best crowning moments in cinematic history take place in the simplest settings, or even completely out of camera view.

For example, in the final payoff scene in Mel Gibson's 1979 film *Mad Max*, Gibson's character has handcuffed the last remaining villain to the undercarriage of gasoline-leaking wreckage. Leaving the villain with a hacksaw and a burning container of fuel that threatens to ignite the wreckage within moments, Gibson drives away. What the audience sees is simply the fireball of an explosion in the background, rather than the wreckage itself exploding. Lowering production costs often requires tapping new levels of creativity that can result in scenes being shot not only cheaply, but cleverly.

Shrinking Locations

The first step toward cutting production costs is to reduce the number of shooting locations. Fitting as many scenes as possible into the fewest number of locations is an incredible time saver, even if it requires rewriting dialogue. As long as the story is being effectively told, your audience will never notice, and certainly won't care. The number of locations in Quentin Tarantino's *Reservoir Dogs* can be counted on one hand. One location—an empty warehouse—suffices for over half the screen time of the film.

By limiting his location shooting, Tarantino was able to stretch the film's relatively lean production budget of $1.2 million. Because the warehouse was integral to the storyline, the fact that the location remained consistent wasn't irritating to the audience. They didn't expect the characters to show up in all sorts of locations.

Minimizing Camera Setups

Rethinking every scene and compiling as many shots as possible into each camera setup is effective for the big screen and cost-effective for your budget. Even a complicated fight scene between two characters can be shot with two cameras and just three setups for each camera. By switching lenses between the cameras, and shooting two takes for each setup, your film editor will have twelve different angles of the fight sequence to work with.

Reducing Players

Cutting cast members may be painful, but the savings can be significant. Make sure that every character in your film is absolutely essential to the story, and be prepared to eliminate any who don't serve a specific purpose. For example, a surly waitress in a restaurant scene can be replaced with a voice-over, using only over-the-shoulder hand-held camera shots of menus, food, and dollar bills being tossed onto a table.

Here's another typical situation. Say, for example, you're shooting an office scene in which your actors are singing a royalty-free "For He's a Jolly Good Fellow." You have extras playing coworkers. If there are fewer than five extras, they must be paid the higher rate for having "lines." Five or more is considered a crowd, and with no individual lines they're paid a regular rate as extras, which is significantly less. These are the types of budgetary situations that you need to be acutely aware of during all phases of filming.

Budget Realities

In the film industry, one of the surest ways to kill a career for producers, directors, and unit managers is to consistently overlook the budget or lose track of where money is being spent. There's a general misconception that most studio productions just naturally go *over* budget. In reality, budgets for studio projects are closely monitored by producers whose primary function is to keep a production financially on track. Those producers answer to studio executives who rely on their oversight, and they'll most assuredly take down an undisciplined director before risking their own career.

ALERT!

When a director insists on spectacularly destroying a dozen new cars in a chase sequence instead of the two jalopies that were designated in the original screenplay, you can be certain that studio executives are going to verify that the extra cost will be more than covered by box office receipts before any approvals are given.

It's also a reality that directors, unit managers, and anyone else who has some say in where money is spent do lose their jobs as a result of blown budgets. Virtually every decision made in regard to going over budget is made with the knowledge that the added expense will pay for itself in increased audience appeal.

Many below-the-line costs are negotiable, and shopping around for the best deals possible is one of the smartest approaches to keeping those costs in line. Among the very best deals for aspiring filmmakers are items that can be borrowed. With a lot of footwork and sincerity, camera equipment, locations, props, laboratory time, and even vehicles can be begged for and borrowed.

Feeding the Troops

Virtually all successful low-budget filmmakers place a high priority on one consistent budget item—food. Whether the cast and crew are being paid union scale, nonunion wages, or absolutely nothing in exchange for experience and bragging rights, everyone will work better, harder, and happier if they're well fed. Major studios spend fortunes on first-class catering for all of their productions, and they do it because it's one of the most cost-effective methods for maintaining a buoyant atmosphere on-set. When it comes time to trim the budget, this is absolutely the last place you'll want to cut costs.

Contingencies

One of the basic factors in your budget that should not be overlooked are funds set aside for *contingencies*. Contingencies are unexpected cost overages that are usually unavoidable during the course of filming. Even the most carefully planned production schedules are subject to changes as a result of bad weather, equipment problems, labor issues, illnesses, and accidents that can add days to your shooting schedule. Ten to fifteen percent of your total budget is a common contingency cost item.

Production Insurance

Another often overlooked line item in an accurate budget is the cost of production insurance. Because filmmaking is generally considered to be a high-risk venture, insurance is not only a sensible business investment, it's mandatory for obtaining most permits and equipment leases.

Productions that are financed through financial institutions will invariably be required to carry insurance coverage. Most knowledgeable investors will also insist on full coverage to help protect their investment. There are many insurance brokers who specialize in entertainment insurance, and they can offer you all necessary policy coverage in a single package. (Rates can vary dramatically, with factors such as higher deductibles often resulting in lower costs.) A reasonable insurance package will add approximately 2 percent to your total production budget.

FACT

If you're hiring hourly, daily, or weekly production personnel who aren't independent contractors, most states require that you purchase worker's compensation liability insurance to cover those individuals in case of accident or injury on the job.

As a rule, be very wary of making undeclared *under-the-table* payment agreements with anyone involved in your production. The reasoning that you or your worker can avoid having to pay taxes is not only a mistake—it's illegal. If a worker is injured on the job without worker's compensation coverage, your production may incur civil lawsuits, possible criminal prosecution, or result in some or all of your existing production insurance policies being voided.

Comprehensive and Property Insurance

Comprehensive liability coverage provides protection for claims of property damage or personal injury when filming on public property. This is generally required for obtaining permits to film on publicly owned roadways and locations. *Property damage insurance* provides protection for damage to rented properties and is usually a requirement when renting or leasing privately held locations, or even locations that are offered free of charge.

Miscellaneous Equipment Insurance

Miscellaneous equipment insurance provides protection for damage to camera equipment, lighting and sound gear, and related equipment that the production owns, rents, or borrows. This is usually required by all rental and leasing companies. Without it, some rental companies will require that their own insurance policies be purchased at the time of rental or leasing. The primary problem with purchasing that insurance on-site is that the rates are non-negotiable and generally higher than the amount you'd pay to your own insurer.

Errors and Omissions Insurance

Errors and omissions insurance provides protection for civil actions brought against a production for plagiarism, defamation of character, or unauthorized use of branded items or locations. It's important that signed releases are obtained from all of the individuals and locations that are filmed and edited into the final cut of the production. Signed clearances are also imperative for music, titles, and virtually every other aspect of the production.

QUESTION?

Do all productions need cast insurance?
The insurance can be expensive, but it may be mandatory for high-profile actors and actresses. As with all insurance, you're better safe than sorry. The more insurance you have, the better you'll sleep at night knowing your entire cast is covered.

The worst-case scenario for lawsuits of this nature can occur if and when a film becomes a blockbuster. In many high-profile productions, injured parties tend to appear in droves at the slightest hint that they've been damaged, appear to have been damaged, or have simply been affected in some way. A well-organized paper trail and attention to detail is invaluable.

Budgeting and Scheduling Software

Most studio productions and reasonably well funded independent film productions utilize budgeting and scheduling software designed specifically for the movie industry. While software is certainly not mandatory, it can simplify paperwork and pay for itself quickly in time savings. These software packages can track every element of your budget, schedule, and production strip boards, and many of the necessary purchase orders, employee forms, and any other related paperwork for any size production. The following program dealers have excellent Web site information that includes pricing and system requirements to run the programs. Some of these software programs can be found at:

- *www.boilerplate.net*
- *www.easy-budget.com*
- *www.enterpriseprinters.com*
- *www.entertainmentpartners.com*
- *www.filmmakersoftware.com*
- *www.junglesoftware.com*
- *www.mindstarprods.com*
- *www.writersstore.com*

Virtually all of these packages are available for downloading off the Internet, and each one is well worth investigating.

Chapter 9

Preproduction: The Birth of a Film

The moment finances are available and the budget is approved, your project can begin the preproduction phase, where schedules are confirmed, department heads recruited, cast and crew members hired, locations verified, and equipment secured. This is the first of many exciting, creative, and nerve-racking phases of filmmaking, and it's the stage that will determine the success of a production. Organization skills, flexibility, and common sense are the keys to maintaining order and keeping all of the major players focused on their number one priority—making your film.

9

Setting Up Shop

In the previous chapters, you learned how to secure financing, create and control a budget, and perfect your production's scheduling. Now it's time to enter another stage of preproduction. This means setting up your headquarters, setting the tone of your production through your director, beginning your initial search for actors, planning and building sets, and deciding upon any other crucial elements that require a long lead time, such as locations and music.

Office space for studio productions is often in a centralized location, and most of the business of making a new film takes place in existing facilities. For independent productions, the first order of business is to retain enough appropriate office space to accommodate executive and business staff. This can range from turning your living room into a command center to leasing office space in a warehouse district.

The important element to setting up shop is to have a single environment for housing business personnel and equipment. Multiple telephone connections need to be installed, and computer hookups should be readily available. Phone lines and e-mail connections will likely be the primary source of communication—and in film production, communication is everything.

Choosing a Director

The director of the film is one of the first creative talents brought on board for film productions, and is usually lined up very early in the process. In the movie industry, the director is second in the chain of command, and answers primarily to the producer. While most directors are given a great deal of creative license for telling the story as they envision it, they seldom have total control over all decisions.

Decisions as to who has ultimate control of creative issues, business and financial issues, and the final cut of the film are generally negotiated and contractually bound at the time a director is hired. Directors who understand financial constraints and diplomacy are generally in the best position to work effectively with producers whose primary function is to deal with the business side of filmmaking.

The Fine Print

If you're directing your own film, you won't need to be as concerned with contractual issues regarding artistic license in the making of your movie. If you're working with a director, you'll need to make certain that all agreements regarding final artistic control of the film are in the contract. Even if your director is your closest friend or relative (*especially* if that's the case), you'll want to make sure the details are in writing.

E ALERT!

> The best way to avoid potential directorial issues is to invest in the services of an entertainment attorney. By drawing up a contract that is designed to protect your film and your investors, you'll ultimately protect your career as a filmmaker.

The worst-case scenarios with directors generally involve creative disputes, budget overages, or falling seriously behind schedule. Creatively, if you become concerned that your director doesn't fundamentally understand the film you want to make, or if he appears to be making a different movie altogether, you'll need to have the recourse to either set him in the right direction or replace him. Also, if your director is burning through the budget too early in the production or the shooting schedule falls behind, you need the power to control the problem.

Know Your Stuff

The director is a storyteller whose number one priority is to know the script, fully understand the story, and recognize what makes that story work. Because of this, many directors work in close collaboration with the screen writer during preproduction, given that the writer invariably has a personal vision of what the story should look and sound like. What sets a great director apart from all others is not only his grasp of a film's concept, but the methods he employs in bringing that vision to life. This includes setting the tone for the entire production and all the cast and crew involved. Every director has his own sense of style, moral and ethical code, industry opinions, and work ethic.

Style and Guile

As a director, the way you conduct yourself and orchestrate your players will become an intrinsic part of your film. A calm approach to directing will help maintain a calm crew. A humorous approach will create levity. A hands-off approach will encourage and nurture creativity in your cast—or it will breed chaos. If you lead well, your cast and crew are sure to follow, and the more organized you are in regard to the script, shots, setups, and all aspects of production, the better your film will be.

Directors tend to fall into two categories, those with a personal approach and those with a viewfinder approach. The more personal style is reflective of a director who pays close attention to the actors, guiding them, with either plenty of advice or limited instruction, to achieve optimal characterization. The viewfinder director is an individual who is less focused on actors and more focused on the camera, special effects, and techniques that will give the film a more stylish appearance. The ideal director is one who combines both approaches to strike the perfect balance.

Previsualizing

Directors by their very nature are dreamers, and dreams can often be hard for others to visualize. Previsualization breaks the script down into the visual elements of each scene. This is most commonly accomplished with *storyboards* and *floorplans*. Major productions usually recruit storyboard artists to draw detailed images of each shot in each scene (see Chapter 11).

These boards have the general appearance of comic strip panels. Artistic talent is helpful for storyboarding, but is not a prerequisite for creating useful drawings. For low-budget productions, the same effect can be created with relatively simple sketches. Storyboards need to be drawn in the same ratio as you're shooting the final film so that all of the elements in the storyboard drawings will translate to the screen.

Storyboard panels can be laid out and videotaped in order with dialogue dubbed in. This can provide a visual sense of the film, and help to identify what's missing in the storyboards or in the story itself.

Each panel should be drawn from the perspective of the camera and indicate the position from which the camera, and ultimately the audience, is viewing the shot. Indicating camera perspective is crucial to compiling the list of shots that will be done from each camera setup. The storyboard panels should also indicate how the scene will be lighted.

After the storyboard is completed with every shot and camera position identified, the storyboard can be duplicated for restructuring as a *shooting storyboard*. This is created by cutting apart the sequential storyboard and pasting it back together in the order of shots to be made from each camera position. Floorplans are drawn as an overhead view of each scene that shows the placement of cast members, crucial set dressings, cameras, and camera angles. Good floorplans are essential for setting up each scene, arranging and fine-tuning the placement of lighting and cameras, and putting your set dressings and cast into position for each camera angle. Storyboards and floorplans will help minimize the number of camera setups necessary for each scene, and will ultimately reduce the time required for setting up lighting and cameras.

The Shot List

A *shot list* is exactly what the term implies, a list of every single shot that will be made from each camera position in every scene. This includes the shots taken after lens changes from each position for closeups, medium shots, and wide shots. The storyboard and the floorplans are crucial for developing the shot list, and the combination of all three of these elements will provide information that will help determine the shooting schedule.

The shot list for each scene is grouped by camera positions and lens changes from each position. Typical shots include:

- **ECU:** Extreme closeups focus on sections of a face, such as the eyes, mouth, and nose.
- **CU:** Closeups show the face and shoulders.
- **MS:** Medium shots show the face and body from approximately the knees and up.
- **WS:** Wide shots show an entire body.
- **LS:** Long shots show the entire body with its surroundings.

- **XLS:** Extreme long shots show characters with a broad view of their background and surroundings.
- **POV:** This refers to the point of view of specific characters as shown by the camera, and what the character is looking at.

Changing lenses during a single camera setup provides a variety of screen perspectives that range from extreme closeups to long-shot views of a scene. The shot list also gives you a checklist for the end of the day to make sure you've got everything covered before moving on.

Finding the Right Players

Bringing the right people into a production will have an effect on the overall mood of your film. A producer will normally handle lining up and hiring business personnel such as accountants and office staff. While a producer often has veto power over all crew members, a director usually has sway over the creative team she chooses to work with, such as the cinematographer, production designer, and film editor. Typically, directors and producers collaborate in choosing and hiring the technical crew and production people who are brought on board for the shooting schedule.

Higher-budget productions usually have a casting director during the preproduction process so he can begin arranging acting talent to fill the parts. In major motion pictures, lead actors are often lined up very early in preproduction, and are even sometimes approached in the conceptual stages of a film production. During preproduction, the casting director collaborates closely with the film's director to ensure that casting is tailored to attract the best actor for each role.

Production Design

The visual mood and atmosphere of the film project is developed in preproduction, often by close collaboration between the director, the production designer, and the cinematographer. The ultimate goal of production design is to translate the director's vision of the script into a workable design that can be effectively captured by the camera.

Set Design and Construction

Film sets are often created entirely from scratch on vacant land or lots. A great deal of ingenuity and craftsmanship is used in building sets, especially on major motion pictures where sets are unbelievably complex. The most critical element of any set is that the images that appear on film look as realistic and convincing as possible. Most film sets are anything but real. Building fronts often have doors that don't open and roofs that extend only a few feet and cover nothing but bare ground. Spaceships have no insides, or even backsides or bottoms, and living rooms and pool halls can't be lived or played in. What's important is that the camera sees enough tangible structural information to create an undeniable sense of realism.

Rome Wasn't Built in a Day, or Even in Italy

Set construction always takes time, and there are stories galore about film crews and casts standing around while the last handful of nails is driven. More than a few motion pictures have begun filming while paint was still drying in the background. Getting the sets designed is the first step in the process, but getting them built and ready for the shooting schedule should come right on the heels of design approval.

Materials and Artistic License

The materials for set construction can come from just about every source imaginable. Major productions will have truckloads of brand-new material dropped off directly from lumberyards. For low-budget productions, salvage yards and scrap piles are gold mines for construction material. As long as the set doesn't fall down or blow away, the materials for construction can be scavenged from innumerable cheap or even free locations.

Paint can be mixed and matched from the seemingly endless supply of partial cans in the garages of nearly every homeowner in America. There's nothing unethical about begging everyone involved in the production for any excess material from home-improvement projects.

Soundstages

Soundstages can be rented or leased for a price, and with that price also comes a number of significant benefits. Most soundstages are fully equipped with electrical outlets for every piece of machinery used in a shoot. The soundstage is also built for recording audio in the best possible acoustic atmosphere. Soundstages can be created from scratch in warehouses or abandoned office space. Virtually any standing structure can be converted into use as a soundstage with enough soundproofing and power. Relatively inexpensive spaces can also be rented or leased for the few weeks that most film productions will take.

Scouting Locations

Scouting locations for shooting is a major preproduction activity. Even in your first meeting, an experienced location scout will have ideas not only about where some of your scenes could be shot, but also about how much a location will cost, how easy going to and from the location will be, what production facilities are available once you get there, and how difficult it will be to get permission and a shooting permit.

A location scout differs from a location manager in that a scout goes out and finds the locations in advance of shooting. If your budget is restrictive, these two jobs obviously can be held by the same person. After you have discussed your shooting needs, the location manager will come back with photos of possible locations. There should be a mixture of "artistic" shots that show the location at its best, and more commonplace pictures that indicate logistical issues such as roads, plumbing, available light, parking, and room for support areas such as dressing rooms, makeup, equipment staging, and so on. Many cities have governmental departments or filming commissions to help in making arrangements for locations.

Are You in the Right Place?

Movie mogul Jack Warner has often been credited with saying, "There is no movie that can't be shot at Griffith Park." Griffith Park, located in Los Angeles, is the largest municipal park in the United States and is home to the famous Hollywood sign. Considering Warner's success with using that Hollywood acreage in such diverse films as *Rebel Without a Cause* and *The Adventures of Robin Hood*, it's difficult to disagree. But modern audiences know there are no eucalyptus trees in medieval England, and the Los Angeles Parks Department is well aware of the monetary value of their most famous filming spot, so you may have several good reasons to look elsewhere.

FACT

Shooting at a distant location requires that the production company arrange for lodging, meals, and per-diem pay (an agreed-upon daily amount) for all personnel who are required to be at the set. Less than fifty miles is considered close enough for the cast and crew to travel to and from their homes, thus not requiring lodging.

Besides the photographic vistas offered by any specific location, there are several other things to be considered. Not the least of these is the cost, since very few property owners are willing to let a small army descend on their land for free. There is also the issue of distance. According to the rules set down by the film industry unions, if a location is less than thirty miles from the home base of a production it's considered a close location. Anything outside the thirty-mile limit is a distant location.

Does It Pay to Stay Domestic?

Much has been made recently about films shooting outside their home countries for reasons other than appropriateness of location. No one can really disagree with the decision to shoot *French Kiss* in Paris or *Sahara* in a distant desert region. But why shoot Middle Earth in New Zealand? How does Toronto, Canada, end up doubling as New York or Chicago? Why go all the way to Romania to shoot a big-budget horror film?

As you might expect, the answer is usually one of finance. Countries such as New Zealand and Canada would like to create a film industry as part of their economy. To do this, they offer extremely low rates and often even tax incentives to production companies that shoot there. The costs of traveling and lodging, among other things, are offset by the lower price.

There have also been situations where "the money" was in another country to begin with. Sometimes the investors were there and wished to have the film made there for reasons of commerce or tourism. There have even been situations where the corporation that owns the studio finds it has funds "locked up" in another country through investments. These investments can only be liquidated or spent in that country, so the decision is made to film within those borders. Some A-list actors or directors insist their films be made in their homelands, purely as a convenience to them. If you want that talent, your film has to shoot on their turf.

Musical Accompaniment

Preproduction is the time to make decisions regarding the musical accompaniment of your film. Music often becomes an indelible aspect of the film, and many musical scores are instantly identifiable with the movies they were written for, becoming very nearly another character in the film. The theme music for *The Good, the Bad and the Ugly* plays in various forms throughout the movie, and is instantly recognizable to almost every fan of Clint Eastwood's early spaghetti westerns. While music is an intrinsic part of the postproduction process, there are many aspects that need to be started early on in the production.

Original Compositions

Sometimes the most creative and least legally contentious approach to giving a film its musical presence is to bring in a *composer* to write music specifically for the film. By contractual agreement, all of the rights to the music composed for a film can belong to its producers. The music can be edited and arranged in virtually any conceivable manner to suit the film, and is designed to match the mood of each scene (see Chapter 16).

Getting the Rights

For filmmakers who plan to use prerecorded music in their film, the process of obtaining rights to that music must be started very early in preproduction. Music recorded prior to 1922 is public domain and can be researched at *www.pdinfo.com*. Otherwise, using a prerecorded piece of music requires two clearances: the *synchronization license* and a *master use license*. The copyright owner of the music provides the synchronization license, which permits the synchronizing of the music to the visual image of the film. The master use license comes from the owner of the rights to a specific recording to be used, usually the record producer. The owners of these rights can usually be found by contacting the American Society of Composers, Authors, and Publishers (*www.ascap.com*) or the National Music Publishers' Association (*www.nmpa.org*).

Prices for these licenses are negotiable, and may be reduced for nonprofit student films and independent filmmakers who plan on releasing their films to film festivals. *Step deals* can also be arranged with independent producers that will allow for increased use rates if a distributor picks the film up for wide theatrical release.

ALERT!

If you're considering sneaking a prerecorded song into your film by some clever means, such as having it play innocuously in the background on the radio in a vehicle scene, think again. You'll be violating copyright laws, which could spell legal disaster for your production.

Stock Music Libraries

Perhaps the most cost-effective approach for obtaining music and the rights to use it in a film production is by going through stock music libraries. Nearly all music libraries market their products on the Internet. Googling "stock music library" on your Web browser will provide more results than you'll ever have time to peruse, but you'll certainly get an idea of how many options you have.

These e-commerce companies offer a wide range of musical styles with relatively reasonable pricing. Some will sell the synchronization rights for their music for a standard fee. Although you won't be buying permanent use or copyrights of the music for any other purposes, you'll have the rights to use this music for your production. Some music libraries also offer step deals, where you can pay a relatively low initial fee, and as your production goes into general distribution, the fees rise in relation to the degree of that distribution. Utilizing stock music libraries can save a considerable amount of time and hassle for securing your musical requirements.

Chapter 10

Essential Crew

A film production crew comprises all individuals involved in the making of a film aside from the actors themselves. The writer, director, or producer may arguably be the heart of the creature, but the crew is its lifeblood. Without specialists, technicians, and organizational masterminds, the creature cannot come to life. Successful crews mean successful filmmaking. When you're making a film, regardless of your budget, there are essential crew members that you must hire to bring your vision to the silver screen.

Hiring Your Crew

Anyone who has sat through the credits of a film can see how many individuals worked on that particular production. For the average Joe making a film in his basement in Ohio, the various job descriptions can be very confusing. On low-budget or independent films, a single individual can hold several different titles, while big-budget productions showcase the work of dozens of standard crew members and highly skilled specialists. Because the size of your crew is linked directly to the size of your budget, it can be tricky to get all the help you need.

Small-budget productions definitely have to cut corners, and this is done in any number of ways. Your cinematographer, for example, may also be your camera operator. An actor may be in charge of his or her wardrobe, pending approval of the producer or director. You may not be able to afford a caterer, so instead you provide bagels and coffee in the morning and make sandwiches for lunch. If you can't afford a full-time medic, you should definitely have a well-stocked first-aid kit on hand and know how to use it. Those are just a few of the things you'll have to compromise on when your budget is tight.

ALERT!

While a short film or documentary can be made with only a few people, a big-budget film may need hundreds of specialists. If you're hiring union labor, keep in mind that individuals will only do the job they are hired for—they won't bend union rules to take on something that isn't in their job description.

This chapter focuses on crew members who are considered essential to the average film production. That's not to say that you have to fill all of these positions, but at the very least you should have an understanding of what they do. Chapter 11 describes additional crew members who are generally hired for bigger budget productions.

So you've got your financing and your script is hot off the press after half a million rewrites—now you really need help. Regardless of whether your crew consists of three or three hundred, your hiring decisions are some of the most important you'll make during your filmmaking journey. Hiring these hardworking folks is not to be underestimated, as they all play a crucial role in bringing your vision to life in one form or another.

The variety and enormity of jobs connected to the filmmaking industry can seem overwhelming, with an intricate web of specialists and tradesmen commingling their verbal, emotional, artistic, scientific, and technological skills toward the same goal. From gofer to gaffer to director, each individual is as diverse, talented, and important as the next. With good common sense and intuition, you can assemble the ideal group of professionals.

Taking One for the Team

By way of introduction, it's perhaps best to think of a full crew as falling into several categories. Management personnel include producers, directors, unit managers, and script assistants. Cinematographers, camera operators, and all of those associated with the visual aspects of the film are part of the photographic team. Everyone involved in sound, such as the editor, boom operator, and foley artists, constitutes the sound unit.

A decorating team includes a broad range of specialists from wardrobe management and costumers to makeup, scenic artists, and set designers. One of the busier groups of individuals are the stagehands, which include construction experts, propmasters, grips, and gaffers.

How Many Do I Hire?

Determining the number of individuals you need to hire for a project requires careful study of the script and all of the film's design and technical elements. Will there be a lot of location shooting? Special effects? Elaborate costumes? Intricate sounds or lighting? All of these things come into play when assembling a crew that can work within the confines of your budget.

Pay for Play

The budget for any production will dictate the direction producers take in searching for production personnel. With a high-budget film, the news that the producers are hiring will spread like wildfire. Professional film production managers usually have access to a great number of potential crew members who are actively looking for work, and will knowledgeably pick and choose the best people for each production role.

Limited-budget film productions don't have the same luxury. The downside to bringing personnel on board for free is that more often than not, you get what you pay for. Reliability is a key consideration, and monetary compensation provides a great deal of incentive no matter what the position or specialty.

Getting the Word Out

There are a number of ways to get the word out that a film production is actively hiring. Trade publications and casting papers generally post notices free of charge. Film schools and colleges with film production classes can also supply a number of interested and reasonably well–skilled production personnel who may be willing to work for minimal compensation.

In major cities like New York City, Los Angeles, Toronto, Vancouver, and San Francisco, there are a number of organizations that maintain bulletin boards containing resumes of experienced production people. There are also Web sites in these areas that list production individuals who specialize in every aspect of filmmaking. The sheer number and availability of hungry and willing crew people in these major filmmaking communities can make locating the film production in one of them a practical financial decision.

Interviewing Potential Crewmates

In general, it's the producer's responsibility to hire crew members. In most cases, the same rules apply to the filmmaking industry as to many other industries. This means carefully checking resumes and references and asking for portfolios or sample film reels when necessary. A potential crew member's salary and duties should be clearly presented and discussed prior to any final decisions being made. It's also important to gauge a person's dedication to her job as well as her attitude toward the production she is about to be hired for.

Independent Contractors

Some production crew members can be hired as independent contractors. These individuals work on a contractual basis, perform various functions and work unsupervised, typically setting their own hours. This can save on paperwork and accounting procedures because they are responsible for their own income tax matters. Location scouts and production designers, for example, can often be independent contractors. Individuals who are required to work a set amount of hours at specific times are considered to be employees and not contractors.

Before hiring anyone, the legal and accounting ramifications regarding income taxes should be carefully discussed with trusted legal and accounting advisors. At no time do you want to be dealing with hazy accounting issues, so make sure everything having to do with employment is crystal clear to all concerned parties.

Union Crews: Pros and Cons

Hiring a union crew comes with pros and cons. One of the pros is that union crews are invariably professionals who are skilled in the varied disciplines of filmmaking. These individuals are used to scheduling and budgetary constraints and work quickly and efficiently. On a big-budget production, the knowledge and experience of union crews can definitely keep production problems to a minimum. Keep in mind that if your film is being made by a union signatory such as a studio, you'll be required to hire union labor.

On the flip side, anyone considering hiring a union crew must research the limitations and regulations attached to that crew. Overtime, meals, pay scale, and duties are just a few of the things that are strictly regulated. On a low-budget or independent film, hiring union crews could be a financial deal-breaker, as each union member is confined to specific duties.

Producers and Directors

Assuming you're not wearing all the hats for your filmmaking endeavor, your producer, director, and writer are arguably the most important people you need to hire. Within those three disciplines are dozens of supervisors and assistants who must complete their assigned duties while also handling the inevitable overflow associated with each position (see Chapter 11).

The Producer

As the name would suggest, the *producer* is in charge of the overall production of a film. This individual must be highly capable and possess the ability to juggle many balls during the entire course of production from start to finish. This includes handling matters pertaining to financing, equipment, and the entire crew associated with the film.

Putting the Wheels in Motion

It is widely recognized in the industry that the producer is the busiest person on a film set. In addition to normal daily proceedings, producers are often responsible for finding financing, acquiring and finalizing scripts, hiring and firing crew members, and distributing a film. During a typical shooting day, the producer is usually the first to arrive on-set and the last to depart.

The term "production" is a bit of a misnomer, given that an entire film is considered a production, so there really isn't a production department in the traditional sense. Rather, there is a production team that covers a wide range of disciplines including overseeing all of the other departments (art, editing, sound, photography, etc.) as well as a staff of accountants.

QUESTION?

When you watch film credits, why are there so many different producers? There are many different production titles such as producer, executive producer, line producer, and unit production manager. These titles are often interchangeable depending on the type of film and the film's budget. Some are working titles, while others are awarded as perks.

A few recognizable and accomplished producers include:

- **Andrew Vajna** (*Basic Instinct 2, Evita, Nixon, Die Hard, Tombstone, Jacob's Ladder, Air America, Total Recall,* the *Rambo* trilogy)

- **Debra Hill** (*The Fog, The Fisher King, Big Top Pee-Wee, Clue, Escape from New York, Halloween*)
- **Frank Marshall** (The *Jurassic Park and Back to the Future* trilogies, The *Bourne* films, *The Sixth Sense, Cape Fear, Who Framed Roger Rabbit, The Color Purple, Poltergeist, Raiders of the Lost Ark*)
- **Gale Ann Hurd** (*Aeon Flux*, the *Terminator* trilogy, *Hulk, Armageddon, Dante's Peak, The Ghost in the Darkness, The Abyss, Aliens*)
- **Hal B. Wallis** (*True Grit, Blue Hawaii, Gunfight at the O.K. Corral, My Friend Irma, Casablanca, The Maltese Falcon, Dark Victory, Jezebel*)
- **Irving Thalberg** (*A Night at the Opera, Mutiny on the Bounty, Grand Hotel, Tarzan the Ape Man, The Champ, The Merry Widow, The Hunchback of Notre Dame*)
- **Jerry Bruckheimer** (The *Pirates of the Caribbean* films, *National Treasure, King Arthur, Pearl Harbor, Crimson Tide, Con Air, The Rock, Beverly Hills Cop, Flashdance*)
- **Kathleen Kennedy** (*Munich, War of the Worlds, Seabiscuit*, the *Jurassic Park and Back to the Future* trilogies, *The Sixth Sense, Twister, Schindler's List, E.T. the Extra-Terrestrial*)
- **Sam Spiegel** (*The Last Tycoon, Lawrence of Arabia, The Bridge on the River Kwai, On the Waterfront, The African Queen*)
- **Saul Zaentz** (*The English Patient, The Unbearable Lightness of Being, Amadeus, One Flew over the Cuckoo's Nest*)

On an independent or lower-budget film, the producer will have his plate full. A consummate professional will be able to accomplish in a day what mere mortals can only hope to accomplish in a month. To suggest these folks arc busy is a massive understatement. Producers range from executives to managers to assistants, each having a slightly different job description depending on the film and most definitely the budget. If you're serving as writer, director, and producer, things can get crazy before you can yell "action."

UPMs and Line Managers

Unit production managers and *line managers* serve directional and motivational functions in the film production from different perspectives. The unit production manager is responsible for maintaining production flow on the business side and keeping a close eye on expenses and the budget. The line producer maintains flow on the set, and helps keep the directors, cast, and crew on track and on schedule throughout the shooting day.

Production Assistants

Production assistants, commonly known as PAs, are a permanent fixture on film sets. As their title suggests, they perform all types of necessary chores, ranging from traffic control to courier service to food service. Sometimes paid, sometimes taken on as interns, these hardworking folks are accustomed to odd jobs. Experienced PAs are often delegated more important tasks, and often they're attached to a certain actor, director, or filmmaker. Also referred to as *gofers* (go for this, go for that), they are generally at the lowest end of the filmmaking totem pole.

Calling the Shots

If you're not serving as director, then hiring one will be one of your most crucial decisions. The director is the creative vision behind a film. It's through their eyes that a script comes to life visually, technically, and musically. Directors work with all of the department heads and especially with the actors, through which the director's vision is ultimately realized.

FACT

It is often assumed that the director is the highest power on a film set. Typically, on a feature film, the director is second in line to the producer. On a television series it is the producer and writers who often have more authority.

When hiring a director it's important to keep in mind that she will set the tone of the production, both on screen and with the crew. Directors are renowned for their creativity and the style in which they control a production. They have a lot to think about and organize, both in their head and in the real world. They are artists in the creative and technical sense, and the role they play in a film is paramount to a film's ultimate success—or demise.

Directors come in all shapes and sizes and varying degrees of experience and paychecks. Their duties are wide in range and scope, as they are hired to do everything from script editing to casting to shot selection and composition. If there's one thing to remember when hiring a director, it is this: A bad director can turn a stellar script into a disaster, and a great director can make even the worst script work on the screen.

Hiring a Writer

As discussed in Chapter 3, a great script is paramount to the success of your film. If you're not the one writing the script for your film, you need to hire someone who can accurately translate your vision into the written word. If you're at the stage where you're actually hiring crew members, then chances are your script has been approved and your film has been given a green light by a studio or production company.

Whether he is on-set or at home, a writer's help is imperative. At all phases of production, scripts are constantly being rewritten and tweaked to the point of sheer madness. For example, if after viewing your film at a test screening the audience hates the ending or a particular relationship, your writer needs to rewrite the necessary dialogue to make the film more palatable. No matter where you're filming or what stage of production you're in, make sure your writer is always available for consultation.

Setting the Scene

Cinematography can create a milestone in filmmaking or a massacre of epic proportion. Think *Lawrence of Arabia* as opposed to *Attack of the Killer Tomatoes*, or *The Sound of Music* versus *Bloodsport III*. What the audience sees on the big screen leaves a lasting impression, and the cinematographer along with a host of production designers, artists, and location experts ultimately create that ambiance.

Cinematographer

As important as a director's vision can be, it can easily become distorted in the hands of an inexperienced *cinematographer*. Also referred to as *director of photography*, or DP, this individual is responsible for bringing a director's creative vision to full fruition in as spectacular a manner as possible. All of the beautiful sweeping scenery, mood lighting, and daring scenes that grace the silver screen come to life as a result of a DP's efficiency.

There isn't enough that can be said about the importance of hiring the best DP your budget will allow. This means careful consideration and screening of all potential candidates, whose specialties include filming, camera equipment, lighting, and visual recording devices. When interviewing potential DPs there are several important factors to bear in mind:

- Resume. The previous work she has done should be closely examined in regard to flexibility and complexity of lighting and camera work.
- Amiability. Is she compatible with the rest of the crew, in particular the director and producer?
- Availability. Does she have a flexible schedule and is she available for the entire shooting schedule?
- Camera experience. What types of cameras and formats has she had experience with? Also, does she have her own equipment, and how much time will it take her to set up the camera and lighting?

If you're on a tight budget, you can do without many crew members, but you can't do without a cinematographer. Most cinematographers are camera operators and often have their own equipment. If this individual is your only camera operator, then her presence is obviously crucial.

Production Designer

The *production designer* is another important crew member to be hired. A consummate artist, this person has the daunting task of creating the overall visual appearance of a motion picture, including the sets, props, makeup, and wardrobe. The production designer works closely with the director, cinematographer, and technical specialists. Their right-hand man is the *art director,* who is responsible for seeing that the production designer's vision is carried out.

Costuming

On most productions, there needs to be someone in charge of costuming. On a very small-budget film, actors can often be in charge of their own wardrobes, but this can be time-consuming and aggravating if the actor's choices are in conflict with those of the director or producer. A wardrobe department with its staff of *costume designers* is typically overseen by a *wardrobe* or *costume supervisor* who works in conjunction with the art director. On a big-budget production, especially a historical period drama, for example, the wardrobe department is crucial. Over the years, many a character has been remembered for their stylish garb and perfectly detailed appearance.

ESSENTIAL

In the 1963 production of *Cleopatra,* Elizabeth Taylor wore sixty-five costumes that appeared in the final screen version. Left on the cutting room floor were scenes featuring an additional forty costumes she wore. In total, Taylor's costumes cost a whopping $195,000, the highest amount ever spent on a single performer's wardrobe at the time.

Wardrobe personnel spend a lot of time and effort making sure an actor's look is consistent with the role he's playing. Some classic motion pictures, like *Gone with the Wind* and *Cleopatra,* and the more recent *Moulin Rouge* are examples of highly stylized films that required talented wardrobe specialists. On a big-budget production, *dressers* are often hired to assist the actors in changing their wardrobe from one scene to the next.

Makeup Artists

The function of the *makeup artist* has greatly evolved over the decades, from Lon Chaney Jr.'s *Wolf Man* to the *Elephant Man* to Jim Carrey's *Mask* and Tolkien's *Lord of the Rings* trilogy. Makeup is no longer just a quick swipe of face power and a hint of lipstick. Instead, makeup artists are creating elaborate characters complete with prosthetic devices.

Reputable makeup artists should have a strong portfolio and the experience needed to maintain script continuity. What this means to the ultimate finished motion picture is that actors consistently have the correct look, hair style, and other appearance-altering mechanisms.

Technicians

Successful filmmaking is a symbiotic relationship between creativity and technical genius. Fortunately for today's filmmakers, technology has taken phenomenal strides, especially in regard to all things digital. Regardless of the technology, however, you still need specialists to handle all of the traditional and transitional equipment. Lighting technicians, electricians, grips, and prop masters all have important roles to play in any production.

Lighting Technicians

Lighting is one of the most critical aspects of filmmaking, as it sets the mood and ambiance of every scene. The *gaffer* works directly with the cinematographer to create proper lighting and ensure that enough electrical power is available to operate all the production equipment, from lighting to cameras. Surrounded by a team of *lighting technicians*, who set up and control the equipment, the gaffer can also be credited as *chief lighting technician*.

One of the most intriguing film job titles is the *best boy*. More often than not, the average filmgoer has no idea what the best boy does or what indeed makes *him* the best. The best boy is the first assistant to the gaffer, and is in charge of additional electrical crew members and all of the electrical equipment. The term "best boy" originated when a crew's "best" member was promoted to a supervisory position.

Pulling Stunts

The *stunt coordinator* plans and helps execute the physical stunts for a film. As well as ensuring that stunts will translate as realistically as possible to the screen, this individual focuses on the practicality of stunts and the safety of the professionals involved in stunt work. *Stunt performers* are highly specialized athletes and actors who perform the physical actions required for stunt scenes. *Stunt doubles* are stunt performers who take the place of specific actors in the film for potentially dangerous scenes. They have the same general physical characteristics as the actors they are representing, and are carefully made up to enhance the visual illusion.

Prop Master

The *property master*, or *prop master*, is in charge of prop acquisitions, prop maintenance, and the distribution of props as they're needed. Whether props are purchased, rented, or created from scratch, they belong in the prop master's domain. On bigger-budget productions, the prop master typically has a staff of assistants, such as an *armorer*, a highly specialized technician whose job it is to monitor and maintain all firearms.

Maintaining Sound Continuity

Continuity plays a huge role in the production of every motion picture. Lighting, sound, music, and editing are arguably of equal importance. Much of a film's ultimate appeal has to do with its editing and all the sounds heard throughout the entire film. You probably have distinct memories of the sound of the rush of fighter jets flying by in *Top Gun*, the hauntingly melodic balalaika dancing through *Dr. Zhivago*, or the frightening footfall of tyrannosaurus rex in *Jurassic Park*. Writers weave intricate tales and directors capture moving images, but composers, editors, and sound technicians ultimately merge their disciplines into an indivisible art form (see Chapter 16).

Mixing It Up

The sound department is one of the most crucial components of film production. Great sound can make a film sing. Bad sound can make an audience run screaming from a theater. Having expert sound technicians is an absolute must in order for a film to prove ultimately successful. The head of the sound department is the *sound designer*, who is responsible for the overall soundtrack of a film. This individual oversees the production's music, dialogue, sound effects, and all of the individuals involved in creating and maintaining a film's sound.

FACT

A production might also have a props builder. A props builder is a jack-of-all-trades who can perform construction jobs and is familiar with electronics, machining, and a host of other disciplines. It is extremely helpful to have a competent props builder around in case anything technical goes wrong on-set.

Sound recordists are audio engineers who record dialogue and all other necessary sounds during film production. They work with any number of microphones and record separate sound tracks that can be manipulated and fine-tuned at postproduction by a *sound editor*. Both the recordist and editor must be technically astute individuals who are familiar with tried-and-true mechanics as well as current innovations in sound technology.

Boom Operator

On occasion, one can see a wayward microphone hovering precariously over an actor's head. The person at the other end of that microphone is a *boom operator*. A member of the sound crew who works closely with the recordist, this individual operates the boom microphone, which is essentially a microphone on a long pole that is either hand-held or mechanically operated. This gives the operator the ability to control where the microphone is placed in relation to the actors and the angle of the cameras.

Knowing the Score

Music is yet another important component of a motion picture, one that in many cases has just as much impact as a film's visual appeal. A film's music sets its tone, whether it's the soft melodic undertone of a love scene or booming crescendos during an epic battle. Music is another character in a film. Imagine the aquatic star of *Jaws* circling menacingly around a potential victim without musical accompaniment. In this case, the unforgettable film score accounted for much of the film's incredible suspense.

The musical component of a film requires the talents of many professionals, from composers to musicians. In charge of the department is the *music supervisor*, who oversees and works with sound editors, mixers, and the *composer*, who creates the musical score that relates directly to the conceptual element of a film. A composer's job can include writing original scores for all of a film's scenes and overseeing musical recordings. Actor and screen legend Charlie Chaplin was so multitalented that he composed the musical scores for all of his motion pictures made after 1931 including *City Lights* and *The Great Dictator.*

Film Editor

Film editing is an intrinsic and highly evolved element of postproduction (see Chapter 16). The *film editor* follows the script to assemble the filmed footage into logical sequences that tell a story. It is most common for directors to have "first cut" privileges. The director usually works in close collaboration with the editor to refine footage and sequences of the production. Although film producers usually have the last word in the version that is released, some directors are powerful enough to demand "final cut" as well.

Chapter 11

All the Bells and Whistles

Every filmmaker's dream is to see her vision come to life on the silver screen. If you're lucky, you can be one of the filmmakers who not only accomplishes that task, but gets to do it with the help of a large budget. In the entertainment industry, as in many other industries, big bucks are just as important as creative and artistic vision. When it comes to producing your film, more financing gives you the ability to enhance your crew by hiring additional managers, assistants, technicians, and specialists.

Enhancing Your Production Team

Now that you've learned about essential crew members, you can begin to understand the various other positions that can be filled when you have the luxury of a bigger budget. This can include management personnel such as a production or location manager, a wide range of production and directorial staff, artists and computer technicians, and all types of specialists. While in a low-budget film, an individual will have to juggle more than one discipline; a higher-budget production allows for crew members to focus on a particular job.

As you learned in the previous chapter, a producer is the individual in charge of overall production. This can be a daunting task for even the best-organized individual. With a healthy budget, you can hire additional production staff who can share the enormity of work that inevitably comes with making a film. This can include a unit production manager, production manager, coordinator, designer, dressers, and assistants who help the production assembly line hum like a well-oiled machine.

Production Manager

In lower-budget film productions, a producer wears many hats. Big-budget endeavors, however, are a different story. If your project has significant financing, you can hire a *production manager* to keep the wheels turning. This individual's primary concern is keeping the shooting schedule on track, overseeing all day-to-day operations, and controlling the film's budget. He also coordinates and oversees all preproduction operations, supervises shooting locales, and creates and maintains the overall and daily cash flow activities, including salaries and equipment. When hiring for this position, it's important to find an individual who can keep a level head at all times in addition to getting the job done.

In general, the production manager reports to the producer and must be extremely organized, an excellent facilitator, and—above all—a delegator. Often production managers hire the department heads. A production manager's support staff can include the location manager, catering crew, transportation captain, and production secretary, among others.

Designers and Decorators

How a motion picture ultimately comes across onscreen is the result of many different creative forces, not the least of which is the design team. Constantly in motion, with a healthy mix of flexibility and spontaneity, these individuals constitute a force to be reckoned with. The *production designer* is the creative guru of this team, the individual responsible for the overall look and feel of a film.

Working directly with the production designer's guidelines is the *set designer*, who creates the construction drawings and blueprints for each set. If you're filming an elaborate period piece or science fiction adventure, this job can be overwhelming. Once the sets are built, the *set decorator* is directly responsible for setting up and maintaining the appearance of sets. This individual ensures that furnishings, curtains, plants, and floor coverings are precisely in place for each scene. In regard to film continuity, these individuals are extremely important.

Additional Producers

On any given film, there are a number of producers listed in the credits. One of the most common is the *executive producer*, which, as far as producers go, has no specific definition. Typically, the executive producer has little involvement in the technical or creative aspects of a film. Instead, she's focused on the film's financial and business dealings. In some cases, she may help secure financing for the production or finance the film herself. It could also be that she lends credibility to a film's distribution, or represents a production company that has a stake in the production. On independent films, investors who contribute more than 25 percent of a film's budget are often awarded the title of executive producer.

QUESTION?

What is a co-producer?
The title of co-producer can mean several different things. Often it's a title given to two or more producers who work as a group and basically split the jobs a producer normally handles alone. It can also be a title given to an actor as a perk or to go along with a raise in salary.

Another common position is *associate producer*, a job description that changes depending on the type of production and the individual's contribution to that production. Commonly, the associate producer performs certain tasks as delegated by the producer or production manager. If, for example, you're working with a production company that has some small involvement with your film, the individuals associated with that company can be given the title of associate producer.

The *production coordinator*, or PC, is a hard-working member of the production crew who often provides the glue that holds the production itself together. When hiring a PC, you should be on the lookout for a highly organized individual who can juggle, among other things, the responsibility of renting equipment, hiring crew members, and finding accommodations for crew and cast.

Assistant Directors

The director is obviously one of the most crucial elements of any film. If you're serving as director, it won't take you long to recognize just how much work is involved, especially if you're on a small budget and have to accomplish all the tasks that would normally be assigned to a host of assistants. A big budget, however, affords you the luxury of hiring any number of assistant directors and unit directors who will not only save you time but relieve you of a significant amount of stress.

Directing Specialties

Assistant directors, or ADs, are individuals whose specialty it is to keep the balance between actual filming and the daily production schedule. Contrary to their title, they aren't actually the director's assistant in the traditional sense. They don't pour coffee or fetch dry cleaning. They do, however, track a film's progress, prepare call sheets, and make sure that everything is on time and within range of the schedule. They also coordinate with actors and crew to maintain shooting schedules.

As with producers, the title of director also has varying levels of assistants. The *first assistant director* is indispensable, especially if you have a long, difficult shoot that requires the use of many different locations or complex scenes that need extra setup time. A good first assistant director can make everything run so smoothly that no one else needs to worry about anything. A *second assistant director* is often hired to help in the preparation of call sheets and also monitor the movements of cast members. The *third assistant director* is issued a variety of tasks, one of which is keeping track of and monitoring the film's extra cast members, commonly known as *extras* or *background actors*.

Second Units

Big-budget productions and television series often have *second unit teams*. Unlike the main filming unit, or first unit, these are small teams of individuals, led by a unit director, and typically include camera operators and a skeleton crew. The job of the *second unit director* and his team is to shoot a film's minor or secondary scenes that contain special effects, action sequences, or *establishing shots* that don't require the use of actors. Say, for example, your two lead characters are walking through the desert. You want to give the audience a sense of the desert by showing a bird's eye view of two people trudging through the sand. Because there are no actual closeups of the actors' faces in that particular establishing shot, anyone could take their place. As a producer, you would assign that sequence to your second unit.

Second units are commonly used in the action genre with scenes involving explosions, fires, car chases—basically any scene where an actor isn't necessary or where there is a high risk factor. Many of the James Bond films contain dozens of scenes filmed and directed by second unit teams.

Second units also film what are called *inserts*, which are either shot simultaneously during a production schedule or during postproduction in the editing phase. Inserts are typically shots showing some type of detail, like a hand turning a doorknob or a candle being lit by someone who is presumed to be the actor, but could in fact be anyone.

Camera Work

All film productions regardless of their budget need the help of a cinematographer. These are the individuals who will ultimately translate your creative vision onto the big screen. On low-budget or independent films, the cinematographer often pulls double duty as the camera operator. If your film is a large-scale production, then you'll be able to hire camera operators who work under the discerning eye of an experienced cinematographer.

Camera Operators

Many cinematographers actually operate their own cameras. Many more do not, and prefer working with cameramen who are skilled in the mechanical function of the camera and understand the expectations of the director and cinematographer. In large productions where the budget permits and the action demands multiple shots, any number of cameras and camera operators may be enlisted.

The *assistant camera operator* is primarily responsible for helping the operator set up the camera, maintaining proper lens focus, and changing lenses for various effects. The *clapper* or *loader* is often referred to as the second assistant camera operator. This individual loads film into the camera, operates the clapper slate for each film take, and keeps records of the scenes and shots. The *still photographer* maintains a photographic record of significant production scenes that are often used for publicity purposes.

QUESTION?

When did women begin to be camera operators in the United States?
Grace Davison, an actress for Astor Film Corp., was the first female camera operator in the United States. She went behind the camera in 1915 to film a number of one-reel comedies.

High-Tech Technicians

Another luxury that a bigger budget can accommodate is the use of digital cameras and specialized imagery technicians. These technicians work with the cinematographer to create and manipulate all sorts of fantastic high-end images that early filmmakers could never have dreamed of. Both the big and small screens have benefited from digital technology, which is constantly evolving and becoming capable of ever more sophisticated feats.

Productions involving digital imagery, however, will require a skilled technical staff, including a *digital image technician* or DIT, who works with either the director of photography or the cinematographer. The DIT's expertise with the digital camera includes image manipulation, continuity, color correction, and quality control. Often a *digital editor* is also needed to further digital enhancement by electronically editing digital images.

Script Supervisors

As most writers, directors, and most assuredly audience members will attest, one of the keys to a successful film is continuity. Keeping things in perspective and in order is the primary concern of the script supervisor. This individual keeps careful notes and monitors which scenes have been filmed and whether there are any discrepancies with the shooting script. Given that motion pictures are usually filmed out of sequence, the script supervisor is of great importance to the overall look, feel, and content of your film. He's also crucial in the halting of bloopers that will haunt your film for eternity.

The 1939 film *The Wizard of Oz*, for example, was rife with continuity issues. For example, in the scene where Dorothy and her companions are walking toward the wizard, Toto is behind them. During the next shot, the little dog is next to the scarecrow. Once at the door, Toto disappears, but then suddenly reappears in front of the scarecrow. Script supervisors are hired to prevent errors like this that detract from the believability of your film.

Storyboard Artists

Developed in the 1930s at Walt Disney Studios, storyboarding continues to be a common practice in the filmmaking industry. Rendered by an artist, storyboards are drawings that portray each scene as written in the script. A complete visual feast, these drawings give the director a reference point for all the visual, technical, and special effect elements of the film as seen through the camera.

Storyboards are often helpful on many levels. For starters, they give cast and crew an introductory representation of how a film will look. This is especially beneficial to those working on animated motion pictures. In addition, storyboards are often used as part of a presentation to potential investors. Visual aids are always helpful when attempting to explain complex action shots, technical elements, unusual characters, special effects, makeup, and wardrobe.

Obviously, the storyboard artist you hire for a particular production should present a portfolio that can be examined and analyzed. In addition to verifying artistic talent, it's important to ascertain whether the individual is flexible and able to work quickly.

Production Specialists

Within the production umbrella and its wide range of departments, there are quite a few skilled individuals you can hire when your budget allows. As you gain more and more experience in the artistic and commercial aspects of filmmaking, you'll clearly recognize the value of specialized technicians and contractors.

Get a Grip

Production members whose job it is primarily to set up and move equipment around a set are called *grips*. A busy group of individuals, these technicians work closely with the electrical technicians. The *key grip* is in charge of the crew that performs the muscle work, moving lighting gear, camera equipment, and virtually all of the other production equipment. A *dolly grip* operates the camera dolly, which is essentially a rolling platform that a camera is secured to. This includes moving and keeping level the tracks on which a camera is placed, otherwise known as a *dolly track*.

Leadman and Swings

An enormous amount of care and time is taken to ensure that sets are accurately and safely built, and subsequently torn down. The *leadman* is in charge of the crew that assembles and disassembles sets. That crew is known as the *swing gang*, and members of the crew are called *swings*. These individuals are highly proficient in carpentry and a variety of additional construction skills. Big-budget films with elaborate sets will likely require a fair number of swing gangs, so their value to the production cannot be underestimated.

Sound Editing

In addition to the essential boom operator and sound recordist, there are two other key members of the sound department who will come in handy. The *sound editor* synchronizes the audio recordings of the film to the screen images in the postproduction editing process. The *foley artist* is adept at creating sound effects that enhance key visual scenes and that are added to the soundtrack during film and sound editing. The sounds of breaking glass, breaking bones, footsteps, slaps, kicks, and punches are usually the work of a foley artist (see Chapter 16).

In 1974, the Universal film *Earthquake*, starring Charlton Heston and Ava Gardner, was shown in Sensurround. Large bass speakers that were placed around a theater emitted high-decibel sound waves that audience members could feel during the powerful earthquake scenes. This sound effect was also used in the films *Midway* and *Rollercoaster*.

Double Take

Having a larger budget also gives your actors a break when setting up time-consuming shots. In this regard, many films generally make use of *doubles* and *stand-ins*. These individuals have the same physical characteristics as the actors they're doubling and are usually used for setting up and lighting scenes while the actor is preparing to actually shoot the scene. They may be seen in the final cut of the film in shots where an actor would be unrecognizable. Stand-ins are similar in that they also fill in for actors during lighting and scene setups, but they are rarely on-set when shooting actually begins.

Bonus Footage

When hiring a crew, regardless of your budget, it's important to secure enough cash to keep cast and crew happy and healthy. This means making sure they're well fed, able to get from one place to another with minimum hassle, and out of harm's way. To accommodate these needs on a large-scale production, you need to hire drivers, caterers, and medical personnel.

Also, keep in mind that in addition to overseeing the needs of cast and crew, there are dozens of other positions that need to be filled when negotiating a big-budget operation. For example, films requiring the use of animals will need animal handlers. Productions featuring air transport will need pilots, or films requiring undersea footage will need divers.

Transportation

As one can imagine, transportation is a key component of the filmmaking process, especially when shooting on location. Not only do the cast and crew need to get from one set to another, but all the equipment needs to be transported in a safe and timely fashion. Typically, a *transportation manager*, or *captain*, is hired to coordinate all of a production's transportation requirements and oversee all of the drivers.

Catering and Food Services

Armies don't travel on an empty stomach, and neither do film crews. Keeping cast and crew well fed will do wonders for morale and keep the production flowing. On a small-scale production, this can be as simple as someone bringing coffee and doughnuts for everyone in the morning. On big productions, where shooting days are long or on location, this means hiring a catering service that can provide cast and crew three meals a day. In this case, the production manager is usually responsible for hiring and scheduling catering services.

Medical Personnel

In an industry where safety is a huge concern, it's important to have some type of medical professional on-set if you can afford one. Many productions typically have a medic available during the entire production, especially when construction or stunt work is involved. This individual can be a nurse, physician, or emergency medical technician who will be available for all medical situations that cast or crew members may find themselves in. Regardless of the situation, at the very least you should always have a fully stocked first-aid kit at the ready.

Animal Handlers

Productions requiring the talent of animals—regardless of how small or large—will need an *animal handler* or *wrangler*. These unique individuals are usually specialists in regard to whichever species of animal they train. Animals can be a challenge to work with, so hiring a talented wrangler is paramount, especially in regard to shooting delays (see Chapter 12).

FACT

The largest cast of live animals in a feature film was 22 million bees used in Irwin Allen's 1978 production of *The Swarm*. And in the 1956 production of *War and Peace*, more than 8,000 horses were used during filming.

Publicists

Once a film is complete or even in preproduction, the element of hype comes into play. In order to generate publicity and excitement about your production, you need to hire a *publicity director* or *publicist* to get the word out. Publicists have all types of strategies and marketing techniques up their sleeve, in addition to having a strong network of media connections. A savvy publicist will know the ropes and be able to reel in a film's target audience by arranging anything from press releases to billboards to interviews.

Chapter 12

Final Phases of Preproduction

There's no question that making a film requires lots of planning from start to finish. Without a doubt, the most important phase of filmmaking is preproduction. You've already learned about financing, budgeting, scheduling, and hiring crew members. Now it's time to further home in on your production, recognize additional personnel, and ascertain which additional specialists you might need, if any. You're also going to begin casting procedures, including finding actors, holding auditions, and finally having rehearsals. Meticulously organizing this final phase of preproduction will get you one step closer to rolling cameras.

Bringing It All Together

The quality of a film depends on dozens of different factors, not the least of which are your director, producer, script, cast and crew, financial resources, and all phases of production. One way to keep yourself in the red and your sanity in check is to perfect everything you need to do in the preproduction phases. There's still much to be done at this stage, but the more perfectly you can accomplish these tasks ahead of time, the better off you'll be when filming begins. Once you've settled on a script, secured financing, scouted locales, and organized your budget and scheduling, it's time to decide on actors and finalize how large a crew you need and can afford.

Big-budget productions obviously require a large crew, which means hiring all the main executives, director, producer, camera crew, art department, writers, production designers, accounting staff, gaffers, electricians, carpenters, wardrobe and makeup personnel, and a vast range of assistants for every department. Your crew list can be endless if you've got the bucks to back you up, but that requires meticulous organization.

Kevin Costner's 1995 film *Waterworld* cost a whopping $175 million to produce, but didn't fare nearly as well as *Titanic* on the domestic market. To date, it has only made about $88 million. Fortunately the foreign market brought the numbers to over $264 million in total gross, but it's still not considered a winner.

The chances of a first-time filmmaker being awarded a $100 million production budget are slim to none. For established filmmakers such as Steven Spielberg, George Lucas, and James Cameron, among others, the box office numbers can potentially be astronomical, so a film's budget is in some cases justifiable. Cameron's 1997 blockbuster *Titanic* had a $200 million production budget in addition to a multimillion-dollar marketing budget. To date the film has grossed over $600 million domestically. When added to the foreign gross, *Titanic* has made close to $2 billion, making it the highest grossing film in history.

Documentaries, no-budget, low-budget, and most independent films will typically have much smaller crews. This inevitably means that each crew member will be wearing more than one hat. If you can afford to hire key crew members such as a producer, or production manager, art director, editor, sound editor, and production designer, you'll be in good shape. Add to the mix a host of unpaid interns and you'll be hopping.

One thing to remember always is that any crew member you hire will need prep time in addition to time spent on the shoot. You must also build in additional time and funding, if available, for the end of a shoot, commonly called *wrap* time. On smaller productions where folks are doing several jobs, this usually isn't an issue; but if you're dealing with union labor, everything will have to be negotiated ahead of time.

Who Are All These People?

During filming, there's always going to be a significant amount of hustle and bustle. You will have to know what each person's job is and how to ensure that everything gets done on time and within your budget. Here is an overall breakdown of the various disciplines:

- **Executives**. This title can represent myriad positions. Executives typically are individuals who have some decision-making power. This could be studio or production company personnel whose power varies depending on the position or attitude of the parties involved.
- **Hands-on personnel**. This group includes all the individuals who are making the movie. At the preproduction level this could be as small a group as the writer, director, and producer. As the production progresses, this would include various department heads such as the production designer, art director, wardrobe director, location manager, best boy, and so on.
- **Office staff**. Under no circumstances should these individuals be ignored, as they are of supreme importance to the filmmaking process. Office staff includes all types of assistants, support staff, receptionists, typists, production assistants, and so on. These individuals keep the wheels turning by accomplishing all kinds of tasks, such

as making sure schedules are distributed, messages are sent and received, and script updates handled.

- **Postproduction crew**. These individuals are the specialists who come in after the major film work is done. At that point, this crew of editors, sound designers, composers, visual effects artists, and second unit crews start working their magic.

At any given time on the set or location, there will be dozens of individuals crossing paths, shuffling everything from paperwork to props. The better organized you are in preproduction, the better organized every department and individual will be when it comes time to begin filming.

Casting Call

Throughout the film industry you'll hear varied opinions about what the most important element of creating a film is. Some say it is a great script; others claim that a film's director is the most crucial element. Then there are those who believe that casting the right actors is the most pivotal decision a filmmaker must make. More often than not, it's a combination of the three.

Casting a film is much like cooking—you need the right ingredients in just the right amounts to create something that's palatable and satisfying. Casting professionals are chefs. They take a director's vision and a writer's story, and concoct a ten-course meal that's worthy of a five-star restaurant. If the recipe is off, however, even a potentially great film could easily turn out to be average.

Setting Realistic Goals

No matter whether your budget is large or small, you have to set realistic goals for your production. Actors, especially A-list players, cost a lot of money. Lesser-known actors don't have the same salary requirements, but they may lack exposure or experience. Casting is a fine line between beauty, budget, and risk, and as such, you need to carefully assess each role and the type of actor you need to make that character successful. Great characters played by the wrong actors can sink a film, no matter how good your screenplay.

The Casting Director

Picture for a moment if Bette Davis had played Scarlett O'Hara in *Gone with the Wind*, or James Cagney had played Ben Hur. How different would those epic films have been with a different cast? Chances are, they probably would have flopped. Fortunately for the viewing audience, those films and hundreds of other classic motion pictures had a cast who possessed the right mix of acting talent that was selected and nurtured. Having the perfect cast can make a motion picture. Having a great casting director (or plenty of clout) will help thwart the tragedies that occur as a result of, say, casting Geena Davis as a pirate or John Wayne as Genghis Kahn.

A *casting director*, or CD, is an individual responsible for finding and auditioning actors for many of the roles a motion picture calls for. CDs work closely with the director and producer as well as the actors and their agents. When hiring a CD it's essential that you find an individual who has a large pool of actors from which to choose, and the ability to mix and match talent to accommodate whatever you or the director are searching for.

In addition, the casting department serves as liaison between the director and actor, and often oversees the negotiations and contracts with agents of actors who are being cast. On a big-budget production requiring hundreds of extras, casting can be overwhelming, so it's crucial to find a CD who is not only well connected but extremely well organized.

Casting directors are pros at matching the right actor to the right role. They immerse themselves in a hunt for established actors while also finding as yet undiscovered talent. They're the matchmakers of the filmmaking industry, and their help is indispensable, especially when it comes to large casts requiring hundreds of extras or specialty films in need of animals.

An organized casting director should have a clear understanding of the director's vision and be able to make casting choices accordingly. The majority of the CD's time is spent sorting through loads of potential actor resumes as well as pouring through her list of resources. A good casting director will have strong relationships with many talent agents and managers and possess excellent negotiating skills when it comes time to recruit actors.

Typically it's a casting director's job to deal with actors and their agents and act as liaison to the film's director. In fact, she usually won't present her actor choices to a film's director or producer until she's got a solid selection to show him. A lot of time is saved when casting decisions are narrowed down and presented in full. This open line of communication is invaluable to a director, who has a busy agenda and little time to negotiate with agents. Casting pros also arrange for auditions, casting calls, and callbacks.

FACT

For his 1978 role in *Superman*, Marlon Brando was paid an unbelievable $3.5 million for less than two weeks of shooting that ultimately became ten minutes onscreen. Four years later in a court case, he was awarded an additional $15 million from part of the film's gross.

Casting directors are also great at assessing potential actors. In making their decisions they'll examine a number of factors, including an actor's experience, range, physical characteristics, and other special talents—for example, martial arts training or stunt experience.

If There's a Will, There's a Way

If you don't have a casting director or can't afford one, then the process of finding talent will fall onto your shoulders or those of your producer or director. Your budget, in that case, will play a large part in casting actors, but don't let that stop you. With the right connections, excellent advertising, or a major dose of luck you could win over any number of A-list actors who might be willing to work within the confines of your budget.

Finding Actors

If you don't have actors busting down your door for a part in your production, then you'll have to make use of other resources such as industry directories, casting companies, and the Screen Actors Guild (SAG). Like a casting director, you can even scout out talent by attending theater productions, visiting acting schools, and watching student films and film shorts. If you find someone of interest, look up their agent or manager and ask for an actor's resume and photos to be sent. You never know when or where you'll find a diamond in the rough.

Word of mouth is never a bad thing in Hollywood when you're searching for talent. Neither is advertising in the trades, magazines, on the Web, or even in your local newspaper. When you're advertising for actors, it's important to be clear about what you're looking for, including level of experience, age range, physical appearance, any particular requirements you might have, and so on. And whatever you do, don't forget to mention a salary (if there is one) or benefits you may be offering, like free food or gas money.

Casting Companies

Most major cities in the United States have some type of casting service that they use for the film, television, and theater industries, and all of them are valuable resources you can tap into. Casting companies are a terrific resource when searching for actors. Nowadays, you could conceivably fill your entire cast list online with a company like Breakdown Services Ltd. (*www.breakdownservices.com*), which takes detailed synopses of the characters in your script ("breakdowns") and posts them to its site for talent agents and managers to peruse.

Online sites such as *www.hollywoodauditions.com* can also prove invaluable. Hollywoodauditions collects resumes and photos of both novice and experienced actors, and compiles them on a CD that is sent twice yearly to production companies and casting directors.

The Screen Actors Guild

The Screen Actors Guild, commonly known as SAG, was formed in 1933. SAG operates much like other labor unions, only its focus is on representing actors. As well as monitoring their benefits, compensation, and working environment, SAG has fought many battles over the decades to ensure that actors' rights are upheld. SAG has the reputation for protecting its members by being tough and enforcing its rules and regulations.

SAG Versus Non-SAG

If you're hiring a union actor, it would behoove you to be well versed in all the union regulations. SAG labor costs money, and in using its talent you are subject to a host of rules, standard rates, and penalties for any disruption of its regulations. The best thing you can do to protect yourself is read all of the fine print to the letter. Only after you fully understand how the union operates should you pursue hiring union labor. But again, it's often worth the effort because you're hiring an experienced professional.

If you're an independent filmmaker with a certain budget, you need to be especially aware of SAG's regulations and its basic agreements. Many of SAG's stringent rules still apply, but over the years it has become easier to acquire union actors for independent films. More in-depth information about the Screen Actors Guild can be found on its Web site at *www.sag.org*.

Non-SAG members are a different story. With these individuals it's up to you to negotiate the deals. If you're on a minuscule budget, chances are you can't afford union labor, so you'll have to hire actors outside its realm. One thing to keep in mind is that even if you hire nonunion labor it's important to still maintain a safe and fair working environment.

Holding Auditions

If you have a casting director, he will be the one who sets up actor auditions. Without a casting pro, the auditions will fall to the director or producer. Unless you're considering an actor whose reputation speaks for itself, you'll want to hold auditions for all of the major roles you're casting.

ESSENTIAL

It's said that Charlton Heston wasn't the first choice for the part of Moses in Cecil B. DeMille's 1956 epic *The Ten Commandments*. The part was originally offered to William Boyd, who played Hopalong Cassidy. After Boyd turned it down, DeMille chose Heston because he thought he looked like Michelangelo's sculpture of Moses.

Actors typically attend auditions with their portfolio, resume, and head shots in tow. If the actors are unfamiliar with your storyline, you may want to give them a short synopsis of your film. There are several types of auditions you can conduct. Sometimes directors will have an actor do a combination of the three types of audition in order to better establish his acting range and ability. These audition types include:

- **Side auditions** have the actor reading an actual scene from the script. These "sides" often constitute what is called a cold reading, or one with little or no time to prepare.
- **Improvisational auditions** are just what they sound like. In this case, you decide on a certain scene and allow the actor to improvise the character. This will give you the opportunity to gauge an actor's personality in regard to a character.
- **Monologue auditions** are a bit different. In this instance, an actor doesn't read opposite another person, instead choosing a single monologue from a different film or theater production. These performances can be more polished, as the actor often has time to rehearse.

Auditions are typically held in a quiet place, where a director can focus on the actor and where the actor can concentrate. If you would like to videotape your auditions, then you'll need a cameraman present.

Callbacks

Once you've run through the audition process, it's time to hold *callbacks*. Think of callbacks as a second-round job interview. After weeding through the initial round of potential candidates, you're ready to get serious about hiring someone. The benefit of callbacks is that you can begin to get a sense of how specific actors would play against each other.

Take this opportunity to mix and match in order to find the perfect combination. If you're casting a western, take note of how the good guy and bad guy match up on a physical level. If you're casting a romance, gauge the potential onscreen chemistry of your two leads. Allowing the actors to audition with one another can make a huge difference to your final cast list.

Remember that hiring actors is much like hiring an individual in any other industry. In addition to experience, you want to assess an individual's work ethic, manners, and personality. If it's someone you're going to be working with for long hours every day, make sure you hire someone you can indeed work with. It's unrealistic to think that there isn't going to be any conflict, as there is at any workplace, but hiring the right people will only make everyone's experience more pleasant.

Screen Tests

Screen tests are basically footage that's shot while an actor is auditioning. This can be footage of an actor on his own, an actor with a reader during a scene, or several actors together. The advantage of a screen test is that videos can be sent on to a director if she isn't present at the auditions. Viewing potential cast members in this way can also afford the director a glimpse of how an actor will appear onscreen.

More than a few of Hollywood's legendary stars have failed screen tests. The enormously popular Shirley Temple, for example, flopped when she auditioned for the *Our Gang* series. Clark Gable was called "a big ape" by Jack Warner when he tested for Warner Bros., and in 1933, Robert Taylor was rejected by United Artists for being too thin.

Rehearsals

The nature of rehearsals largely depends on the director, the type of production, and the experience of the actors involved in that production. Typically, all productions will at least have a cast *read-through*, which involves all of the actors sitting together and literally just reading the script out loud. The benefit of read-throughs is that they give the director and the actors an opportunity to immerse themselves in the script, gain insight into their roles, and gauge how their lines should be delivered.

Inexperienced actors will need more rehearsal time, so that must be built into your schedule. Obviously, the more rehearsal time you allot, the better off you'll be when it comes time to film the actual scenes. Actors who don't know their lines cost valuable production time. On the other hand, you don't want to over-rehearse. Part of the believability of film is that dialogue sounds real and not forced. Over-rehearsing your actors can sometimes cause crucial dialogue to become stale.

Scenes are typically shot out of sequence. For this reason, it's important to rehearse the film in sequence at some point so that everyone sees the big picture and confusion is avoided as to the film's proper sequence. This will also help those working on the film to maintain the film's continuity.

Dealing with Agents

Agents represent individuals in the entertainment industry and are licensed by the state. They're wheelers and dealers who typically get a percentage of an actor's salary, usually around 10 percent (see Chapter 5). In general, it's the casting director who deals with an actor's representation. If you are dealing directly with an agent, make sure you fully understand the contracts you're presented before signing anything.

Extra Help

When you're making a film you're going to need every bit of help you can get. In some cases, that means finding actors with a particular specialty, age range, or skill with animals. If your film requires the use of animals or child actors, there are strict rules that must be adhered to, and more than a few inherent problems to be acutely aware of. There are also very few films made these days without the use of extras, which translates to more time, money, and, most assuredly, top-notch organization. Fortunately, there are now many casting agencies and animal actor resources for you to research.

Working with Minors

We've all seen child actors on the silver screen, and we know how powerful their performances can be, whether it's Shirley Temple in *Bright Eyes*,

Drew Barrymore in *E.T. the Extra-Terrestrial*, or Haley Joel Osment in *The Sixth Sense*. One might think that child actors are a dime a dozen, but in truth, they can be difficult to find. In addition, there are a host of considerations, not the least of which is that they're kids: they require naps and have short attention spans!

Inherent to the problem of hiring child actors is that children are protected under child labor laws that greatly limit the amount of hours they're allowed to work. These rules vary according to state but must be strictly adhered to. In many cases, they also include rules regarding a child's education. Another thing you have to consider when casting a child is the content of your film. If your film contains controversial elements, everyone involved in representing the child actor—especially the parent—should be clear on what the child is expected to do. Youngsters who have experience will often be more receptive to direction as opposed to those who lack screen time.

Finding Fido

Many a director's patience has been tried when filming animals for a motion picture. Not only do the animals have short attention spans, but they're often unpredictable. Even Lassie had her moments. Animals require supervision in the form of a trainer or animal wrangler. All kinds of domestic and exotic animals are hired for motion pictures and are trained to perform under all types of circumstances.

If you've got a few animal roles to cast and your German shepherd is giving you the brushoff, you can contact an agency that specifically represents animals. The Hollywood Animals Animal Actors Agency (*www.animalactorsagency.com*) is one such service that can provide animal actors for your production. Another service is Animal Actors International (*www.animalactors.com*). The most important thing is to be very clear with animal handlers and their agents what you expect from the animal, and to ascertain if it can be done in a timely and predictable manner.

Casting Extras

Several films have used a staggering number of extras for various scenes. When filming *Gandhi* in 1981, director Richard Attenborough used approximately 300,000 extras for Gandhi's funeral scene, which was shot in a single morning with the help of almost a dozen camera crews. So you're making a film with a cast of thousands—where are you going to get the thousands? With the technological enhancements of digital filmmaking it's now possible to exponentially increase your numbers, but chances are you'll still need a few extras to fill out your background. Whether it's street scenes or boxing matches, extras complete a picture. Without them a film would look empty.

Be careful when you enlist the help of volunteers. Not everyone takes your production as seriously as you do. On shooting day, the extras you lined up may decide they have better things to do and leave you with costly delays and scheduling nightmares.

If you're on a small budget, then you'll probably need all the help you can get in the form of family, friends, relatives, your mail carrier, and your mother's entire bridge club. And that's okay as long as you're clear about what you require—for example, how long your extras will be standing under a blazing sun, or sitting in a stadium, or escaping a torrential downpour. It's also nice if you can at least offer your extras lunch or even provide monetary compensation.

Big-budget films often make use of local sources, especially when filming internationally. Military personnel, students, and all types of groups have been employed as extras. In director Mel Gibson's 1995 film *Braveheart*, for example, Gibson made use of the Irish territorial army, the F.C.A. In the 1945 Nazi-produced film *Kolberg*, almost 200,000 soldiers were pulled from their wartime duty to play Napoleonic soldiers.

Chapter 13

Science in the Art

Referring to filmmaking as an art over-simplifies the breadth of talent and resources that are required to produce a movie. Filmmaking is the orchestration of many separate and distinct art forms, combined to form a single visionary showpiece. Capturing the imagery of every scene onto film is one of the most technically demanding and constantly evolving art forms in the filmmaking process. In order to best capture their subjects, filmmakers must evolve with technology and begin exploring the digital world.

From Sprockets to Terabytes

The digital age has made a great impact on the way motion pictures are made, a fact that is especially evident when it comes to camera work. Filmmaking is currently in the midst of a growing and inevitable shift away from shooting onto film. One of the fading arguments for using traditional film cameras is that film has a look or feel that can't be duplicated digitally. While this is most certainly still the case when the imagery of large-format film is compared to consumer-grade and entry-level digital camera equipment, experienced cinematographers and camera operators who use high-end professional digital equipment are quickly eliminating the distinction.

Evolution of the Camera

The light bulb and phonograph may be Thomas Edison's most famous inventions, but he can also be credited with the creation of the world's first commercially successful motion picture camera, which he patented in 1891. Several earlier devices had been created that enabled the illusion of motion to be captured on film. The tongue-twisting Phenakistiscope and Zoopraxiscope were capable of projecting images that produced the appearance of movement, but they relied on a series of still cameras to create their images.

During this same time, the Eastman Kodak company had designed and marketed consumer-oriented single-shot cameras that utilized rolls of film that could be hand-wound through relatively simple mechanisms. Edison's team of creative geniuses realized that the same concept could be applied to a motorized camera that would automatically wind and shoot multiple frames of film in rapid succession.

Black Maria

The result of Edison's effort was a motion picture camera that utilized rolls of film thirty-five millimeters (35mm) wide. The camera was given its own home in the world's first motion picture studio, unofficially dubbed the *Black Maria* (pronounced ma-rye-uh), which you learned about in Chapter 1. The studio was constructed to pivot on a single axis in the center so that the entire structure could be swiveled to face the sun, which provided the light required to shoot the scenes within.

The camera Edison's team developed was called the *Kinetoscope*, and the device on which films were viewed was the *Kinetograph*. The Kinetograph was a single-user mechanism that would trigger a worldwide amusement industry and encourage America's hunger for inexpensive entertainment. The cinema was born.

FACT

The Kinetograph gradually gave way to projection systems that displayed films onto screens that dozens of patrons could view at the same time. From these humble (and very profitable) beginnings, the technology of filmmaking and film cameras has grown in sophistication, speed, and image capacity.

Cinematography

The art of cinematography encompasses both the technical function of cameras, lenses, filters, and various films and the visual effects that can be achieved by manipulating all of those elements. Much of the art consists of framing and focusing images through the camera lens, and lighting scenes to achieve a director's visual expectations.

In the budding days of filmmaking with hand-cranked cameras and limited lighting sources and techniques, many motion pictures resulted in a fairly crude look by today's standards. To modern audiences, the jerky feel and highly contrasted appearance of early silent films can make them seem more like home movies than the highly conceptualized, state-of-the-art entertainment they were at the time. In some cases, this raw appearance worked to a filmmaker's advantage, as with F. W. Murnau's haunting presentation of vampire Count Orlok in the 1922 silent film *Nosferatu*.

In the 1930s and 1940s, as film cameras, lenses, and lighting methods became more sophisticated, black-and-white filmmaking, classic *film noir*, often presented visually stunning imagery. Detail, depth of field, and use of light and shadow resulted in some of the finest cinematography in history—imagery that stands up well to this day. Classic films such as *Casablanca*, *Citizen Kane*, and *The Maltese Falcon* are brilliant examples of filmmaking as art, not just for world-class casts and screenplays, but for the sheer beauty of the cinematography.

In modern filmmaking, the craftsmanship of cinematography and camera work are more important than ever. Astronomically expensive special effects and intensive postproduction computer wizardry only serve to highlight the art of the camera as it's used on the set in front of live actors and action.

Choosing a Camera

Selecting a camera involves considerations of cost weighed against expectations. Along with determining the most appropriate camera to use in a production, choices must be made regarding film stock, lenses, and filters. Then there's the matter of transferring the finished footage into the appropriate format. For the wide screen, the only choice is to transfer film to 35mm prints for running on standard theater projection equipment. Going directly to videocassette or DVD sidesteps this expensive transfer process, but it also limits the opportunity to screen the film theatrically.

Super 8

In the early 1930s, *8mm cameras* were designed as a cheap consumer-oriented alternative to larger film sizes by slitting 16mm film stock right down the middle. *Super 8* film cameras have been around since 1965, when Kodak introduced an upgraded version of the 8mm format. By eliminating the magnetic soundtrack tape on the edge of the film, the usable image area was increased by a substantial 40 percent.

Significant graininess results when Super 8 film is transferred to videotape, and becomes impossible to ignore when blown up to 35mm prints for theatrical release. Although Super 8 cameras are abundant and can be acquired for next to nothing, the drawbacks in cinematic quality usually outweigh the low cost. For film productions that are intended for distribution, the Super 8 format is probably not the ideal investment.

16 Millimeter

When people today discuss shooting with 16mm film, they're either referring to *standard 16* or *Super 16* sizes. Standard 16mm cameras and film result in box-like screen images that don't easily transfer to the rectangular dimensions of 35mm prints without significant cropping on the top and bottom of the images.

Most filmmakers believe that their budget is the determining factor in choosing a film format. A production budget of approximately $200,000 is a benchmark figure that is considered to be sufficient when deciding whether or not to use 35mm film.

Super 16 film is 40 percent wider than the standard 16 size, and correlates very well to the rectangular-size ratio of 35mm prints. Many feature films are shot on 16mm film, and with good cinematography, the audience is rarely the wiser. The real value of the standard 16mm format is that cameras are relatively common, inexpensive, and easy to acquire. Filmmaker Robert Rodriguez shot *El Mariachi* entirely on a borrowed 16mm camera. Modern film for 16mm cameras is extremely high quality, and it stands up well when blown up to 35mm print sizes for theatrical distribution.

Worldwide Standardization

Since the time of Thomas Edison's filmmaking empire in the early 1900s, 35mm has been the standard size film for feature films. The reasons for this are a combination of chance, availability, and economics. Edison's early motion picture camera utilized rolls of *still* camera film that were 70mm wide. Edison ordered rolls of this film split in half lengthwise for his project testing and development. The resulting 35mm film proved to be the ideal size for his first Kinetoscope. By protecting product patents and eventually obtaining a virtual stranglehold on the film industry in later years, Edison's 35mm format became the worldwide standard for professional filmmaking. That distinction remains true to this day, and virtually all theater projectors in the entire world are designed to handle only 35mm print stock.

Lenses

Camera lenses feed the imagery of a scene onto the film in the belly of the camera. High-quality lenses are masterpieces of technology and are built to extremely demanding standards of craftsmanship. Quality lenses add dramatically to the cost of camera equipment, but the level of excellence they add to your final product is worth every cent. The focal length of a camera lens determines the image that is captured on film or on a computer disk. Lenses are identified by that focal length in millimeters.

Wide

Wide-angle lenses capture a great deal of imagery from left to right in the camera perspective, and can be helpful for low-lighting shots because they gather a great deal of available light. The effect of wide-angle lenses is to increase the apparent distance between the foreground and the background. Wide lenses are seldom used for closeups because they tend to distort head shots by widening faces, making the nose protrude and the ears seem too far back.

Medium

Medium lenses are used to capture a normal range of imagery with a wide range of depth. The medium lens is often used for closeups and medium shots because they produce normal-looking images with a realistic field of depth.

Telephoto

Telephoto lenses will shoot past unwanted images in the foreground, and tend to flatten and compress perspective by shortening the apparent distance between the foreground and background. Of all the lenses, telephotos usually require the most light in order to perform effectively. Some productions are filmed entirely with a good-quality telephoto lens as the only lens.

The Magic of Filters

Adding filters to camera lenses can create a different dimension because they can remove a predictable amount of light from the spectrum. This can be an important consideration if you're using film manufactured for sunlight shooting conditions in an indoor set that's artificially lit. There is a wide range of filters that you can choose from, depending on the onscreen atmosphere you're striving to create.

Types of Filters

Filters are designed to produce or reduce a number of effects during shooting. Filters can be adjusted to accommodate for shooting indoors with outdoor film, and to reduce the brightness and atmosphere of outdoor shots. They can also be used to create specific color effects, or to change the overall tint of images.

QUESTION?

What do you use if you have too much natural light?
For outdoor scenes with too much natural light, neutral density filters are often used to help reduce the amount of light that's allowed to travel into the camera. Neutral density filters have little effect on color, and can be used without concern for color shifting onto the film.

For shooting outdoor scenes with a significant amount of haze or smog, *skylight filters* are often used to help counteract the haze. These filters can be either slightly pink or yellowish in appearance. Because they have virtually no unpleasant effect on images shot outdoors, they're often left on the camera lens in all outdoor settings as added protection to the actual surface of the lens.

Graduated filters are partially neutral density filters and partially clear. The neutral density half of the filter is positioned to reduce the harshness of the sky on a bright day without affecting the ground-level action. You can use graduated filters in the same way to create the illusion of a night sky while shooting in broad daylight.

Polarizing filters are designed to selectively remove excessive light. By rotating a polarizing filter, reflections from window surfaces and the surface of water can be greatly reduced and sometimes entirely eliminated. Care must be taken to ensure that the filter doesn't also completely remove the appearance of the window or water.

If you're attempting to reduce harshness and hard lines, you'll want to use a *diffusion filter*, which gives your image a soft, dreamlike quality. Diffusion filters are often used when shooting digitally, and help negate the inherent overly sharpened and often jagged edges of digital images. *Color compensation* filters are used to specifically alter the color of the imagery onto film. If, for example, you want your film to have a warm sepia tone, you'd use one of these filters. The eerie effects of fluorescent lighting can also be corrected with color compensation filters.

Matte Boxes

Matte boxes are square framed boxes that are fitted around the camera lens. They're designed to hold lens filters and prevent light leakage. Filters can easily be slipped into matte boxes in specially sized slots. In the case of polarized filters, the filter slot is designed so that the filter can be rotated to achieve the best polarizing effect for the lens.

Stocking Up on Film

Raw film stock is the term used to describe unshot motion picture film. Camera film is manufactured in wide rolls and then sliced into widths for its intended use, from 8mm up to 70mm. Roll lengths can vary from fifty feet to 2,000 feet. To help ensure consistency throughout a shoot, many filmmakers (those who have the funding to do so) prefer to buy recently manufactured raw film stock from the identical production batch. Given the very high quality-control measures from batch to batch during the manufacturing process, this step isn't mandatory. The most important criteria for you to pay attention to are that the camera film you're using is fresh and from known suppliers with strict handling procedures.

Virtually all camera film for commercial and feature film reproduction is *negative* film that requires processing and transfer to a *positive* film format for viewing through a projector. *Reversal* film is manufactured in positive format, and can be projected immediately after processing. You would choose reversal film if only one copy of your film is needed, or if the time between filming and processing for viewing needs to be limited, as is often the case with news footage.

Negative camera films are manufactured in a wide selection of "looks" and *film speeds*. Film speed is adjusted by altering the film emulsion and its sensitivity to light. Speeds are chosen to provide latitude for various lighting conditions. The look of camera films can range from films with deep and intensely saturated color to films that accurately convey very fine, sharply detailed images.

Going Digital

Digital filmmaking equipment runs the gamut from inexpensive consumer cameras to expensive high-definition (HD) cinema cameras that appear to capture exactly what the human eye perceives in real life. Digital cameras put images directly onto digital videotapes that can be loaded onto computer hard drives for editing.

Pros and Cons

Shooting digital video is much less expensive than shooting and processing with traditional film equipment. Film costs are basically eliminated, although video does require transferring to 35mm film prints for theatrical release. Also, because videotapes can be used over and over, and unwanted or unusable images can simply be erased, there's no waste of film. One of the great advantages is time savings—you can see what you've shot within minutes of shooting it.

Video images can produce noticeable defects. Because digital images are made up of tiny square pixels, hard edges can often look jagged and rough. The brighter areas in images, such as skies and windows, can become completely *blown out*—a stark and disorienting bright white. The sharpness of video can also appear to be a little too real and too crisp, lacking the organic softness of shooting to film. Many of these issues can be minimized by using filters to avoid overexposing highlights and to soften the sharpness of video. Good exposure techniques are helpful for reducing jagged edges.

The Creative Debate

There are many strong arguments for using traditional film cameras for feature filmmaking. In the 16mm format, cameras are relatively abundant and inexpensive, and 16mm film is much less costly than 35mm film. The downside is that the cost of blowing up 16mm film to 35mm prints for theatrical distribution is significant for a feature-length film. Arguments for starting filming with 35mm gear is that there are no additional laboratory costs for blowing up the image for theatrical release. It's argued that those cost savings can be absorbed into leasing 35mm equipment, purchasing 35mm film stock, and paying for processing during production.

The position that digital filmmaking is here to stay is undeniable. With state-of-the-art cinematography techniques, high-end digital filming today rivals the results of shooting with film. As digital technology advances and prices continue to drop, it's inevitable that traditional camera film will sooner or later be replaced.

Chapter 14

On the Set

All your preproduction planning is done, your cameras are loaded, your cast and crew are in place, the coffee is hot, and the bagels are fresh. What else could you possibly need before you start shooting? For starters, you'll need props, sound, lighting, and setups for all your special effects, all of which take time and require the help of many crew members. The production phase of filming may seem like the most glamorous, but as any industry pro can attest, it takes plenty of hard work and supreme planning.

Got Props?

The function of props in a film seems so obvious as to not require a definition. For this reason, important details sometimes get overlooked. A prop is anything that an actor will touch, pick up, or interact with. A vase on a table is only set dressing until your hero dusts it for fingerprints. A box of chocolates is ornamentation until your romantic heroine opens it and takes a bite. No matter how small your film, or how inconsequential any prop may seem, it's important to know early on if it will have to be borrowed, bought, or rented. If you're making a historical drama or a science fiction epic, the task gets harder, since some or all of the props may have to be specially designed and built.

Once everything has been accounted for, it is the job of the *prop master* to make sure each actor has the appropriate prop when the scene begins, and to collect the props when shooting is done. Careful organization is essential, to prevent loss and to help keep track of which props were used in case reshoots must be done days or even weeks later. Even in a small film, it's important that someone be assigned those duties before shooting commences.

The Importance and Science of Sound

In many respects, the role of sound in a film is as crucial as the visual imagery. Not only does it convey information in the form of dialogue and sound effects, but the proper use of sound can set a mood and help establish the surroundings before an actor enters or a word is spoken. There are many important elements to sound in film, and in order to truly understand it, you must familiarize yourself with the science on which it's based. You also need to recognize the part that sound plays in the production and postproduction process and the techniques your specialists employ.

Sound is created by vibrations. Vocal cords, guitar strings, breaking glass, and crashing cars all create a disruption that vibrates through the air, creating compressions and rarefaction until they reach our ears. Sound itself is defined by four parts: wavelength, harmonics, resonance, and amplitude.

Wavelength

Put simply, the faster the vibrations, the shorter the distance between compressions and the higher the *frequency* and *pitch*. Frequency is the number of compressions per second. This means that low-frequency sounds have a longer wavelength; high frequencies correlate to shorter wavelengths and create a higher pitch.

The *cycles* from the beginning of one compression to the beginning of the next are measured in *hertz* (Hz). The average human ear is capable of detecting sounds from 15 Hz at the low frequency up to 20,000 Hz.

ALERT!

The musical accompaniment to your film should always be appropriate to the scene itself. For example, a symphony orchestra plays at about 75 dB, while a rock group can easily reach 90 dB. But be warned, at about 120 dB, sound becomes painful. Keep this in mind for the final mix, especially when including dialogue.

Harmonics

The source of any sound vibrates at its *fundamental frequency* and at other frequencies called *harmonics*. Harmonics are always a higher frequency, rising in multiples of the fundamental. If the fundamental is 200 Hz, the next harmonic would be 400 Hz, and the next would be 600 Hz, and so on.

Resonance

Most string instruments have large, hollow areas to help intensify and prolong the sound produced by the strings. The space in our nasal cavities, chest, and lungs produces a similar effect when we speak. This intensifying effect is called *resonance*. The natural *resonant frequency* is determined by the physical parameters of the vibrating object. Any object, from your skeleton to a suspension bridge, can be made to vibrate if acted upon at its resonant frequency.

Amplitude

The actual measurement of sound is defined by two parameters: the scientific and the psychological. The scientific measurement of amplitude is often confused with its psychological equivalent of *loudness*. Amplitude is measured in *decibels* (dB). A rise of 10 dB results in a perceived doubling in loudness.

Sound Equipment

To the average Jane making a film in her attic in Cleveland, the concept of sound and all the equipment involved in sound recording and mixing can appear overwhelming. But if you break down the components and examine their various functions in context, you'll find that sounds are a fascinating study. When it comes to your film and recording sound, the microphones are your ears, the recorder serves the function of your brain, and the tape is your memory.

Recorders

On consumer-level tape recorders, there are three heads that read across the tape. One erases any existing data while the other two record and play back new information. Professional recorders, however, also have a *synch head* for laying down a synchronization track, which allows the camera and recorder to be timed together. Professional recorders will also have either a *volume unit* (VU) *meter* or a *peak program meter* (PPM) to aid in setting the appropriate input levels.

Digital and Analog Sound

Most film recording is done using one-quarter-inch (6mm) *analog tape* or the smaller *digital audiotape*, commonly called DAT. Various qualities of analog tapes are available, using different types of magnetic media. The aim is to get the best signal while reducing system noise and dropouts. The tape passes over the recording head at a rate of seven and one-half inches per second, allowing for fifteen minutes of recording on a standard reel. This process is slightly different for digital recording. Instead of recording the sound itself, a digital system records information about the sound's waveform. That information is fed to the playback unit, which recreates, rather than replays, the sound. This eliminates the system noise associated with analog tapes.

With some of the medium-priced digital equipment, the sound travels from the camera straight into a recording computer via an inexpensive high-speed connecting cable called *FireWire*. While budgetary concerns may make this an acceptable option, compressing the audio down to FireWire compatibility and then expanding it back again to edit the sound results in a loss of quality. The audio signal can be so degraded by the time it reaches the editing room that it's impossible to raise the volume without raising the system noise.

The company Sound Devices makes a good four-channel Time Code Recorder that records to a forty-gigabyte hard drive that's commonly used in the film industry. Fostex also makes a field recorder that features a time-code device.

Ideally, audio should go through a mixing board but then split off to a DAT recorder or *hard drive recorder* rather than to the camera that feeds the computer. This will mean using a *time base corrector* (TBC) that creates a time-code with the audio that corresponds with the video time-code. The audio is always best when left in multitrack form, then mixed, mastered, and married back to the video in the master-to-tape process.

Microphones

There are almost as many types of microphones as there are opinions as to which are best. In the broad sense, microphone designs fall into one of two categories. *Directional microphones* will pick up sounds from a limited area. The designs vary depending on the *pickup pattern* or the shape of the area to which they are sensitive. These are extremely useful in settings with lots of background noise, such as a city street location, or in an interview situation when you want to hear the subject's voice clearly and distinctly without any ambient sound.

Omnidirectional microphones pick up sound in a nearly 360-degree sphere. This can come in handy for recording a conversation between two or more people around a table, for example. Assuming the rest of your set is as quiet as possible, a single mike can simplify filming (and keep equipment rental costs down).

Sound Versus Noise

The difference between sound and noise is like the difference between a daisy and a thistle—they're made of the same basic stuff, but you don't want both of them in your bouquet. The inherent difficulty in excluding all noise is that no recording equipment is perfect. Couple that with the abundance of ambient noise surrounding us no matter where we are, and you've got a host of issues to conquer.

System Noise

For decades it has proven impossible to eliminate all the *system noise* that results from imperfections in recording equipment. Because of these inherent flaws, both microphones and analog tapes add a noticeable background hiss to any sound recording. Fortunately, the new generation of digital recorders and DAT tapes reduces equipment noise to negligible levels.

Ambient Noise

Everywhere we go, we're surrounded by *ambient noise.* Fluorescent lights, chirping birds, the hum of a refrigerator, and the distant drone of traffic are a few examples of the natural and continuous sounds of our everyday environment. On one hand, you want to get rid of them as much as possible; on the other, you want to be sure to record them.

When filming anywhere except in a completely controlled soundstage, you cannot help but have background ambience or *room tone.* Because the ambience is unique to that location, be sure to record several minutes of room tone, with no dialogue, movement, or anything that'll interfere with the pure background noise. This will prove invaluable at the editing stage, by providing you options if it becomes necessary to rearrange synchronized sounds.

Other than recording a track of room tone, you want to minimize ambient noise as much as possible. One way to do that is *redubbing*. Also called *looping* or *automated dialogue replacement* (ADR), this is the process of recording or replacing voices during editing, long after the film is done. It's a difficult task at best, and one that soaks up precious editing time and money.

A far easier way than redubbing to get around ambient noise is by using a highly directional microphone. When properly positioned, this microphone will pick up the dialogue or other sounds you want while minimizing background noise.

It may also be necessary to muffle the cause of the noise. Refrigerators, for example, can be turned off during shooting. Film cameras not only make a lot of noise as they sprocket the film past the gate, but they're often close to the subject, and therefore close to the microphone. In order to avert this problem you'll need to invest in specialized camera covers called *barneys* and *blimps*. If you're keeping it simple, try throwing a blanket over the equipment. This usually works well enough, as long as you remember to remove it between takes to keep the camera from overheating.

Microphone Placement

The ideal place for the microphone is three to six feet from an actor. Not only is the actor's voice stronger the closer you place the microphone, but it also allows the recordist to lower the incoming volume, thus lowering any system noise. The danger of putting the microphone too close to the actor is the possibility of creating a hiss on any spoken "s" sounds or popping caused by a "p" or "d." This can be minimized with the use of a foam cover over the microphone.

Things That Go Boom!

Separate from any pyrotechnics work, a *boom* is a long pole, mounted or held so that the microphone is just out of camera range. It's important for the boom operator to work closely with the camera operator and the best boy to make sure the microphone is not seen and doesn't cast a shadow. Shadows can be eliminated by moving the boom to a new position, such as below the subject, pointing upward.

Lavalier and Radio Microphones

Sometimes it's simply impossible to have a microphone close enough to hear an actor without it being in the picture. For these shots you might want to consider a *lavalier* microphone. The lavalier is about the size of your fingertip. It can be clipped to an actor's clothes, or even taped to their skin to avoid the noisy rustle of fabric. The difficulty lies in the long thin cord that connects the microphone to the recorder. In some cases, this can be threaded through the subject's clothes, out of sight until it reaches the floor. But keep in mind that this limits the actor's movements and the director's choice of camera angles to avoid revealing the cord.

A better solution is the use of small *radio microphones*. These have a small transmitter that can fit in the subject's pocket or clip to the back of a skirt. Each microphone has its own frequency and its own feed into a mixing unit, which is attached to the recorder.

Controlling the Recording

While most professional audio recording equipment is designed for ease of use, it's important for the sound recordist to constantly monitor the recording for the best possible quality. This monitoring system requires the use of several different pieces of equipment, including a volume unit meter, peak program meter, and a host of additional mixing and cabling devices.

Volume Unit Meter

The *volume unit*, or VU, meter measures signal amplitude as an approximate average. The meter is marked with a red or black area to indicate when distortion occurs. When recording any sound, it's the goal of the recordist to avoid distortion. Since the VU meter measures an average, it's best to keep the indicator as close to the distortion area as possible without crossing into it.

When using a radio microphone on location, be sure to check for nearby power lines or broadcast sources on the same frequency. You don't want your romantic and elaborate outdoor wedding scene to be interrupted by the crackle of a railroad dispatcher.

Peak Program Meter

The *peak program meter*, or PPM, measures the peak signal level. This means the indicator should be allowed to cross into the distortion area without being allowed to "peg" all the way to the right side of the meter. That would indicate signal distortion.

Deciding Whether to Mix

All this talk of watching the needle and keeping it within a specific range doesn't mean the recordist continually adjusts the volume controls. Also called *potentiometers* or *pots*, these should be set during a volume test before filming begins. Once set, there should be no need to adjust them while recording. Doing so can result in unwanted fluctuations, making it difficult to match sound during editing.

Cables and Connections

Most recording problems during filming arise because of defective or incompatible cables or connections. If one piece of equipment has DIN plugs and the other requires XLR connectors, a lot of time and money can be lost while the correct equipment is tracked down. A difference in *impedance* can also create difficulties when recording. If your microphone and your recorder have different impedance levels, distortion can occur. While some recorders have a variable impedance switch, it's easier to check beforehand to confirm that the equipment is compatible. A ratio of five-to-one is acceptable. It's always a good idea to keep several cable adapters in your recording kit to quickly and easily avert an audio disaster.

Lighting Techniques

We've all seen the moment when the heroine emerges from the gloomy mansion into the daylight, symbolizing the beginning of her new life. We've also seen the warm glow of a couple having a romantic dinner, and the menacing face of a vampire appearing from the shadows. Lighting is necessary to expose film—to alter the emulsion and create an image—but with a little bit of care, it also creates a mood.

The Upshot of Lighting

Proper lighting is a balance between *exposure*, *sensitivity*, and *contrast*. A quick way to determine this is the use of a *pan glass*. Looking through this small, hand-held lens shows the scene you're filming at a higher contrast, effectively mimicking how the image will look on film. Your cinematographer can then make adjustments before shooting.

The intensity of light being given off by a particular source is measured in *foot candles* (fc), which is the amount of light received from a standard candle one foot away. In metric terms, the distance is thirty centimeters and is called *lux*. Since we rarely look directly at a light source, most of the light we see has been reflected off all of the objects around us. The reflectivity of a surface or surfaces determines the foot candles that make up the high and low range of your shot.

Knowing the Surface

A smooth surface is said to be *specular* because it reflects the light more directly. A rough surface, such as fabric, absorbs much of the light, and the specularity is more diffuse, reflecting smoothly in all directions. It's crucial for various departments, such as set dressing and wardrobe, to work closely with the camera crew well in advance to determine if there will be problems with reflections during filming.

The Setup

The major components of setting up the lighting for any shot come down to three broad categories: *key light, fill light,* and *back light.* The key light is the primary source. It should mimic the *motivating light* in both intensity and direction. For instance, if there's a large window in a room, the key light may simulate sunlight coming through that window.

Fill light refers to a nondirectional, softer light, often placed in a position opposite the key light in relation to the camera. Its job is to "fill" the shadows caused by the key light, softening the subject to more realistic ambience. The back light, as you might guess, is one placed behind the subject, aimed toward the front. While this will create shadows on the front of the subject, it will also generate a sense of depth and emphasis.

FACT

Warmer colors such as yellow, orange, and red can make the audience feel comfortable or even physically warm. Moving the lighting into the greens and blues creates a sense of coolness.

The secondary thing to consider when lighting a scene is color. Since color is by definition light, white light is made up of equal parts of red, green, and blue (RGB). These colors can be separated out by use of colored bulbs or by putting a colored transparency between the light source and the subject. This can be important, not only for matching or imitating a particular motivating light, but to communicate mood or even ambient temperature.

Available Versus Practical

Whether you choose to utilize the available light of a location or the practical light provided by household lamps and streetlights, odds are you'll end up using professional lighting equipment to enhance or simulate the real thing. In this regard, there are several considerations, including housings, reflectors, and bulbs.

The Basic Housing

The structure of the lighting instrument is called a light housing. *Open-face* housings are simply a bulb in front of a reflector. These are lightweight and provide an even spread of light. The bulb of the *Fresnel* light is behind a lens that amplifies and focuses the beam. The housings are larger and heavier than open-face units, but provide a better quality of illumination. The light from the *parabolic aluminized reflector* (PAR) is comparable to the headlight of a car. Because the bulb, parabolic reflector, and lens are all fixed in the housing, the beam cannot be altered.

Reflections

While reflections on your set may be bad, reflectors in your lighting unit are crucial. Often shaped for a specific purpose, they bounce the light out of the housing in a particular direction and manner depending on their shape. Common shapes and their uses are as follows:

- Parabolic reflectors surround the bulb, creating a highly directional, highly intense beam.
- Flat or curved reflectors in a broad light are usually dimpled, and produce a more diffuse beam.
- Bounce light is not a reflector in a housing, but rather a method of pointing a light at something on the set and allowing the light to "bounce" back onto the subject. The reflecting surface can be an object made for this purpose, or simply the wall or ceiling of the room itself.

Bounce light provides a quick and effective way to light a room evenly and softly. As such, it's often ideal for documentary-style filming.

Getting Radiant

At the center of every lighting unit is the *bulb*. A far cry from a sixty-watt reading lamp or even the huge bulbs of previous generations, modern bulbs are smaller, cooler, and more lightweight. It's important that you understand the types of bulb and their functions. These bulbs include:

- Tungsten lights, which are very big and bright. Usually used as floodlights, they have a very limited life span, especially in terms of brightness and color stability.
- Quartz-halogen lights, which are tungsten-based but do much better at maintaining a consistent amount of light and color balance.
- Carbon arc lights, which create a spark between two carbon electrodes to create a light strong enough to match daylight. The units themselves are big and heavy, and the electrodes must be trimmed and replaced about every thirty minutes.

Hydrargyrum medium-arc iodide, or HMI, is a mercury-halide arc lamp. HMIs are the new solution to many of the old problems. The mercury-arc discharge lamps are only at full power for a fraction of every second, keeping them cooler while making them more efficient than quartz lights. One difficulty is the large, heavy ballast that accompanies each unit. Another big drawback is the price. It would be cheaper to buy an entire quartz-halogen light head than to replace a single HMI bulb.

Be sure that everyone working on your film is extremely careful when dealing with very high voltages and extremely hot lights. Never think that lighting a set is as simple as flicking a switch. Be sure your gaffer has had sufficient training, and that your power requirements don't exceed the limits of your shooting facility.

Special Effects

Special effects are often confused with visual effects. Trick photography or computerized spaceships fall under the category of visual effects. Things like smoke, fire, fog, and fake blood, however, are all part of the magic of special effects that can be done right on the shooting set. For this reason, they are also referred to as practical effects.

Up in Smoke

If a car blows up or a rock band catches fire, you're seeing the work of *proximate pyrotechnics*. These are the non-fireworks type of effects that can be done on stage, in front of the camera. These include smoke, flames, flashes, and explosions. Please be aware that pyrotechnics is not a place for experimentation or on-the-job training. These materials are, by their very nature, extremely hazardous. If your film calls for something to catch fire, to spark, or even to just fill a room with smoke, seek out the advice of a certified pyrotechnician as early as possible.

While actual *squibs* or exploding bullet hits come under the heading of pyrotechnics and stunts, there are safer solutions that have been used effectively for decades to simulate a person being shot. Packets of fake blood, for example, can be worn under an actor's clothes. When the character is "shot," the actor clutches where the bullet supposedly entered, thereby releasing the blood.

In Michael Mann's *Manhunter*, a character is shot directly in the forehead, on camera. Makeup artists Doug Drexler and John Caglione Jr. came up with an elegant solution by having the actor stand perfectly still during the shot. A thick dot of red makeup was placed in the center of his forehead, and the actor fell down. When the "before" and "after" segments were edited together, the effect is seamless.

Recreating Weather Conditions

One of the simplest and yet trickiest effects to pull off convincingly is that of warm breath in a cold environment. If your actors can handle cigarette smoke, have them inhale a small amount just before a closeup. The smoke is released as they speak, but you should try to cut-away as quickly as possible. Not only because there will be no smoke on their second line, but also because cigarette smoke behaves differently from steam and the audience will notice. If the actors continue to "act" cold on the medium and long shots, no one will notice the lack of cold breath.

Having smoke show up on camera may require a slight back-lighting, so be sure to consult with your cinematographer as early as possible, and allow for camera tests a day or two before shooting.

While filming Frank Capra's 1937 classic, *Lost Horizon*, small pieces of dry ice were placed in mesh containers that the actors held in their mouths to create the effect of warm breath in a cold climate. One of the actors got so frustrated with the device that he took the ice out of the mesh and popped it directly into his mouth. The frozen carbon dioxide immediately burned off half of the man's tongue.

One piece of effects equipment that a beginner can use with just a little practice is a *fog machine*. Small ones are available for purchase or rental from many party supply stores. The "smoke" is perfectly safe to breathe, although those with asthma or other respiratory conditions are best advised to spend as little time as possible in the area of the fog to minimize irritation.

Stunts

Even if your film has no car crashes or shoot-outs, it's vital to carefully plan and rehearse anything that involves jumping, falling, throwing, or even running. For example, in the 2005 indie film *Fixed*, a scorned lover throws a vase at her boyfriend as he walks off camera. After several takes, everyone was getting tired and a bit too relaxed. The safety guy missed catching the vase and it hit the actor in the head. Several scenes had to be re-shot to explain why the boyfriend had a bandaged ear.

When dealing with stunts, always consult a professional, and never lose sight of the fact that stunt work is extremely dangerous. The last thing you want as a filmmaker is for your actors to get injured. You need to hire a stunt team to take the big risks.

Chapter 15

Visual Effects

It might be a thundering starship or a majestic steamship, a flower that blossoms before our eyes or a flock of geese taking flight on cue, a well-trained owl or a hungry tyrannosaurus. Or it may be a throng of ecstatic soccer fans or a solitary ghost. Sooner or later, the need will arise for a moment that is too difficult, too expensive, or simply impossible to shoot in real life. This is when a filmmaker turns to visual effects.

Inside the Camera

Unlike special effects such as smoke or pyrotechnics that happen during shooting, a visual effect is a trick. It's a filmmaker's sleight of hand that makes an audience see what the filmmaker wants them to see. Like a painter, a visual effects artist relies on the fact that an audience has limited perception of the two-dimensional world shown on a movie screen. As viewers, our eyes and brains are always striving to "fill in" the third dimension of depth. The visual effects artist uses lighting, color, false perspective, hard and soft focus—anything to convince viewers to believe the alleged reality they're seeing.

In the most general terms, visual effects fall into three categories:

- Those created inside the camera
- Those created on-set
- Those created in postproduction

Some of the least expensive but highly effective visual effects are done right inside the camera itself. This includes maneuvers such as overcranking and undercranking, reversing shots, changing lenses, and controlling exposures.

Overcranking and Undercranking

One of the easiest effects is the use of slow and fast motion. Professionally, this is called *overcranking* and *undercranking*, terms left over from the days when the camera operator would turn a crank to control the speed at which the film moved through the camera. Film normally moves through the camera (and later through the projector) at a rate of twenty-four frames per second. Overcranking ups the camera speed so that more frames pass by the lens each second. When projected at the normal rate, what took one second to shoot at forty-eight frames per second is slowed to two seconds of projected screen time. The action slows down by a factor of two.

Higher cranking rates translate to slower action. Some highly specialized cameras can shoot at rates of single frames per hour, effectively stopping time to watch the construction of a building or the bloom of a flower.

The more common equipment rarely goes above eighty frames per second. Conversely, undercranking slows the film through the camera so the resulting action is accelerated.

Simple tricks can have great emotional impact on your viewer. We've all seen the moment when the young wide receiver dives for the winning touchdown—always in slow motion. Another perfect example of this is the running scene on the beach in *Chariots of Fire*.

These manipulations can also be useful in practical ways. For example, what if the script calls for a high-speed chase, but your driving location is only safe for thirty miles per hour? If you undercrank to eight frames per second, your car is suddenly going ninety miles per hour!

When shooting miniatures, slow motion helps small objects appear larger. Huge submarines move slowly through the water and large creatures are often ponderous. As a general rule, the larger you want something to appear, the slower it should move. Remember, it's all about what your audience expects to see and what they're allowed to perceive. If you're using digital editing equipment, it may be possible to speed up or slow down the action electronically. There are quality concerns to be aware of, however. Undercranking can cause blurring and overexposure, and overcranking may result in stuttering or jerkiness in the image. It's always best to shoot camera tests before spending time and money on the real thing.

Reversing the Action

While running the action backward is most often used for comical effect, it can also come in handy for dramatic moments. If a shot calls for a quick zoom into a tight shot, it can be tricky getting the exact framing you want at the end. By running the film backward, you can begin with the closeup, then quickly pull back. When projected normally, the zoom will have a powerful effect.

For example, in the first *Mission: Impossible* film, the camera performs an amazing fly-in on a speeding train, finally stopping on a closeup of the right window. The primary photography for this was accomplished by using a helicopter, beginning with the shot framed on the window, then flying away to the wider view. The visual effects team simply reversed the shot (and digitally added their visual effects coordinator into the window behind Vanessa Redgrave!).

Utilizing the Lens

As described in Chapter 13, many specialized lenses are available to help you achieve specific results. An object moving toward you never seems to get any closer when viewed through a telephoto lens. A fisheye lens creates the rounded, bulbous look often used to depict the viewpoint of someone mentally ill or disoriented by drugs. Extremely low angles are possible using a periscope-mounted lens. Experimentation with different lenses can be fun and open your film to several creative possibilities.

Camera Rigs

The *Hot Head* camera is one that can be controlled remotely. This allows it to be used in places where it would be too dangerous for a camera operator, such as on the street in front of a speeding car. If the Hot Head is attached to a long, extendable arm, it's called a *Luma crane*. This crane can reach places where a full camera rig and operator wouldn't be able to go, such as in and out of windows, suspended off the roof of a building, or from the ceiling of an enclosed room.

FACT

One of many memorable scenes from *The Blues Brothers* is when the prison doors open to reveal John Belushi for the first time. White light pours around him, creating an almost celestial quality. The blinding white effect is called solarization and it's created by purposely over-exposing the film.

One of the most versatile and useful camera rigs is the *Steadicam*, which consists of a hard, inflexible harness worn by the operator with a mounting arm attached to it. The arm is balanced to compensate for the weight of the camera, allowing the operator to walk, run, climb stairs, or circle a room while keeping the camera itself level and steady. Proper use of a Steadicam requires some physical strength and hours of practice, given that these cameras are extremely heavy.

Magic on the Set

Before deciding to spend millions on high-end effects, stop and determine whether your visual effect can be achieved right on the stage. There are a host of tricks you can employ to add flair to your scenes without your audience even batting an eye and wondering how it was done. These include the methods of front and rear screen projection, the use of miniatures and false perspective, and even stop motion animation.

Rear Screen Projection

In the 1933 film *King Kong*, Robert Armstrong as Carl Denham was throwing gas bombs at King Kong on a soundstage in Hollywood. But the "gigantic" monster was in fact thirteen inches tall, filmed using *stop motion animation*, and added to the shot using *rear screen projection*. Rear screen is just what it sounds like—previously shot footage that is projected from behind onto an opaque screen with a high transmission factor. This means that it allows light to shine through to the other side. The screen is placed at the back of the scene with actors and set pieces in front.

QUESTION?

Where do you most commonly see a rear projection shot?
You're most likely to see a rear projection shot out of the rear windshield of a car. The actor faces forward and pretends to drive while the street moves behind him.

In the case of *King Kong*, the monsters fought or charged from the back of the scene, but always stopped just short of the real actors. Usually a row of rocks or bushes was used to hide the base of the screen, and to help tie the projection in with the actual set. The key to good rear screen projection is matching the color balance and vanishing point with the "real world" elements. If your camera is too far to one side, the distant perspective will not match the audience's eyeline. If the color or contrast coming through the screen is incorrect, it'll look faded and fake, and the effect will be blown.

Front Screen Projection

Front screen projection is a similar gimmick to rear screen, but is much more difficult to accomplish correctly. The benefit, however, is that front screen projection can provide a sharper image for the effects footage. The best screen for this purpose is called *Scotchlite* and is made of glass and silver beads. It's highly reflective and produces a bright, sharp image.

With the screen placed at the back of the set, a half-silvered mirror is set in front of the camera at forty-five degrees, with the reflective side facing away from the camera. The camera should be able to see through the back of the mirror and see the set. Offstage, a projector is set in line with the forty-five degrees so that the image projected at the mirror is reflected up onto the screen. If the alignment is correct, the camera should record a seamless image of background and foreground elements. Direct lighting should be kept off the screen, since this will diminish the brightness of the image.

Shadows are the tricky part of front screen projection. When the actors and set pieces are in position, their shadows should fall directly behind them, hidden from view of the camera. If the actor moves at too much of an angle, a shadow will appear around the edges. If the projected image has too much motion or contrasting elements, it may be visible on the actor. Your shooting schedule should allow several hours for testing and rehearsal.

Onstage Miniatures

The most famous, even "classic," use of miniatures on a set is Godzilla smashing his way through Tokyo in the 1954 version of the film. The balsa and polystyrene buildings are highly detailed, adding a great sense of realism to the destruction. But there can be smaller examples of onstage miniatures.

In his 1996 short film *Father Time*, director Jamie Neese included a scene where a commercial jetliner is frozen in mid-air. Actor K. C. Marsh has a great comic moment as he does a very slow take to find the giant aircraft floating directly above him. When asked how he achieved this tremendous effect with no budget, Neese explained that he mounted a toy airplane, no bigger than a foot across, directly in front and slightly above the lens. With the actor standing several feet away, they rehearsed until Marsh had the perfect eyeline, looking up as if the plane were over his head.

Stop Motion Animation

Arguably one of the most painstaking methods of filmmaking is *stop motion animation*. A fascinating forte, stop motion animation melds artistic skill and mechanical wizardry. The earliest version of King Kong was first sculpted in miniature on a posable armature skeleton. The animators would position the miniature in a set constructed to the same scale, and then shoot one frame of film. The miniature was then moved ever so slightly, along with any leaves, trees, airplanes, dinosaurs, or natives that were in the scene. A second frame was then shot. The miniatures were moved again for a third frame, and so forth. At twenty-four frames per second, you can imagine how long it took to create such a shot, and in 1933, this was state of the art.

FACT

If you watch the 1933 King Kong closely, you'll see his fur move in odd ruffles, as if caught by strange, random breezes. These are the nearly unavoidable "fingerprints" left by the animator as he moved the miniature.

Filmmakers like Ray Harryhausen and Henry Selick became masters of their own styles of stop motion. Harryhausen's army of skeletons in the 1963 film *Jason and the Argonauts* is still a landmark piece of filmmaking. The skeleton fight alone was shot at the rate of thirteen frames per day. In 1993, Selick revitalized stop motion almost as a genre of its own in director Tim Burton's *The Nightmare Before Christmas*.

The difficulty and the artistry in stop motion is the ability to time the movements into smooth, realistic action. In modern times, this has been made easier by the aid of computer-controlled robotics and camera mounts. When a miniature is photographed one frame at a time, it's not moving while the shutter is open. There's none of the blurring that occurs naturally when filming a moving object. With robotics, miniatures can be made to move just the tiniest bit, timed to the opening of the camera. The camera itself can be fixed to a movable mount, controlled by the same computer. The object and camera move at the same time, resulting in a natural-looking blur and a more realistic effect.

False Perspective

As a filmmaker, you want to utilize an audience's unconscious efforts to interpret the two-dimensional movie screen as a three-dimensional world. One simple trick to accomplish this is to take advantage of *perspective*. Perspective is the concept that the farther away objects are from us, the smaller and closer together they seem to be. For example, if you film a shot of a road going toward the horizon, the road appears to narrow the closer it gets to the horizon. The same goes for mountains, which in reality are thousands of feet high, but seem no bigger than our thumbnail on the big screen.

Let's say you have a small shooting space, but you want your set to appear large. One place to start is having converging lines on the floor and/ or ceiling. Since the lines obviously don't extend to the horizon or *vanishing point*, they'll never meet. But having them even a little bit closer together at the end farthest from the camera than they are at the near end will make the audience believe the room is bigger than it is.

The same can be done with columns, tall window frames, or vertical molding to make a room seem taller. A good example of this is the main street of Disneyland, which is lined with old-fashioned storefronts. The street level is built to normal scale, but the second and third floors of the exterior facade are each constructed at a slightly smaller scale than the one below it, giving the buildings a tall, stately appearance.

Another way to play with perspective is by having larger objects in the foreground and smaller ones in back. This may be as simple as a tall potted plant near the camera and smaller ones in the background. In *Star Trek: The*

Motion Picture, the engineering set was made to look bigger, not only by having the floor tilt upward in the background, but also by using shorter actors in the back and taller ones closer to camera.

Effects in Postproduction

By far, the large majority of visual effects today are created in postproduction, usually at specialized effects labs called optical houses or effects houses. In 1931, the invention of the optical printer allowed filmmakers to take pictures of pictures, effectively enabling them to duplicate sections of their film while adding or subtracting elements. If you want a better closeup, you zoom in the optical printer's camera on the subject. You could also rotate the camera to tilt the shot, or photograph each frame more than once, effectively creating a stuttering slow motion. Parts of the scene could be masked out (also called matting) so that other elements could be photographed in their place.

The increase in computing power available to the average consumer, along with the advent of more affordable software for creation and editing of visual effects, has brought the optical house into the computer age. Nearly everything can now be done digitally. For example, in Robert Zemeckis's 1994 Best Picture *Forrest Gump*, Tom Hanks's character, Forrest Gump, was inserted into various historical film footage to give the appearance that Gump was actually in the scenes.

Real World Versus the Digital World

Photographic miniatures have long been a staple of visual effects, using real-world materials to match the look of a full-sized object. The recent innovations in computer graphics imagery (CGI) has expanded the palette of the visual effects artist into realms that were previously impossible. Three-dimensional, or 3-D, computer graphics are created entirely in the "virtual" world using specialized 3-D software. Though the computer monitor, like the movie screen, is only a two-dimensional medium, geometric data is represented in a three-dimensional construct, using shadows, highlights, and perspective, among other aspects. But whether it's a plastic model on a stick or a computer-generated landscape, the basic steps remain the same.

Modeling Basics

Creating realistic miniatures is a true balance of art and technology. For decades, models were built from clay, metal, wood, rubber, or plastic. They not only had to look real, they often had to operate like the real thing. Propellers had to spin and lights had to blink and power lines had to blow up.

ALERT!

When purchasing a previously built 3-D model, be sure you're also buying the rights to use that model in your film. Models that replicate copyrighted objects such as the starship *Enterprise* or *Star Wars' X-Wing* may be fun to practice with, but cannot be used in a commercial venture.

Sometimes even the term "miniature" seems out of place when you consider that models such as the submarines in *The Hunt for Red October* or the overturned fuel truck in *Terminator 2: Judgment Day* were each several yards long. Models of cities often take up an entire soundstage, but it's their large size that allows them to be so convincingly detailed. Using a computer, 3-D models can be built "full size" since there's no limit to the size of the imaginary place in which they're constructed. Every 3-D application uses slightly different tools or construction metaphors, but the techniques usually come down to one of four methods.

Solid Geometry

Objects are pieced together from smaller objects, comparable to adding shapes of clay to one another. In their most basic form, the objects are cubes, spheres, cones, pyramids, and prisms.

Polygonal Models

Shapes are defined by the arrangement of *polygons* along the surface. Usually the polygon is a simple flat triangle. Multiple triangles placed side by side form edges or curves, like a geodesic dome. The smaller the polygon, the smoother the surface. Perhaps a more familiar example would be a soccer ball, which is a sphere made up of several five-sided polygons. Keep in mind, the more polygons you have, the better your object will look, but it will also take up more computer-processing power. Try to find a compromise where it looks good and your computer won't crash.

Subdivided Surfaces

This is defined as the limit of an infinite refinement process. Basically, it means you can begin with a rather blocky shape made up of big subdivisions. You can divide those into smaller subdivisions, then smaller again, and so on. With each successive refinement, the surface of the object becomes smoother. But like polygons, the more subdivisions you have, the more computer power it will take.

NURBS

An acronym for non-uniform rational B-spline, NURBS is a way of expressing complex curves in a standardized mathematical formula. This is important if you're the designer of a car or boat and you want the builders to get the shape just right, but you don't need to understand the math in order to use the NURBS function in most 3-D software. There are usually metaphorical tools to let you shape objects the way you want while the computer handles the number crunching.

Finessing Your Model

Once a model is built, the next step is to add texture, color, shading, transparency, reflectivity, specularity, or any of the seemingly endless list of characteristics that would make an object appear real. Many 3-D applications have built-in surfaces. To make the bumper of a car shine, for example, you only have to highlight the appropriate parts of the object and then select "chrome" from the preset choices. Once the basics are set, you may want to add scratches, dirt, or "rough spots" to add an extra layer of realism.

Building the model may also involve giving the object a *skeleton*. This is a collection of *rigs* that, though invisible in the final product, will make it easier to control movement and shape if the object is to be animated. For those who prefer to film models but not build them, several companies and individuals offer completed 3-D models for sale, usually via the Internet. While the prices may seem steep at first, when compared to the time spent building the model, they are usually quite reasonable.

Shooting and Scene Layouts

Once you've created your models, you're ready to photograph them. In the case of physical miniatures, this means positioning the model in a fixed location or on a movable mount, usually in front of a monochromatic background. The model is photographed, sometimes several times for different lighting or motion "passes." If multiple models are required for one scene, such as a squad of fighter planes attacking a battleship, each model may be filmed separately, then composited, or pulled together, into one scene with the others, along with any extra passes that were required.

If the entire effects sequence is being created digitally, the process is somewhat different. CGI models are arranged in what is called a *scene layout*. This is equivalent to placing actors and scenery on a stage. Once in their positions, both the object and the camera can be moved in relation to each other, and to the world at large.

Digital Models

One advantage of digital models is that the visual effects artist has options regarding shooting. Each model can be filmed or *rendered* individually and composited later, as you would do with physical miniatures. The other choice is to set up an entire scene at once, including landscape, buildings, 3-D characters, clouds, trees, lighting, shadows, and so on. and then render the entire thing at the same time. Digitally rendering everything at the same time may seem simpler, but it takes much more computing power and limits your freedom when it comes to editing.

For example, if you're shooting a tractor-exploding sequence and realize the tractor should explode half a second earlier, you'd need to render the entire scene again, which might take hours. But rendering just the tractor, or even simply adjusting the existing explosion in the editing room, may only take a few minutes.

Digital Movement

If a digital scene involves movement (as compared to a still image), you'll most likely use a technique called *keyframing*. Remember how with stop motion the animator had to move the model in every frame? In computer animation, you only have to set up *keyframes* at certain points in a sequence. For example, let's say your script calls for an airplane to go into a barrel roll as it flies past the camera. For the first keyframe, you begin with the plane in an upright position, 100 meters away from the "camera object." At a point five seconds later in the sequence, you move the plane to 100 meters on the other side of the camera, and you rotate it 360 degrees on the long axis, just as if it were doing the roll in real life. This is the second keyframe. The computer will calculate the change in position and axis between the two keyframes and then fill in the airplane's correct placement and attitude for every frame in between.

Of course, this is a highly simplistic example. To make this look at all real would require careful timing and adjustment to the movement curve. If you're just getting started, practice with very simple shapes that render quickly. Once you're confident in your skills, use the final model, but begin with simple test versions such as *wireframe* or *animatics* until the motion is perfect.

It's a good idea to practice with different styles of lighting and even shoot several tests to make sure it matches other footage. Be certain you are happy with the look and the emotional feel of the scene before any final shooting begins.

Another key element that you must consider is lighting. Whether real or digital, proper lighting can mean the difference between an imposing aircraft carrier and a bathtub toy. This is even more important if the effect will be added to existing footage shot on a stage or location.

Compositing

The final step is to put all the pieces, or *elements*, of your effect together. This is called *compositing*. Compositing can be thought of as layers of film stacked atop one another. If you're compositing your exploding-tractor footage, one layer has the background. The next has a moving stream. One has a farmhouse and another has just the smoke coming from the chimney. The topmost layers might be the tractor, then the explosion elements.

To keep all the layers clearly delineated from each other, each is defined by solid black areas called *matting*. The matte area can be used to define either the area that will be visible on that layer or the area that will be transparent, letting the layers behind show through. Each element layer and its accompanying matte layer can be moved, re-timed, color enhanced, brightened, dimmed, or adjusted in almost any way without altering the other layers.

Many 3-D software programs can create matte lines for you using *alpha channels* or other automatic settings. When using physical miniatures, mattes are often drawn by hand, or at least indicated manually, and then filled in by an editing computer later. To simplify this process, you would film your subject in front of a monochromatic background in a process traditionally called *blue screening*.

Blue Screens

When it comes to using blue screens, the truth is that the background screen doesn't have to be blue. Often it's green, or even orange. The strategy of using a single, vibrant color is to make it easier for the person (or computer) creating the matte to distinguish between what images remain and what needs to be matted out. So the choice of color is determined by the colors used in your scene. For example, if your evil alien has blue skin, you probably want to shoot him in front of a green screen. If the shot involves green grass and a blue sky, then orange might make things easier.

Television newscasts use a low-quality version of this in a process called *chromakey*. Controlled by a video mixing board, the camera is instructed to not "see" a specific color. A second image fed from a computer or even another camera is then keyed in to replace that color. If the weatherman is standing in front of a green wall, and the chromakey is set to that green, the weather map will appear behind him. If he makes the mistake of wearing the wrong color necktie, it might look as if he's being strangled by a low-pressure system.

Rendering in CGI

Since there's no film camera inside the digital world of your computer, the 3-D software program will provide an object that represents the camera. This can be pointed and moved just like a real camera. There will be settings for focus, zoom, and aperture, as well as special lenses and filters to match anything done in the real world. Once you're satisfied with your scene layout, there are several options for rendering:

- Wireframe or animatics let you quickly see the relationship of the objects to each other.
- Open GL renders a bit slower, but still fast enough for an easy check of color, shading, and shadows.
- Ray-tracing provides the most full realistic results.

As it renders, the computer saves the frames on a hard disk, either as individually numbered files, an image sequence, or a digital film file such as Quicktime or Windows Media. These can be replayed at a higher frame rate (usually the standard of twenty-four or thirty frames per second) to create the illusion of motion.

ALERT!

While ray-tracing results in a better image, it can take from a few seconds to several days for a single frame, depending on the complexity of your scene. That's why it's a good idea to do a test render in wireframe before going on to ray-tracing.

To more accurately portray the way the human eye perceives the behavior of objects on film, the software can add effects like motion blur, lens flare, and depth of field. Rising technology and falling prices have brought quality visual effects within reach of any filmmaker willing to take the time to learn the basics, and to experiment with just how much the finished product can be enhanced by visual effects.

Natural Effects

Besides film and camera behavior, natural effects are available on some software systems. *Volumetric effects* such as fog, clouds, and dust alter the way light passes to the camera. *Particle effects* can simulate rain or fire. To stay on schedule with a film containing several complex visual effects, an optical effects house will make use of a *render farm*, which ties several computers together, working on the same sequence simultaneously. For even larger films, studios will employ several effects companies, each assigned a different part of the film.

Chapter 16

Postproduction

Once your footage has been shot, your film will enter the postproduction phase. Now you must edit the film to its best commercial and artistic potential. In doing so, you have to create the right ambiance through sound and music—two subtle disciplines without which a film would be empty. Many a film has been saved or slaughtered in postproduction, so to assure yours is a winner you need to give careful thought to the choices you make and the ultimate visual and aural appeal you want your film to exude.

Creative Choices in Editing

As a filmmaker, your goal is to bring your vision to life. All of the creative aspects, technical choices, characters, emotion, action, suspense, and ultimately the entire story fall on your shoulders when your film graces the silver screen. Add to the pressure the aspects of financial gain, scheduling, all stages of production, and a film's distribution and reception, and you've got a recipe for success or a disaster.

The editing phase of production can be scary. It's at that point that you begin to revisit some of the aspects of your production and wonder if you've shot enough usable footage, or if there's anything you've missed that is crucial to your storyline. Many a film can be born or broken during the editing stage. The thing to always remember is that editing a film has as much to do with trusting your instincts, or those of your *film editor*, as it does with the technical process itself. When editing, you always want to keep yourself focused, because the way a film is edited can have great impact on its final cut. Always ask yourself, "What story am I telling? Is the film being edited in such a way as to convey that story through its dialogue, pace, action, emotion, flow, and suspense?"

ESSENTIAL

When you're filming, it's important to monitor the number of usable sequences. If you're not certain that you've filmed enough, film extra so you won't get caught short when editing. Even if a shot seemed perfect, a director may ask for "one more take for protection." It's far more expensive to reshoot extra footage after your sets and actors are gone.

Successful films have mastered the concepts of creativity and continuity while at the same time showcasing expert cinematography, effects, and perfect casting. It's the film editor's job to follow the script and assemble all the emotional storytelling elements you've created to form a cohesive finished product. It's also your job to make sure that the film stays true to your vision and intent.

Daily Checkups

One of the benefits of editing a film is making use of what are commonly called *dailies* or *rushes*. Dailies constitute raw film footage that a director and film editor can view after a day's shooting schedule has ended. Dailies are also a great benefit to other departments, such as makeup and wardrobe, and individuals, such as the script supervisor, who need to monitor the continuity of a film and its actors. At the end of the day, it's always a good idea to view the previous day's shot list as well. That way, you're constantly in sync with what's been filmed before you continue filming. This affords you the opportunity to make any changes or adjustments to various scenes before it becomes too costly to do so.

Test Screenings

Another way to ensure that your film has been edited correctly is through *test screenings*. Before your film is actually released, the studio or production company will show it to a select audience, who will then answer questions and offer opinions. This process can be extremely helpful, especially if the audience recognizes problems that can be fixed by re-editing sequences or editing in additional footage.

Some filmmakers rankle at what they see as "studio interference." But director Frank Capra used to take his own films to local theaters, and then sit in the balcony with a tape recorder, letting the microphone hang over the front railing. In doing so, Capra captured the sounds of the audience shuffling in their seats, coughing, talking, and so on. Hearing those sounds in conjunction with the film gave him a sense of timing. Ultimately, he found that his testing methods were far more useful than questionnaires.

Linear Versus Nonlinear Editing

In the past, traditional film editing was done in a linear fashion. The film was literally cut into long strips divided by scene and take, and then glued or taped back together to create a film in logical sequence. This was time-consuming, tedious, and highly specialized work. All or most of any given scene had to be completely shot before editing could begin.

The biggest drawback with linear editing was that the process itself destroyed the film. Splicing "used up" several frames, and if anything went on the now-infamous "cutting room floor," it would most likely never be seen again. As technology improved, this handwork was made obsolete. In the digital era, editors have shifted gears, using *nonlinear* systems that give them the flexibility to work on scenes, and even traditional frames, out of sequence.

FACT

In Howard Hughes's 1930 film *Hell's Angels*, an incredible 2 million-plus feet of film was shot during the four-year production schedule. Unedited, this footage would've run for twenty-three days nonstop. The edited film ran for two hours and fifteen minutes, an incredible accomplishment for the film editor given the sheer amount of footage.

There are many advantages to the nonlinear editing system. For starters, it allows the editor access to any given frame, scene, or even groups of scenes at any time. Since the raw footage is kept intact while perfect digital copies are used to create the edit, the editor can return to the original take at any time. The first nonlinear editing system used on a feature film was on Martha Coolidge's 1993 *Lost in Yonkers*. The entire film was edited using Avid Media, which enabled the editor to view the film in the "real-time" rate of twenty-four frames per second.

The method is also computer friendly. Most programs allow you to quickly edit scenes from low to high resolutions with little time delay. These programs are now so common that everyone from professionals to first-time filmmakers can afford and master the software. Programs like Adobe Premiere and Final Cut Pro are popular choices. Or if you're just getting started, standard Windows and Apple operating systems come with free applications such as Movie Maker and iMovie.

The Effectiveness of Sound

As noted in earlier chapters, motion pictures are filled with sounds, both natural and unnatural. Every sound from chirping crickets to cars crashing to electrical wires humming is enhanced and perfected by a sound specialist. A finished film will include a wide range of sounds that have been recorded or manufactured by these individuals. As a filmmaker, you need to pay special attention to the sounds associated with every scene of your film. No matter how big or small your budget, you need to have someone who is adept at recording, editing, and mixing sound (or at least a friend with a tape recorder).

Individuals who compose the sound department, including editors, recordists, and foley artists, are skilled technicians. They work with film editors and the music department to give you the best possible sound and sound effects for your film. In Chapter 14 you learned about the science of sound. In this section, you'll learn about perfecting sound at the postproduction phase.

Ambience and Dominance

Sound effects can be classified in several different ways. *Background sounds*, commonly referred to as ambient sounds, are recessive noises that you can hear throughout a film—the soft gurgle of a brook during a hiking scene, or frogs croaking, or wind blowing. By contrast, there are *dominant sounds* that relate to something you're seeing onscreen, like a gun being fired or cars crashing. *Manufactured sounds* are the type you would expect to hear in a science fiction movie in order to create a certain unnatural aura. *Specialized sound* effects such as paper crumpling or cloth ripping are created by a foley artist.

You Don't Know Jack?

Chances are you've never heard of Jack Foley, but you've definitely heard his work. A true motion picture legend, Foley developed many of the techniques used for sound effects in film. Having begun his career in silent films as a screenwriter and stand-in, Foley later helped Universal Pictures revolutionize the world of sound as we know it today. Because of his pioneering efforts, sound effects professionals are known as *foley artists*. Watching a foley at work is a fascinating study. Part artist and part inventor, these individuals work in studios surrounded by all types of everyday implements, articles of clothing, weaponry, and even various foods.

Foleys are unique specialists who usually come on board during the postproduction phase. Most of the sound effects you hear during a film are the result of a foley artist's innovative work. These sounds run the gamut from footsteps to doors opening and closing to leaves rustling to the unnerving crack of bones breaking.

Snap, Crackle, Pop

All of the sound effects created by foley artists are unique and can be tailored to any movement, action, or dialogue. The sound of horses' hooves, for example, is made by hitting together a pair of hollowed-out coconut shells. To create the sound of bones breaking, the artist snaps a stalk of celery. The sound of hitting a watermelon becomes the sound of one actor punching another. All of these sounds are recorded and given to the *sound editor*, who mixes and compiles all the sounds during postproduction.

Making Music

When you think of music in film, what do you think of? The menacing *da-dum-da-dum* as a great white shark speeds toward a skinny-dipper in *Jaws*? Or the sound of drums during a canoe chase in *Last of the Mohicans*? Or perhaps Wagner's "Ride of the Valkyries" as helicopters invade the shore in *Apocalypse Now*? Music is a crucial component to any motion picture. It sets the tone and balance of your overall soundtrack and it helps elicit emotional response at peak times throughout your film.

QUESTION?

Where can I find sound effects libraries?
If you surf the Web you'll find dozens of sites dedicated to sound effects, like *www.soundideas.com*; you can join many of these for a fee and begin downloading sounds. Other sites offer collections that can also be purchased.

If you're on a very tight budget and have friends who can play instruments, you can always ask them to lend a hand. You can also check out music libraries that feature royalty-free tunes, like *www.cssmusic.com* or *www.musicbakery.com*. For a nominal fee, you can find everything you need to make your film sing.

If you have the budget for a music department, then you'll need a *music supervisor*. This individual works with a *composer*, oversees all musicians involved in creating a film score, and deals with all details necessary to secure rights to songs (see Chapter 9). What you ideally want to have in a composer is someone who's both creative and adept at bringing out the subtle and dominant themes of your film. Most films have up to an hour or more of music, and that requires talent to keep the threads of your film tightly wound.

The Big Score

The background music of any film is called the *film score*. Written by a composer, it's meant to match what's happening on the screen in an effort to create a mood or provoke emotion. Often these scores are performed by an orchestra, or can include original or prerecorded songs (some of which you'll need to negotiate rights for). All of the music compiled together becomes part of your film's soundtrack. The film industry has been graced with the talents of many prominent composers who have scored hundreds of films and television series. They include:

- **Bernard Herrmann** (*Citizen Kane, The Birds, Psycho, North by Northwest, Vertigo, Fahrenheit 451, Cape Fear, Taxi Driver, Journey to the Center of the Earth, The Ghost and Mrs. Muir, The Day the Earth Stood Still*)
- **Danny Elfman** (*Spider-Man, Big Fish, Charlie and the Chocolate Factory, Corpse Bride, Sleepy Hollow, Men in Black, Mission Impossible, Batman, Dick Tracy, Edward Scissorhands, Beetlejuice, Chicago*)
- **Hans Zimmer** (*Pirates of the Caribbean: The Curse of the Black Pearl, Driving Miss Daisy, Twister, Thelma & Louse, The Lion King, The Prince of Egypt, Gladiator, The Ring, Black Hawk Down, Batman Begins, The Da Vinci Code*)

- **James Horner** (*Troy, Aliens, A Beautiful Mind, Deep Impact, Titanic, Casper, Braveheart, Apollo 13, Patriot Games, Field of Dreams, Willow, Star Trek II* and *III, Cocoon, Mighty Joe Young*)
- **Jerry Goldsmith** (*Alien, The Omen, Planet of the Apes, Patton, Coma, Poltergeist, Chinatown, Basic Instinct, The Mummy, Congo, Total Recall,* most of the *Star Trek* films, and the *First Blood* trilogy)
- **John Williams** (*Close Encounters of the Third Kind, The Poseidon Adventure, Superman, Schindler's List, Jaws, E.T. the Extra-Terrestrial, Home Alone, Harry Potter,* and all the *Star Wars, Indiana Jones,* and *Jurassic Park* films)
- **Max Steiner** (*Gone with the Wind, Casablanca, King Kong, Mildred Pierce, Dark Victory, The Treasure of the Sierra Madre, Key Largo, The Jazz Singer, Bringing Up Baby, Jezebel*)

Incidental Music

Incidental music is the term used for the musical score that's written specifically to accompany the "feel" of scenes in a film production. Well-edited incidental music is often so subtle that it's not noticeable, and is almost never intrusive. The inclusion of incidental music is designed to punctuate key moments in scenes, and to elicit emotion, suspense, and excitement from your audience. Romantic interludes, explosive action scenes, and lead-ins to dramatic exchanges are often accompanied by musical material of corresponding intensity and pacing.

If you plan to use any music written or recorded after 1922, you're required to contact the copyright holder and secure permission. Don't think that even a small local band will be so "flattered" to find their song playing in your film that they won't sue you.

To help understand and appreciate the impact and intent of incidental music, sit through a few of your favorite movies, paying specific attention to the various ways background music is manipulated to sustain the action onscreen. Skillful use of incidental music can help turn a good film into a great film.

Needle Drops

The term *needle drop* was first used by disc jockeys to describe how they can drop a phonograph needle in the exact place they want a song to begin playing. The term has since been adopted by the filmmaking community. In terms of your soundtrack, it refers to pre-existing songs, usually currently popular music, that is "dropped" into a film to highlight a story point or character moment. Lawrence Kasdan's classic 1983 film *The Big Chill* is good example of needle dropping.

Going Public

The best source of information for acquiring music that's in the public domain and royalty free is the Public Domain Music Web site at *pdinfo.com*. If you're in the hunt for John Philip Sousa's "The Stars and Stripes Forever," for example, you're in luck. All songs written before 1922 are considered public domain in the United States, and if you visit the site you can not only obtain the sheet music for a nominal fee but also purchase royalty-free CDs or DVDs, or simply download what you need straight to your computer.

Credit Due

Every film has a set of titles and opening and closing credits that runs at the beginning and end of the film. These credits list all of the individuals who participated in your film's production, from actors to accountants to assistants. This is an opportunity to give credit where credit is due and let everybody and their mother see their name on the silver screen. Creating the opening and closing credits can be as plain or elaborate as you can afford. Some films have a simple scrollbar as a closing credit that moves from the bottom of the screen to the top, others include jokes or even bloopers. More recently, filmmakers have been eliminating opening credits altogether, instead running an extended credit list at the end.

If you're a filmmaker on a tight budget, you can have an optical company or title house create very basic titles and credits for a reasonable price. If you've got a big budget, you'll still need to plan for your titles and credits, because it's easy to go overboard. Titles that are designed optically with special effects such as fade-ins, drop shadows, or animation are primarily used on larger budget operations due to their expense.

When compiling a list of credits, be sure to check everyone's title and the spelling of everyone's name. Then double check them. You'll also need to establish the order in which you'd like the credits to run, paying close attention if certain contracts call for an actor or crew member's name to appear in a certain position.

Unions, Guilds, and Credits

The order of the credits, specific job titles, and often the exact wording itself is usually spelled out by the professional filmmaker's unions or guilds. For example, the opening credits of a feature film almost always appear in the same order:

- Production company name
- Director's film credit (e.g., "A Mike Nichols Film" or "A Spike Lee Joint")
- Names of stars (the order of which is rigorously negotiated)
- Producers (executive, associate, co-)
- Department heads (cinematographer, composer, costume designer, production designer)
- Writer's name
- Director's name again

To paraphrase a well-known negotiator, the rules of entitlement are more like guidelines. Everything can be negotiated, or even waived. The best example of this is what the Directors Guild sees as a hard-fought battle over many years, one in which they insisted a director's name be shown at the beginning of every film. In 1977, however, a young upstart director decided that the beginning of his movie should be so big that no one's name should come before the film's title—not even his! When the director's union threatened to kick him out, he moved 400 miles north of Hollywood and began his own production company. Today, George Lucas is one of the most successful film producers, and the pride and joy of the Directors Guild.

As a filmmaker, the important thing to remember is that you cannot change the rules on your own. You can't decided which actor's name goes first or that it would be groovy to withhold the name of your surprise guest star until the end credits in order to maintain the surprise. All these things must be talked out and settled very early on in the film process. Officially, everything should be in writing before any work begins. Even casual mistakes have resulted in arbitration and lawsuits.

Chapter 17

Getting It Out There

Aside from the profound personal artistic satisfaction that is derived from completing a motion picture, the primary objective of any filmmaker is to get her film in front of an audience. This can be done in several different ways, all of which require patience, tenacity, and, in some cases, legal assistance. Marketing and distributing a film are part of a filmmaker's job. Film festivals, independent distribution, and studio distribution and marketing deals are yet another big part of the filmmaking game. With a bit of luck, you're sure to be a winner.

The Distribution Challenge

As with every other aspect of filmmaking, getting a film distributed can present a substantial and frustrating challenge. There are never any guarantees, but the upside to this challenge is that if you've a created a really good film—especially one with commercial potential—you'll be able to get it screened by people who can get it distributed. A film in the can is infinitely more valuable than a concept or a screenplay, and it's difficult for any major cinematic player to turn down the opportunity to "discover" you after you've done all the work.

Probably the best way to get your film noticed is to enter it into a film festival. Major festivals are heavily attended by studio representatives, agents, managers, and the press, who are all hungry to discover new talent and potentially profitable film projects. Very few commercially viable films slip through the bigger festivals without attracting attention.

Film festivals provide some of the few remaining venues in the world for screening 16mm prints, which for a filmmaker can save tens of thousands of dollars in postproduction costs. For a film with good commercial possibilities that receives positive exposure and publicity in festivals, major distributors will happily pick up the cost of transferring 16mm film negatives to 35mm film prints for general theatrical release.

FACT

A number of films such as Robert Rodriguez's 1992 indie film *El Mariachi* and Steven Soderbergh's 1989 hit *sex, lies and videotape* were jump-started at film festivals, and launched the careers of their makers.

There are scores of regional film festivals in the United States that can provide good publicity and audience response. While regional festivals usually don't attract nearly the same attention in professional filmmaking circles as the major festivals, they can still provide invaluable exposure. You can try to invite as many distributors and buyers to your screenings at festivals as possible, but be aware that many of the major players are loath to being accosted by overeager filmmakers. Even at festivals, you can't force, or necessarily even expect, anyone to watch your production. If your film is good, it will generate its own publicity and buzz.

If you're planning on submitting your work to the *crème de la crème* of film festivals such as Cannes, Sundance, New York, and Toronto, be warned that the competition for inclusion can be stiff. Web sites for a few of the festivals that will be described are:

- Sundance Film Festival: *www.sundance.org*
- Slamdance Film Festival: *www.slamdance.com/filmmaker*
- Cannes: *www.festival-cannes.fr*
- Toronto: *www.e.bell.ca/filmfest*
- Telluride: *www.telluridefilmfestival.com*
- Dances With Films: *www.danceswithfilms.com*
- Moondance: *www.moondancefilmfestival.com*

If you're convinced that your film has the chops to stand up to vigorous competition, it's well worth the time and effort to get it screened at one of these.

Sundance

The Sundance Film Festival in Park City, Utah, has become the best-known and largest independent festival in the United States, and one of the most elite in the world. Since 1978, the festival has been screening and analyzing all varieties of independent films and documentaries. A prominent figure in the annual event is actor Robert Redford, who helped bring Sundance into the public eye. In 1985, the Sundance Institute took over as managers of the festival, and it has now become a much anticipated journey that entertainment industry professionals make every January.

Hundreds of films are entered into the Sundance Film Festival each year, and judging and audience expectations are both demanding and sophisticated. Having your film accepted into this festival is a major accomplishment. (See Appendix E for more information.)

Slamdance

The Slamdance Film Festival is also held in Park City, Utah, and has filled a gap vacated by the increasingly elite Sundance gathering. Slamdance is designed specifically for independent filmmakers and is a great domestic venue for premiering a good low-budget production. Slamdance entries can experience invaluable industry buzz, publicity, and audience response.

Cannes

The Cannes Film Festival in France is the premier high-profile international festival, one that annually attracts entries from all over the world. Major film distributors and producers flock to Cannes with their most lavish and expensive productions, and show their films amid true Hollywood glamour. Having a low-budget independent film accepted for the Cannes film festival requires excellent production values and a fair amount of luck.

Toronto

The Toronto Film Festival in Toronto, Canada, is North America's second-highest profile festival next to Sundance, with an emphasis on worldwide independent entries. Audience and judging sophistication are also very demanding, and acceptance alone is a high compliment to any production.

Telluride

The Telluride Film Festival in Telluride, Colorado, showcases only a few dozen feature films and shorts. Telluride launched many well-known independent films, such as *Sling Blade*, *The Crying Game*, and *My Dinner with Andre*. Telluride is unique among film festivals in that it's not a competition and no prizes are awarded. It is one of the most highly regarded film festivals in the country.

Dances With Films

Dances With Films in Los Angeles, California, mandates that *none* of their entries have known actors, directors, producers, or writers. Begun in

1998 as an alternative to the politicized elitism of many major film festivals, Dances With Films can be the perfect venue for the first-time filmmaker.

Moondance

The primary and ongoing mission of the Moondance film festival is to reach out to female writers and filmmakers from six continents and from a wide diversity of ethnic and linguistic groups. Based in Boulder, Colorado, the festival organizers seek to inspire and invigorate the creative potential of filmmakers to perceive, conceptualize, and produce their works for the benefit of the world society.

Film Festival Formats

The film festival scene is recognizing that many excellent films are being produced by independent filmmakers who may not have the substantial postproduction funds that are required to transfer digital images to a large-film print format. One of the great benefits to entering your film in festivals is that many of them can screen films directly from DVDs. Not all film festivals have the capacity for digital or videotape screening, but the trend is growing and will continue to do so.

The ultimate result of the technological advances that allow for effective digital screening is that in the future, virtually all theaters will be projecting wide-screen feature-length films directly from DVD or similar electronic formats. There's every likelihood that digital films will eventually even be transmitted via satellite to wide-screen theatrical venues. The economic and creative benefits to independent film production and distribution will be explosive and permanent.

Film Festival Categories

Film festival entries are placed into competition by genre and category. Genres run the gamut from comedy to drama to science fiction and fantasy. Festivals also screen entries under specific categories that cover virtually every type of film production. Categories will usually include the following:

- Black comedy
- Comedy
- Coming of age
- Commercials
- Drama
- Dramatic comedy
- Experimental
- Family
- First feature-length film
- Horror
- Low-budget independent
- Mockumentary
- Other narrative
- Period
- Romantic comedy
- Science fiction
- Screenplay
- Thriller
- Urban
- Western

Many festivals permit entry of a film under several genres, but the choice is generally left up to you when you prepare your entry forms.

Producer's Representatives

A good *producer's representative* is usually a freelance sales agent with connections to film festivals, film buyers, and distributors. Producer's reps charge negotiable fees for their services, which are usually a percentage of any sales they make with your film production. That percentage will vary depending on the representative you're considering working with, and can be as much as 25 percent of your financial deal with a buyer.

Before making an arrangement with a producer's representative, be sure to check his background and ask for references. Ethical reps will be happy to prove their past performances to you. Be wary of any who balk at supplying references. Some may claim that they're unable to provide names of their clientele by citing so-called confidentiality agreements, but that's hogwash. Satisfied customers are always happy to recommend people with whom they've had positive business dealings, and producer's representatives are no exception. Producer's representatives are listed in *The Hollywood Creative Directory*.

Independent Distributors

There are scores of film distributors in the United States. The largest independent film trade association is the Independent Film and Television Alliance (IFTA). The IFTA has a membership of more than 150 professional companies that are involved in the financing, production, and distribution of independent films worldwide.

The mission of the IFTA is to provide marketplace services and worldwide representation for the independent film and television industry. In the past thirty-five years, IFTA membership companies have produced or licensed over half the films that have won the Academy Award for Best Picture. These films include *Gandhi*, *Amadeus*, *Platoon*, *The Last Emperor*, *Driving Miss Daisy*, *Dances with Wolves*, *The Silence of the Lambs*, *Braveheart*, *The English Patient*, *Shakespeare in Love*, *Chicago*, and *The Lord of the Rings: Return of the King*.

IFTA runs an excellent Web site with a complete member list that includes information and a profile of each member's professional activities regarding their production and distribution interests. The membership list also provides links to member Web sites. For more information, go to *ifta-online.org*.

The Hollywood Creative Directory produces directories for virtually every aspect of filmmaking. They also produce the *Hollywood Distributors Directory* that lists 2,000 independent companies with many thousands of names and contact information. The directory is sold in book form and can be ordered via the Internet. *The Hollywood Creative Directory* also has a fee-based online directory service. These directories are worth their weight in gold to anyone interested in the filmmaking industry. Additional information can be found at *www.hcdonline.com*.

Be sure to check the references and past performance of distributors before you sign with them. Don't be afraid to ask for references. If a distributor refuses to provide you with at least a short list of satisfied clients, or offers feeble excuses for why they can't do so, run. You deserve to know a distributor's track record before entering into any business arrangement, and if they've got a good record, they'll be proud to share it with you.

Major Distributors

The major film distributors in the United States are also the major studios. Even if they've had nothing to do with your production, if you can get your film into the hands of the right people, and if those people believe it will sell well at the box office, they will distribute your film. However, it can be difficult, if not impossible, to simply make an appointment with a studio to screen your film. If you're an unknown with an unknown film in your hands, very few studio executives will be willing to spend any time viewing your project.

FACT

South Park's creators, Trey Parker and Matt Stone, were launched into the stratosphere by producing an animated Christmas card for a studio director who paid them a few hundred bucks for the project. The tape featuring the card bounced around Hollywood until it was noticed by the Comedy Central network.

One method of getting your film into the hands of studio decision-makers is to transfer your film to DVD, which can be done fairly inexpensively if your editing and cinematography are sound. By duplicating the DVD onto dozens of copies, you can hand DVDs out to virtually anyone you can find who has some sort of access to studio executives. Junior directors, production assistants, secretarial staff, or anyone with a connection can get the ball rolling and get your film noticed.

Personal P.R. and Self-Distribution

If your film is good enough, sooner or later one of those DVDs will be viewed by someone who'll be delighted to bring it to the attention of someone else who has enough clout to pursue discussing a deal with you. This process is a combination of the trickle effect and the "six degrees of separation" concept that suggests that anyone involved with a studio in any capacity is only a few steps away from the top. People at the bottom of the Hollywood chain have no possible way of directly reaching those in charge of major studios. But folks at the bottom of the ladder know people who know people who can put you in contact with the right people.

Many independent film producers choose to self-distribute their films. This can be a difficult path to take, but it can have its rewards. Small theaters and art houses are often willing to screen independently distributed films, often for a theater rental fee and a percentage of the box office receipts. Renting theaters to screen your own film is known in the industry as *four walling*. In this situation, you'll be responsible for promoting and publicizing your film, which can include placing ads in local papers and printing posters.

If you can get a reviewer interested in seeing your film and writing about it, publicity can be generated free of charge. Unless you have good connections, however, getting your film reviewed can be a dicey proposition. The best thing you can do is get the word out to the media in the form of a press release or personal call. Remember though, you run the risk of getting a bad review as well as a good one.

When you find an interested distributor, you'll be offered a contract for the rights to distribute your film. Distribution contracts are notoriously complicated, and are also often lopsided in favor of the distributor. Be aware from the beginning that you'll need qualified legal counsel before signing anything.

Your Legal Watchdog

There are many attorneys who specialize in entertainment law and understand the fine points of distribution contracts. You will be well served by doing some serious homework before selecting an entertainment attorney to handle the legal work of a distribution agreement. Your contract will be the deciding factor in whether or not your film production, your investors, and, of course, you will see profits, regardless of whether your film becomes a hit. Your attorney will be your closest ally in securing a beneficial distribution deal, so hire the best legal help you can find.

Distribution contracts should explicitly define the finances a film produces in terms of *gross* and *net* returns. Gross returns are all of the income that a film generates. Net returns are the funds that are left after the distributor deducts their share and expenses and other profits from the total gross. It's important that the amount of money to be used for the expenses of distributing your film be negotiated up-front, preferably with the aid of your attorney. This will help dissuade distributors from simply racking up sometimes unsubstantiated distribution expenses to the point that you never see a penny of net returns.

The cost to your distributor for distributing your motion picture can be substantial. The first cost, and one that you'll be interested in negotiating, is the advance that you'll be paid. This advance is an up-front payment for the film, and will generally be deducted from profits before you are paid any further. For feature films with strong commercial value, the advance can and should be substantial. Expenses will also include the cost of marketing the film, which will entail designing and printing magazine and newspaper advertising, posters, and promotional mailings and flyers. A promotional movie trailer will also be edited and printed from the production footage.

Chapter 18

Studio Strategies

There are many factors a studio has to consider when preparing to release a film. They need to ascertain when they should release it, and how many theaters it should play in. They also have to decide whether to first release the film domestically and then internationally or to initially release it worldwide. Other movies that are scheduled for release near their film's planned release date also have to be examined. These are just a few of the strategies that studios must consider as they work to make their movies box office leaders.

How Studios Operate

It's a widely held theory that movie studios operate on fear. This is not entirely wrong. With millions of dollars at stake, jobs on the line, and investors and stockholders clamoring at the door, the studio executive has very good reasons to be afraid. Her job is to predict the viewing habits of a highly unpredictable audience. Part of the formula is to see what films are currently successful, or were successful in the past. Given the volatility of the industry, decisions made in this film guessing game are what make or break careers.

Studio executives must also live in the future. It takes an average of three years for a film to go from script to screen. This means that studios must determine what an audience will like three years from now. Action films are a safe bet. Romantic comedies seem to do well consistently. But what about the occasional offbeat film? Will anyone go to a movie about two unsympathetic guys on a wine-tasting road trip? Or what about the big-budget risk? Who wants to see a film about a ship that sank ninety years ago, when the audience already knows how it ends?

Made with a budget of $6 million, *The Terminator* grossed $38 million on its release in 1984. *Terminator 2: Judgment Day*, released in 1991, grossed almost $205 million, doubling its $102 million budget. The jump in profit helped spawn the 2003 sequel *Terminator 3: Rise of the Machines*, which had a $200 million budget but earned only $150 million.

To the average filmgoer it seems that on occasion the studios are copying each other. One releases an action movie and another is right behind. One comes out with a comic book hero brought to life, and another will soon have a competing superhero bounding across the silver screen. Remember that movies are planned long before they are released. A wave of similar movies is the result of marketing plans that foresaw a certain pattern and made films that were expected to be popular. A blockbuster in a specific genre will likely send the studios running to make a comparable movie—one they hope will be even better and bring in more box office revenue.

If a movie has done well, a studio may decide to follow it with a sequel or, as seems to happen often, a trilogy. *Back to the Future*, *Jurassic Park*, *Star Wars* (which, after its original trilogy, spawned a trilogy of prequels), and *The Terminator* are just a few of the movies that have given us familiar characters and storylines. Sometimes these sequels are successful, but not always.

Sometimes real-life events can affect which films are made. If a war breaks out or a tragedy occurs, people feel a surge of patriotism, and films will be made that reflect that feeling. The studios constantly monitor what people are watching, and attempt to green-light films that they believe audiences will want to see in the near future. As a filmmaker, you're constantly playing the odds. A concept brought to a studio's attention that happens to fit a mold of what they're currently looking to fill will be more likely to find its way to the screen.

Rolling the Dice

Studios will sometimes take a risk and produce a movie that seems very unlikely to succeed. These scripts makes their way to the right person at the right time, and that person is willing to roll the dice and green-light the production. This can be either a huge success for a studio or an expensive disaster. Because there are no guarantees either way, a movie that fits a pattern is more likely to be made than one that shows up out of left field. But when a studio opts to take a chance on a small film like *Sideways* or a niche movie like *Shakespeare in Love*, it can sometime pay off with a surprising blockbuster.

In 1975, 20th Century Fox released a feature-film version of a rock musical that began as an experimental theatrical production on a small London stage. *The Rocky Horror Picture Show* flopped. But on April 1, 1976, a Fox advertising executive named Tim Deegan convinced the Waverly Theater in Greenwich Village, New York, to begin showing the film at midnight on weekends. As a result of Deegan's tenacity, a huge cult following has grown up around the rebirth of *Rocky Horror*. The film that flopped has grossed $113 million to date in the United States alone.

Jockeying for Position

Once a movie is made, a studio has to decide on its best possible release date. Is it a family movie that needs to open when children aren't in school? Is the studio hoping it'll be an Oscar contender? Are there other similar movies about to be released by a competitor? These and many other factors have to be considered when studios make release-date decisions.

Domestic and Foreign Releases

A film's *domestic release* indicates its release in the United States. When a movie is released outside of the United States it is called a *foreign release*. A studio may schedule the foreign release to coincide with the domestic release, or it may release the film internationally at a later date.

Domestic and foreign audiences may not always like the same movies, although they often do. Traditionally, action films are profitable, given that they have an easier time overcoming the language barrier. An example of a movie that flopped in America, but ultimately came out in the black due to overseas receipts is Kevin Costner's *Waterworld*. Released in 1995, the movie was a dismal failure domestically. Despite its $175 million budget, it earned only $88 million. But foreign audiences enjoyed the film, and internationally it earned an additional $176 million.

Winter Release

If a movie is going to be considered as a candidate for an Academy Award, it will be released during the winter months. Although any movie that opened during the previous calendar year is eligible for an Oscar nomination, it's strategically assumed that movies that have opened as close to the cutoff date as possible will more likely be in voters' minds when they receive their ballots in January.

A Thanksgiving weekend release is often planned for a family movie, or for a film that studios hope will be a blockbuster. Traditionally, people are off work and out of school that weekend, and studios release movies hoping to entice families. *National Treasure*, *Home Alone*, and *Toy Story* are just a few movies that have enjoyed profitable Thanksgiving release dates.

Which movie had the biggest Thanksgiving weekend opening?
For the five-day holiday weekend, *Toy Story 2* had an $80 million opening weekend in 1999. In the year 2000, M. Night Shyamalan's *Unbreakable* grossed over $46 million. And in 1998, Pixar's *A Bug's Life* generated over $45 million.

Summer Release

A summer release is often planned for a movie that the studios believe will be a family movie, blockbuster, or both. Children are out of school, and vacations allow people more leisure time. The Fourth of July weekend has become known as a blockbuster movie release date. That weekend has proven successful for many films including *Independence Day*, *Forrest Gump*, *Men in Black*, *Jurassic Park*, *The Sixth Sense*, *Twister*, *Jaws*, and the first two films of the *Pirates of the Caribbean* trilogy. Summer blockbusters are often action/adventure films designed to draw in the young adult and teenage viewership. The largest box office summer release was the 2006 film *Pirates of the Caribbean: Dead Man's Chest*, which during its opening weekend grossed almost $136 million. As of August 2006, it had grossed over $401 million domestically and over $922 million worldwide.

Box Office Blockbusters

Blockbusters are the movies that everyone has to see, and nothing makes a studio happier. *Titanic*, *Star Wars*, *Lord of the Rings*, and *Harry Potter and the Sorcerer's Stone* are just a few of the elite group of films whose tickets sell out again and again. No one knows for sure why certain films make so much money. What is it about *Star Wars* that touched a nerve in the collective audience?

Approximate box office figures compiled from Box Office Mojo (*www.BoxOfficeMojo.com*) as of August 2006 showed that the top ten all-time domestic film leaders are:

1. *Titanic* (1997, $600 million)
2. *Star Wars* (1977, $460 million)
3. *Shrek 2* (2004, $441 million)
4. *E.T. the Extra-Terrestrial* (1982, 1985, 2002, $435 million)
5. *Star Wars: Episode I—The Phantom Menace* (1999, $431 million)
6. *Spider-Man* (2002, $403 million)
7. *Pirates of the Caribbean: Dead Man's Chest* (2006, $401 million)
8. *Star Wars: Episode III—Revenge of the Sith* (2005, $380 million)
9. *The Lord of the Rings: The Return of the King* (2003, $377 million)
10. *Spider-Man 2* (2004, $373 million)

The top ten all-time worldwide grosses to date are:

1. *Titanic* (1997, $1.8 billion)
2. *The Lord of the Rings: The Return of the King* (2003, $1.1 billion)
3. *Harry Potter and the Sorcerer's Stone* (2001, $976 million)
4. *The Lord of the Rings: The Two Towers* (2002, $926 million)
5. *Star Wars: Episode I—The Phantom Menace* (1999, $924 million)
6. *Pirates of the Caribbean: Dead Man's Chest* (2006, $922 million)
7. *Shrek 2* (2004, $920 million)
8. *Jurassic Park* (1993, $914 million)
9. *Harry Potter and the Goblet of Fire* (2005, $892 million)
10. *Harry Potter and the Chamber of Secrets* (2002, $876 million)

So-called experts have claimed that James Cameron's 1997 film *Titanic* broke every rule of good screenwriting, that the acting is lazy, the characters are uninspired, and the story is familiar beyond reason. It should have been a very expensive flop. The ticket-buying public disagreed. Costing $200 million to make, the movie grossed over $600 million domestically and almost $2 billion worldwide, making it the number-one hit movie ever, both internationally and domestically. In second place is the original *Star Wars*; combining its three releases (1977, 1982, and 1997), it grossed over $460 million domestically.

Box Office Bombs

On the opposite side of the coin are the movies that bomb at the box office. People don't go to see them, or word of mouth from those who do go keeps everyone else away. In some cases, these flops may be films that have fair box office attendance, but the cost of making the movie was so great that the box office receipts aren't enough to justify production costs. Either way, box office bombs don't generate enough interest or income and they can and do happen—even to A-list actors and directors.

FACT

Adjusting the gross box office receipts for inflation, *Gone with the Wind* becomes the number-one blockbuster of all time. Its $198 million gross in 1939 becomes $1.293 billion when adjusted to the 2006 average ticket price of $6.40.

For example, despite starring the very popular "It couple" Ben Affleck and Jennifer Lopez, 2003's *Gigli* was a disaster at the box office. Costing $54 million to produce, the movie generated only $6 million in ticket sales. Some other notable box office bombs include:

- *Around the World in 80 Days* (2004, budget $110 million, domestic gross $24 million)
- *Cutthroat Island* (1995, budget $92 million, domestic gross $10 million)
- *Heaven's Gate* (1980, budget $44 million, domestic gross $1.5 million)
- *Judge Dredd* (1995, budget $90 million, domestic gross $34 million)
- *K-19: The Widowmaker* (2002, budget $100 million, domestic gross $35 million)
- *The Postman* (1997, budget $80 million, domestic gross $17 million)
- *Red Planet* (2000, budget $75 million, domestic gross $17 million)
- *Wyatt Earp* (1994, budget $63 million, domestic gross $25 million)

Sometimes a movie that does very well inspires the studio to do a sequel. This can be a great thing for the studios and fans of the original film. Or it can be catastrophic. In the latter category, consider the 1992 Sharon Stone film, *Basic Instinct*, which cost $49 million and grossed almost $118 million domestically. In 2006, *Basic Instinct 2* was released and earned less than $6 million on its opening release, not even putting a dent into its $70 million budget.

Chapter 19

Going It "Alone"

Filmmakers as a group are instinctively independent. They have a vision and they want to show that vision to the world regardless of how it gets done or on what scale. Independent filmmakers are a breed apart. They're bold and controversial, and stare adversity in the face, but for good reason—making a film on your own is no easy feat. If you have the will, there's a way, but be prepared for a long and bumpy ride.

19

What Exactly Is an Independent Film?

The concept of making an independent, or indie, film has become a bit blurred over the years. The term itself is slippery, given that most major studios now have branches that are deemed "independent," when in fact filmmakers and their productions are under the studio umbrella. The classic definition of independent filmmaking means funding (usually on a shoestring) and producing a film outside the auspices of a studio. What often confuses things is that there have been independent studios, like New Line Cinema, Miramax, and Hemdale, that distributed independent films. All three of those studios have now been absorbed into larger entities. With each passing year, the lines between true independent filmmaking become slightly more fuzzy, especially given the high-profile publicity accompanying films like *Shakespeare in Love*, *The Passion of the Christ*, *Pulp Fiction*, *Sideways*, and *Capote*, among others, which are considered to be indies.

A common view of what industry professionals still deem an independent film is one that someone makes himself, but distributes through a studio. Given that the studio didn't finance the project, the film remains independent while at the same time reaping the benefits of being distributed by the studio to a mainstream audience.

Independent films are sometimes commercially viable, but almost always contain artistry in the form of raw characters, emotion, humor, and trauma all bound together by unconventional storylines. In many cases, they're directed by first-time filmmakers, most of whom have to cut corners and make more than a few personal sacrifices to get their work recognized. The indie route is a path paved with grand visions and great intentions, and it's laid the groundwork for more than a few famous filmmakers.

Evolution and Revolution

The formation of most major studios before and during Hollywood's Golden Era made it hard for independent filmmakers to thrive. As with most big business conglomerates, the studio monopoly had control of everything from ticket prices to film stock to censorship. These constraints spawned a new breed of creative individuals who were determined to make their own films their own way, without the support of what were previously independent studios.

Nanook *and* Nosferatu

Filmmaker Robert Flaherty spent time living in the area around Canada's Hudson Bay. By 1913, he began ignoring his day job, instead filming the sights, sounds, and daily life of the Inuit Eskimo tribe. In 1922, *Nanook of the North* was released and quickly became the first commercially successful documentary/feature. That same year marked the arrival of F. W. Murnau's classic silent film *Nosferatu*. Undaunted by threats of legal action, Murnau sidestepped an adaptation of Bram Stoker's *Dracula* and created not only one of the most compelling indie films, but one of the most haunting films in history.

Indie Pioneers

During the 1940s and '50s many low-budget and B movies were made. It wasn't until the monopoly of the major studios was broken up in 1948 that independent productions truly began to see the light of day. One of the indie genre's greatest assets is Roger Corman, who during his long career has directed more than fifty films and produced several hundred. Along the way, he also mentored budding directors including Ron Howard, Francis Ford Coppola, and Martin Scorsese. Known for his seriously low budgets and notoriously quick shooting schedules, Corman has become a hero to many budding filmmakers. One of the more famous legends associated with Corman is that his 1960 low-budget production of *Little Shop of Horrors* was filmed in three days.

Miners striking at a zinc mine in New Mexico were the subject of indie pioneer Herbert Biberman's 1954 classic *Salt of the Earth*. Biberman was renowned for being one of the infamous Hollywood Ten. In 1947, when he refused to respond to questions regarding the Communist Party, he was cited for contempt of Congress.

Actor, writer, and director John Cassavetes is often considered a pioneer of independent filmmaking. Those unfamiliar with Cassavetes often remember him as Mia Farrow's husband in *Rosemary's Baby*, but to filmmakers his devotion to indies is legendary. In 1959, with money raised through his family and friends, among others, Cassavetes filmed the controversial film *Shadows*, which focused on a black woman who begins dating white men. His more notable works include *A Woman under the Influence* (1974), *The Killing of a Chinese Bookie* (1976), and *Gloria* (1980).

Mad Cops and Pink Flamingos

In 1968, moviegoers were utterly terrified by George Romero's indie flick *Night of the Living Dead*. Starkly filmed in black and white, the movie set the stage for dozens of future zombie movies while at the same time giving independent filmmaking a boost. In the 1970s, several soon-to-be-famous filmmakers made their mark on the indie scene. In 1971, George Lucas showed audiences a bleak look at the future in *THX-1138*, starring Robert Duvall. The following year, John Waters humorously broke what some consider to be the taste barrier with his $12,000 divine classic *Pink Flamingos*. Mentored by John Cassavetes as well as Corman was filmmaker Martin Scorsese, who in 1973 brought us to the *Mean Streets* of New York's Italian neighborhoods.

All manner of freak and fright was featured in indie films of the day. Newcomer David Lynch spent five years filming his practically no-budget film *Eraserhead*, which was released in 1977. Two years later, George Miller made amazing use of his estimated $400,000 budget, showcasing his post-apocalyptic cop *Mad Max*, which grossed almost $9 million domestically. Also on the indie scene was director John Carpenter, whose mindless

Halloween killing machine Michael Myers branched out into a permanent horror franchise.

Sex, Lies, and Success

After decades of fighting for independence, the indie genre finally started to hit the mainstream during the 1980s. Films like Spike Lee's *She's Gotta Have It*, Sam Raimi's *The Evil Dead*, James Cameron's *The Terminator*, and Jim Jarmusch's *Stranger than Paradise* let audiences know that indies were here to stay. Also entering the independent scene were brothers Joel and Ethan Coen, whose homage to *film noir*, *Blood Simple*, set the benchmark for their future endeavors, including *Miller's Crossing*, *Raising Arizona*, and the Oscar-nominated *Fargo*.

ESSENTIAL

Indie filmmaker Tobe Hooper got creative in 1974 with his *Texas Chainsaw Massacre*, which featured a family of cannibals. Considered to be one of the scariest movies ever made, the film was allegedly financed from the profits the production company had made as a result of its 1972 porn film *Deep Throat*. To date, Hooper's film has grossed over $30 million.

By 1989, two indie films tipped the scales in regard to high-end exposure. Filmmaker Michael Moore showed his mettle in the documentary *Roger and Me*, which focused on his hometown of Flint, Michigan, and the economic crash that followed the closing of an automobile plant. Moore's bold style caught critics' attention, just as it would with his later films *Bowling for Columbine* and *Fahrenheit 9/11*.

That same year, newcomer Steven Soderbergh hit the ground running with the hauntingly brilliant and voyeuristic *sex, lies and videotape*. With its seductive shots showing characters filming other characters, the movie proved to be mesmerizing enough to generate over $24 million in domestic sales. With a Best Screenplay Oscar nomination to round out his success, Soderbergh helped breathe life into the indie world by forcing the major studios to sit up and take notice.

Gaining Ground

The past two decades have seen indie films gaining serious momentum. In 1992, a newcomer named Quentin Tarantino catapulted the status of independent films when he made *Reservoir Dogs*. Tarantino had originally estimated spending about $30,000 for the production, until the screenplay came to the attention of Harvey Keitel. With Keitel's influence, the budget shot up to $1.2 million, and a shooting script was written in two weeks. With a stellar cast including Keitel, Tim Roth, Michael Madsen, and Steve Buscemi, the film finally proved to audiences that outsiders could play the Hollywood game. *Reservoir Dogs* only grossed $2.8 million domestically, but it brought Tarantino to the forefront as a director, and he continued with the huge hit *Pulp Fiction*, along with *Jackie Brown*, *Hostel*, and the *Kill Bill* volumes.

As the years passed, indies continued to grow in popularity, many receiving critical acclaim and award nominations. Four out of the five Best Picture nominees at the 1996 Academy Awards were independent films not funded by major studios. *The English Patient*, *Fargo*, *Secrets and Lies*, and *Shine* received multiple nominations, with Anthony Minghella's *English Patient* ultimately winning Best Picture.

The Coen Brothers

Joel and Ethan Coen created a wave of audience appreciation and critical acclaim with their first film production, *Blood Simple*. The film was an indie masterpiece, an edgy, black-and-white thriller packed with dark humor, creepy camera angles and lighting, and clever dialogue. The Coens' filmmaking techniques are a resurrection of the *film noir* genre at its finest, with characterizations of relatively average people becoming entangled in schemes that grow increasingly complicated and out of control. Most of the Coens' films strongly emphasize local cultural idiosyncrasies and dialects, as showcased in the Minnesota and South Dakota locations featured in the 1996 film *Fargo*, and the pronounced Southern influence of *O Brother, Where Art Thou?*

As quirky and violent as the Coen brothers' productions are, they nevertheless gather broad audience appeal with characters whose motives are often portrayed as sympathetic and naive, such as William H. Macy's character Jerry Lundegaard in *Fargo*. Even after setting in motion an unbelievably self-serving and ultimately deadly scheme, somehow you just can't help but feel sorry for the guy.

FACT

The Coens aren't lacking in the humor department. Their quirky film *Raising Arizona* is often listed as one of the top comedies ever produced, and in 1996, *Fargo* won an Oscar for Best Screenplay. Joel Coen's wife, Frances McDormand, also earned a Best Actress Oscar for her portrayal of Marge Gunderson.

The Coen brothers have produced a steady stream of commercially successful films that include *The Ladykillers* (2004), *Intolerable Cruelty* (2003), *The Man Who Wasn't There* (2001), *O Brother, Where Art Thou?* (2000), *The Big Lebowski* (1998), *Fargo* (1996), *The Hudsucker Proxy* (1994), *Barton Fink* (1991), *Miller's Crossing* (1990), *Raising Arizona* (1987), and *Blood Simple* (1984).

The Passion of Publicity

Mel Gibson's 2004 film, *The Passion of the Christ*, was a blockbuster long before it saw wide theatrical release. Alternately viewed as a profoundly inspiring cinematic rendition of the last hours of Jesus by vocal religious advocates, and an anti-Semitic slasher flick with a happy ending by equally vocal critics, the controversy over *Passion* generated astonishing publicity and hype through virtually every source of worldwide media.

Much of the film's controversy centered around concerns in the Jewish community that the perception of ancient Jewish participation in the crucifixion would be exacerbated by the graphic violence Christ suffered at the hands of Roman torturers. Although the story is one of the oldest and universally well known in history, the swelling of anti-Semitic claims produced a media frenzy that any publicist and film production would love.

The Passion of the Christ was considered an unviable box office risk by most Hollywood producers and distributors partly because the dialogue was in Aramaic and Latin. Much of the hype surrounding the film was Gibson's own investment of a reported $8 million in funding to complete filming. Although impressive, this amount was probably not much of a stretch for Gibson, who is one of the most commercially successful actors in film history.

Predictably, all of the critical tongue-wagging and positive religious posturing produced virtually no worldwide backlash against the Jewish community, and probably resulted in only limited permanent religious conversion. With an estimated budget of $30 million, the storm of controversy has produced an astronomical worldwide box office take of nearly $600 million.

Miramax: An Independent Film Distributor

In 1979, brothers Bob and Harvey Weinstein founded Miramax with the intention of distributing films with edgy subject matter. Named after their parents Miriam and Max, Miramax was prepared to take significant risks in choosing films with difficult themes and tailoring marketing strategies to suit each film's strengths. Their publicity and advertising strategies, and the quality of films they released, have resulted in an impressive series of critically acclaimed and commercially successful pictures.

Independently produced films distributed by Miramax include many Oscar winners and Oscar-nominated productions such as *The Aviator, Finding Neverland, Chicago, Gangs of New York, In the Bedroom, Chocolat, The Cider House Rules, Shakespeare in Love, Life Is Beautiful (La Vita É Bella), Good Will Hunting, The English Patient, Il Postino (The Postman), Pulp Fiction, The Piano, The Crying Game,* and *My Left Foot.*

ESSENTIAL

Allegedly filmed with a Wal-Mart camcorder, the 1999 indie *The Blair Witch Project* sent audiences to the edge of hysteria. Made on a budget of $25,000, it went on to gross almost $250 million. Considered to be the first true independent blockbuster, *Blair Witch* got a significant boost as a result of Internet advertising.

In its time, Miramax was responsible for releasing twenty-four nominees for Best Foreign Language Film. In total, their releases won sixty

Academy Awards, with 249 nominations, and they produced a number of films that were thought to be commercially questionable but proved to become hugely successful, including Oscar-winning Best Pictures *The English Patient, Shakespeare in Love*, and *Chicago*.

In 1993, Miramax Films was purchased by Walt Disney Studio Entertainment for $80 million, which is considered a bargain price by today's standards. In 2005 Buena Vista Motion Pictures Group took control of Miramax. The Weinstein brothers then formed a new production company, The Weinstein Company, and retained the Dimension Films label.

Taking the Indie Route

Unless you're incredibly lucky, well connected, or independently wealthy, the chances of your film hitting the big time are very slim. That said, however, it doesn't mean that if your goal is to go commercial, it can't be done. With enough hard work, business savvy, patience, tenacity, and a few well-placed industry professionals, it is possible to obtain a measure of success.

What it all comes down to is your goal as a filmmaker. If you want to become a blockbuster movie-maker, then that's certainly a goal to strive for. If you're happy in the low-budget realm, that's good, too. If you're unwilling to give up any measure of control, you are not alone. There are innumerable filmmakers in the world who are perfectly happy never having to deal with a studio and the politics and complexities associated with any higher-budget production.

The Pros

What most independent filmmakers will tell you, if they're being honest and realistic, is that going the indie route is exceptionally stressful and frustrating in regard to time and financing. What they'll also tell you is that it's probably the best job you could ever hope to have. Being in control of your cinematic vision is a powerful feeling, especially if you're not concerned with budget and you're simply creating films through innovative means for the sheer pleasure of it. Many indie filmmakers can't quit their day jobs, but as with any truly artistic endeavor, they don't necessarily need to. As long as they have some funding to feed their creative hunger they can continue to make innumerable films.

The Cons

Every perceived "perfect" job has its downside, and the world of independent filmmaking is no different. Creative endeavors aside, making an indie film is tough work. Without significant financing, everything has to be done on a shoestring budget, and that inevitably makes each aspect of a production exponentially harder than it would be on a typical film production. Even on the most basic level, you need a camera, a computer, software, a script, a few willing friends, and some form of transportation to get you to your locations. As an indie filmmaker, you can certainly do everything on the cheap, and beg, borrow, barter, or charge up your credit cards, but in reality any amount of excess funds you have will get used up quickly.

The other sad reality is that most independent films rarely get the exposure necessary to further someone's career. Many indie filmmakers spend years working on their films, only to have them seen by a handful of friends and family members. Filmmaking is an intensely collaborative medium, a fact that makes going it alone an option that has to be carefully considered.

Filmmaking on a Shoestring

Low-budget films are typically considered to be those made for under $500,000. Depending on who you talk to, that limit could be as high as one million. Most indie filmmakers would give their right arm for a budget of $50,000, and many have made commercially profitable films for far less. In true rags-to-riches style, Sam Raimi's 1983 cult horror film *The Evil Dead* grossed $2.4 million worldwide. By 2002, Raimi's blockbuster film *Spider-Man* became the first motion picture ever to make $100 million during its opening weekend.

The 2002 film *My Big Fat Greek Wedding*, which was independently produced by Tom Hanks' Playtone Company, has the distinction of being the most profitable motion picture in history in relationship to its budget. With a production budget of $5 million, the quirky romantic comedy has grossed almost $370 million worldwide.

Organizations for Independent Filmmakers

The Independent Film and Television Alliance (formerly known as the American Film Marketing Association) is the largest and arguably the most powerful organization designed for the production and distribution of independent films. In 2005, film companies associated with the IFTA were involved with the production or distribution of forty-three of the 110 Academy Award nominees.

The IFTA represents hundreds of film companies from the United States, Canada, Europe, Australia, and Asia, including Alliance-Atlantis, Capitol Films, Carlton International Media, Crystal Sky, Filmax, Focus Features, Franchise Pictures, FremantleMedia, Goldcrest Films, Good Times Entertainment, HBO, IAC, Intermedia, Liberty Entertainment, Lions Gate, Lola Films, Miramax, Morgan Creek, New Line, NU Image, Overseas Filmgroup, Pathé, StudioCanal, Summit, TF1, Troma, and Wild Bunch. The IFTA can be accessed on the Internet (see Chapter 17) for a complete listing of their affiliated companies along with contact information.

Documentaries

Documentary films raise issues and explore facets of the human existence in sometimes startlingly realistic contrast to fictional cinema. From the harsh wilderness story of a neurotic animal-rights activist in *Grizzly Man* to the cheeky, self-indulgent, and self-destructive *Supersize Me*, documentaries are invariably independent productions made by determined filmmakers. Documentaries are to "reality TV" what symphony orchestras are to kazoo bands.

FACT

The March of the Penguins, distributed by Warner Independent, has enthralled audiences worldwide, grossing $77 million since its release in 2005, the second highest documentary box office earnings behind *Fahrenheit 9/11.*

Documentary filmmaking has reached unprecedented audience acceptance in the film industry. Michael Moore's controversial film *Fahrenheit 9/11* won the top prize at the Cannes Film Festival in 2004, and has grossed nearly $120 million to date. Moore's 2002 documentary, *Bowling for Columbine*, has earned nearly $22 million.

Guerrillas in the Mist

There is a growing contingent of hardcore independent filmmakers who gleefully ignore traditional production protocol and shoot movies either their way or no way. Guerrilla-style filmmaking is often done on the run, shooting in unauthorized locations with little regard for permit processes and usually no regard for municipal codes or restrictions.

This freestyle approach to filmmaking often results in exciting cinema, although the commercial marketability of these endeavors is questionable. For many filmmakers with a rebellious nature, commercial success isn't the motive. The motive for guerrilla filming is often simply the personal satisfaction of just picking up a camera, getting out there, and making a film.

Indie Films and SAG

The Screen Actors Guild has consistently monitored and adjusted pay scales in response to the growing number of independent low-budget films being produced. Depending on the actual budget and the intentions and affiliations of film producers, using SAG actors is often within financial reach.

For films produced by enrolled film school students, SAG union actors can defer 100 percent of their salary. While few name actors will bother working on a student film for zero compensation, it's possible to find talented union actors who are willing to help out with a project they like and a screenplay that they love. Most actors are eager to broaden their acting horizons, and if your script is well written, there's no reason not to pursue union talent.

ESSENTIAL

For short films of thirty-five minutes or less, and with budgets of less than $50,000, SAG actors can also defer 100 percent of their salaries. The same cautions apply here that apply to student films. The benefit is that you don't have to be enrolled in a film school to take advantage of the opportunity.

For feature films with budgets of less than $200,000, SAG union pay scales are $100 per day. Unemployed union actors would rather find work on low-budget films than flip burgers, so there's no reason not to explore this avenue. You can get very good, professional actors for a reasonable fee, and most of them can prove to be extremely helpful on a film set. Particularly if you are a relatively inexperienced filmmaker, union actors can bring a lot of valuable knowledge and expertise to a production.

Chapter 20

Filmmakers of Legend

It's every filmmaker's goal to be recognized for the vision he or she has brought to the silver screen. Not only is it a major accomplishment, but it's a testament to their legacy, something that will stand the test of time and be seen by generations to come. All filmmakers strive to become the best, and more than a few have achieved status akin to the actors who starred in their productions. To see how high you can go, you need to see how far those before you have gone.

Epic Filmmakers

As films became more commonplace in the 1900s, and as the public began to enjoy them more and more, the simple viewing of a short film of reality became passé. Audiences developed a voracious appetite for the medium and wanted to see bigger and better films. It fell upon the early filmmakers to forge a path into this new world. Some made changes that would alter the face of filmmaking altogether, and they continue to do so to this day with style and panache.

Since the beginning of the Hollywood era, certain producers and directors have created movies so monumental that they cannot be forgotten. Many of these filmmakers have developed directing styles or innovative techniques that have changed the face of movies. They created films that for one reason or another have become legendary. They are the epic filmmakers whom we can never forget.

Orson Welles

Orson Welles was an actor, writer, producer, and director who helped usher in the modern era of filmmaking. Prior to his film activities, Welles was a popular radio star, teaming up with John Houseman to produce *The Mercury Theater on the Air*. On Halloween night 1938, the Mercury Theater presentation of *War of the Worlds* frightened many listeners into believing that aliens were actually landing in New Jersey. This drama resulted in Welles being offered a three-picture deal with RKO Pictures in 1940. The first of those films was *Citizen Kane*.

Other notable Welles films include *Journey into Fear*, *The Stranger*, *The Lady from Shanghai*, and *The Third Man*. Welles never got along well with studio executives. Disillusioned with Hollywood, he spent the majority of his directorial career in Europe.

Citizen Kane was a commercial failure, but in making it Welles used many innovative techniques that helped change the face of filmmaking. It was the first film to use low camera angles as well as deep-focus photography, which allows objects both close and far away in a scene to be in sharp focus. The film also employed new makeup effects that enabled a young actor to portray an older man and still retain normal facial movement.

Cecil B. DeMille

Cecil B. DeMille's career spanned silent films to radio and eventually talkies. He's best known for his epic works, and for being a larger-than-life storyteller. DeMille had a reputation as a showman, and many of his movies featured huge casts of extras. His epic productions could never be made today, because the cost would be prohibitive.

During his illustrious career, DeMille produced and directed more than seventy feature films, and brought to the viewing audiences spectacular effects for the time, including train wrecks, the destruction of a pagan temple, and the parting of the Red Sea. *The Ten Commandments*, *Cleopatra*, *The Crusades*, *Samson and Delilah*, *When Worlds Collide*, *The Greatest Show on Earth*, and *The War of the Worlds* have all become legendary films. Cecil B. DeMille is the source of many Hollywood legends. During one film, he reportedly told a Paramount executive who was complaining that it would cost too much to film a battle scene with thousands of extras that he had the problem covered. "We'll use real bullets," DeMille said.

Stanley Kubrick

Stanley Kubrick was a controversial filmmaker who made several movies that became cult classics. His first critically acclaimed film was *The Killing*, which was noted for its use of nonlinear time. That film brought Kubrick to the attention of studio executives, and in 1957 he directed the United Artists production of *Paths of Glory*. Kubrick next filmed *Spartacus*, starring Kirk Douglas, then went to England where he directed the controversial *Lolita*.

Kubrick would remain in England for the rest of his life, and from there directed the cult classics for which he has become best known, namely *Dr. Strangelove*, *2001: A Space Odyssey*, *A Clockwork Orange*, *Barry Lyndon*, *The Shining*, *Full Metal Jacket*, and his last film, *Eyes Wide Shut*, starring Tom Cruise and Nicole Kidman. Kubrick chose many controversial themes for his movies, and was known for his innovative lighting and camera techniques. He also was known for his unrelenting demands on cast and crew.

David O. Selznick

David O. Selznick produced more than eighty films in his life, but is most famous for *Gone with the Wind*, which earned the Best Picture Oscar in 1939. Selznick was not known for being particularly easy to work with. Before its final release, *Gone with the Wind* went through three directors and fifteen scriptwriters. Selznick made history by becoming the first producer to win that honor two years in a row, when *Rebecca* became the Best Picture of 1940. Selznick worked for MGM, Paramount, and RKO studios, as well as his own Selznick International Pictures Studio. During his career, he signed such high-powered talent as Alfred Hitchcock, Joan Fontaine, Vivian Leigh, and Ingrid Bergman. Other notable productions of Selznick's include *Spellbound*, *The Third Man*, *Duel in the Sun*, and *A Farewell to Arms*.

Akira Kurosawa

Akira Kurosawa was a Japanese filmmaker whose films were more popular in the West than in his native country, mostly because of his adaptations of Western genres and authors including Shakespeare and Dostoyevsky. Kurosawa was a true film innovator, whose works served as the basis for many future filmmakers.

Kurosawa's films are known for showcasing his compassion for his characters and his admiration for nature. He supervised the editing of many of his movies, and wrote the screenplays for most of them. Among his works were *Rashomon*, *Seven Samurai* (which was remade in the United States as *The Magnificent Seven*), *Yojimbo*, *The Hidden Fortress* (the inspiration for George Lucas's *Star Wars*), *Ran*, and *After the Rain*. In 1989, he was awarded a Lifetime Achievement Oscar.

Class Acts

Certain filmmakers distinguish themselves by becoming associated with a specific kind of film, working within a specific genre, or presenting their movie in a particular way. In films such as *Some Like It Hot* and *The Apartment*, Billy Wilder produced classic comedies that have withstood the test of time. Walt Disney took animation and made it a legitimate form of film. Preston Sturges took the screwball comedies of the 1930s, added dialogue that was far ahead of its time, and moved the comedy genre to a higher level. Those filmmakers, who became synonymous with a certain style, are the class acts of Hollywood.

Walt Disney

Walt Disney arrived in Hollywood with a suitcase, twenty dollars, and an abundance of talent and optimism. By the time of his death in 1966, he'd become a legend in animation and animated films as well as feature-length family movies.

FACT

Walt Disney produced more than 550 short and full-length features during his life, and his characters and movies are beloved by children of all ages. Films such as *Sleeping Beauty, Cinderella, Dumbo, Bambi*, and *Pinocchio* are classics that never lose their luster.

In 1938, after winning Academy Awards for two of his short cartoon features, Walt Disney presented *Snow White and the Seven Dwarfs*, the first full-length animated movie. The success of *Snow White* allowed Disney to build a new studio, and soon more animated features were released. In 1950, *20,000 Leagues under the Sea* became Disney's first live-action feature film.

Alfred Hitchcock

Known as the "Master of Suspense," Alfred Hitchcock directed more than fifty films, the majority in the thriller genre. He began his directing career in England during the age of the silent films, coming to America in the 1940s. Hitchcock's films are revered for their never-ending suspense, dark humor, and inventive camera angles.

As a filmmaker, Hitchcock had many plot devices and themes that he enjoyed using over and over. He made full use of the principles of mistaken identity, ordinary people being put into extraordinary situations, and the use of what he called a "MacGuffin," which constituted a detail that motivates the actions of characters within the story but is actually unimportant to the story itself. Hitchcock's films are synonymous with suspense. *North by Northwest*, *Psycho*, *The Birds*, *Vertigo*, and *Frenzy* are but a few of his masterpieces. The fun thing about Hitchcock is that almost all of his films feature a staircase, the drinking of brandy, and a cameo appearance by Hitchcock himself.

Frank Capra

Frank Capra is known for films that are inspirational and humanitarian in nature. Among them are *It Happened One Night*, *Mr. Deeds Goes to Town*, *Mr. Smith Goes to Washington*, *Lost Horizon*, *It's a Wonderful Life*, *Arsenic and Old Lace*, and *Pocketful of Miracles*. Capra made audiences feel good and experience a renewed sense of faith in humanity. He was a master at connecting with his audience by eliciting emotion, and his films remain loved today for just that reason.

Ron Howard

From Opie to the Oscars, Ron Howard has charmed audiences for many years. He's directed comedies such as *Night Shift* and *Splash*, action-adventure films including *Apollo 13*, *Backdraft*, and *Ransom*, and dramas including *The Da Vinci Code* and the 2001 Oscar-winning Best Picture *A Beautiful Mind* starring Russell Crowe and Jennifer Connelly. Howard has proven his versatility and ability to please theatergoers over the years, and will undoubtedly continue that practice for many years to come.

Clint Eastwood

Clint Eastwood began his Hollywood career as a television character actor. As Rowdy Yates on the legendary western series *Rawhide*, he became a household name and set the stage for his career as a film cowboy in many spaghetti westerns like *A Fistful of Dollars* and the classic *The Good, the Bad and the Ugly*. While branching out as an actor to include roles as cops and other tough guys like Dirty Harry Callahan, he also moved into the directing field.

In 1992, the western *Unforgiven* won Eastwood a Best Director Oscar. After that, he went on to direct *The Bridges of Madison County*, *Space Cowboys*, *Mystic River*, and *Million Dollar Baby*, which earned him his second Best Director award at age seventy-four.

Kings of Comedy

Sometimes making an audience laugh can be a difficult job. What one person finds funny, another may not. The slapstick comedy *Airplane!*, directed by David and Jerry Zucker and Jim Abrahams, is very different from Rob Reiner's romantic comedy *When Harry Met Sally . . .* , and neither seems much like Ivan Reitman's *Ghostbusters* or Frank Capra's *Arsenic and Old Lace*. Yet all four movies are comedies that are still revered by audiences. A filmmaker who can consistently "make 'em laugh" has done a difficult job well. Making a comedy that transcends the passage of time is a tall order, and the filmmakers who've succeeded with that job are kings of the comedic genre.

Hal Roach

Hal Roach is known as one of the top two comedy producers during the early years of Hollywood. He began his Tinseltown career by working as an extra in silent westerns until 1914, when, using money from an inheritance, he formed Hal Roach Studios. Some of the best comic actors in the business, like Will Rogers and Laurel and Hardy, were part of his studio. Roach's studio was the first to go to an entirely color production schedule, and the first studio to produce films exclusively for television. He produced the Laurel and Hardy shorts, as well as the *Our Gang* series, and feature films including *Topper* and *Of Mice and Men*. At the 1983 Academy Awards, Roach received a Lifetime Achievement Award.

Woody Allen

Woody Allen started out as a standup comedian and scriptwriter for shows such as *The Ed Sullivan Show*, *The Tonight Show*, and *Your Show of Shows*. In the mid-sixties he wrote his first screenplay, *What's New Pussycat?*, and directed his first film, *What's Up, Tiger Lily?* His early movies, including *Bananas*, *Everything You Always Wanted to Know about Sex (But Were Afraid to Ask)*, and *Sleeper*, were slapstick comedies, teeming with one-liners.

Allen's 1977 classic *Annie Hall* was a more sophisticated comedy that won four Oscars, including a Best Director win for Allen. Some of his other successful movies include *Manhattan*, *Stardust Memories*, and *Hannah and Her Sisters*. Allen frequently appears in his movies, often portraying a neurotic New York writer.

Mel Brooks

Like Woody Allen, Mel Brooks began his career as a standup comic and writer for television comedies, including *Your Show of Shows*. In 1965, he caught his first big break when he created the innovative comedy series *Get Smart*. Brooks then moved on to movies, and quickly discovered that his film niche was satire and parody. His films have since become comedy legends. *Blazing Saddles*, *Young Frankenstein*, *History of the World: Part 1*, *High Anxiety*, *Spaceballs*, *Robin Hood: Men in Tights*, and *The Producers* (twice) are timeless comedic masterpieces. Brooks developed a talented group of actors that he enjoyed working with in many of his films. Gene Wilder, Dom DeLuise, Harvey Korman, Cloris Leachman, and Madeline Kahn have all starred in at least three Brooks comedies. He is also a member of a select group of filmmakers: He's one of the few industry professionals who have won an Oscar, an Emmy, a Tony, and a Grammy.

Action Filmmakers

From westerns to fantasies, war stories to outer space adventures, and historical re-enactments to futuristic travels, there are hundreds of action stories and filmmakers who do them well. Immensely popular with viewing audiences, these movies are often the top moneymakers for studios, production companies, and directors themselves. These filmmakers often become big names in Hollywood, and as a result, have the luxury of being selective about the projects they work on.

John Ford

While John Ford directed films in several genres, it's the western for which he's best known. Ford's powerful imagery of the beauty of the land combined with his clean, simple direction makes his films the epitome of the American western. He also had a long-standing film relationship with John Wayne, whom he directed in more than twenty films including *The Quiet Man*, *The Wings of Eagles*, *Stagecoach*, and *The Man Who Shot Liberty Valence*. Ford's style of filmmaking has influenced many directors, and he won four Best Director Oscars for *The Informer* (1935), *The Grapes of Wrath* (1940), *How Green Was My Valley* (1941), and *The Quiet Man* (1952).

Steven Spielberg

Named "Most Influential Person of His Generation" by *Life* magazine in 2000, Steven Spielberg is often called the most powerful figure in the film industry. From his early action-adventure movies like *Raiders of the Lost Ark*, *Jaws*, *Close Encounters of the Third Kind*, *E.T. the Extra-Terrestrial*, and *Jurassic Park* to the more emotionally charged stories of *Schindler's List*, *Amistad*, and *Saving Private Ryan*, Spielberg has shown that his filmmaking brilliance is not limited to a particular style of movie.

How much did Steven Spielberg earn for directing the award-winning movie *Schindler's List*?
Nothing. Spielberg asked that he not be paid for doing the epic World War II saga, which won the Oscar for Best Picture in 1993.

Spielberg has been nominated six times for Best Director and has won the honor twice, for *Schindler's List* in 1993 and *Saving Private Ryan* in 1998. His films often deal with lost innocence or seemingly ordinary people who find themselves in extraordinary circumstances. Spielberg has arguably become the premiere producer/director of Hollywood, and his films have influenced countless future filmmakers.

George Lucas

George Lucas, a close friend of Spielberg, is also considered to be a film innovator. His films clearly showcase his love of storytelling, and often feature characters who prove that mankind can overcome all perceived limitations. Lucas began his career with *THX 1138*, followed by the immensely popular *American Graffiti*. In 1977, he wrote and directed *Star Wars*, a film whose enormous popularity spawned two sequels and three prequels. As a result, he created the production company Lucasfilm Ltd., whose subsidiary Lucas Digital Ltd. comprises sound and visual effects subdivisions Skywalker Sound and Industrial Light and Magic, among the most respected in their fields.

Francis Ford Coppola

Francis Ford Coppola is a sometimes controversial director, producer, and writer who has had many box office successes, and a number of box office bombs like *Finian's Rainbow* and the 1984 Richard Gere film *The Cotton Club*. Coppola is best known for his legendary *Godfather* trilogy, *Patton*, *Apocalypse Now*, and more recently *Bram Stoker's Dracula*.

Problems have often followed Coppola during his career. *Apocalypse Now* began filming in 1976 and the film wrapped fourteen months later, rather than following the scheduled thirteen-week shoot that was originally planned. During that time the film's budget almost tripled, making all concerned parties extremely nervous. For all Coppola's efforts, *Apocalypse* was named Best Picture of 1979. After the enormous financial failure of *The Cotton Club*, however, Coppola was forced to become a director for hire.

James Cameron

James Cameron is best known for his action movies including the *Terminator* trilogy, *The Abyss*, *True Lies*, and *Titanic*, and the spectacular special effects he showcases. It was in *The Abyss* that Cameron first used computer graphics imaging (CGI), and it won the film the 1989 Academy Award for Best Visual Effects. In 1997, *Titanic* won a second Visual Effects Oscar along with awards for Best Picture and Best Director. The most expensive and largest-grossing film to date, *Titanic* used both CGI and scaled sets to great advantage.

Pushing the Envelope

Some filmmakers have the courage to make films that are not mainstream and in some cases are downright controversial. This requires a belief in what you're doing and the ability to convince others that the controversy will play well to an audience. Not everyone can make movies that go against the grain, but those who can do it well often find themselves listed among the great filmmakers of their generation.

D. W. Griffith

Born in 1875, D. W. Griffith began his film career as an actor in silent films, but eventually moved into directing at the then-struggling Biograph studios. Griffith made more than 450 shorts for Biograph, and developed and perfected many filmmaking techniques, including cross-cutting, tracking shots, the running insert, flashbacks, and the closeup. With all that innovation, he wanted to make feature-length films, but when Biograph wasn't interested, he left to pursue feature filmmaking.

D. W. Griffith directed for more than twenty-five years and was honored many times for his innovations in filmmaking. Unfortunately, the controversy surrounding his films didn't work in his favor. The racist label he acquired after *The Birth of a Nation* would follow him throughout his career.

In 1915, Griffith released the controversial *The Birth of a Nation*, a Civil War–era film that was highly successful, but considered to be extremely racist. He followed this film with *Intolerance: Love's Struggle Throughout the Ages*, a commentary on intolerance and its effects during four different historical eras.

Roger Corman

Roger Corman is known for creating movies replete with strange characters, social commentary, special effects, and new talent, all filmed in a matter of days on a shoestring budget. Films such as *Swamp Women*, *Machine Gun Kelly*, *Little Shop of Horrors*, *The Wild Angels*, and several Edgar Allan Poe classics like *The Pit and the Pendulum*, *The Raven*, and *The Masque of the Red Death*, were each shot in less than three weeks' time and with very limited funding.

In 1970, Corman formed New World Pictures, which became the largest independent production and distribution company in the United States After selling New World in 1983, he formed Concorde/New Horizons, where he continues to release successful and inexpensive productions. Corman's studios have been a training ground for directors and actors such as Francis Ford Coppola, Martin Scorsese, Jack Nicholson, Robert De Niro, and Dennis Hopper.

Spike Lee

Spike Lee is a highly intelligent and talented filmmaker whose movies examine urban life, crime, poverty, race relations, and political issues. Lee doesn't shy away from controversy, and has found himself and his films at the center of a controversial storm more than once. His movies, such as *Do the Right Thing*, *Jungle Fever*, *Malcolm X*, and *Summer of Sam*, often depict the struggles between the African-American and Caucasian communities. Lee has often stated that he feels blessed to have the opportunity to express some of the views of African-Americans.

Quentin Tarantino

Quentin Tarantino is an actor, screenwriter, producer, and director whose films often feature bloody violence and nonlinear timelines. Having started out as an independent filmmaker, Tarantino wrote *True Romance* in 1993, then went on to write and direct *Reservoir Dogs*, *Pulp Fiction*, *Four Rooms*, *Jackie Brown*, and the *Kill Bill* movies. His films are complex and often brutal, and one way or another, audiences definitely have strong opinions about his work.

Ang Lee

Born in Taiwan, Ang Lee has become an important contemporary film director. Lee began his filmmaking career in 1992, with a trio of films featuring Taiwanese-American families that explored the differences in traditional versus modern family relationships. In 1995, he struck gold with an adaptation of Jane Austen's *Sense and Sensibility*, for which he won a Golden Globe for Best Picture and an abundance of critical acclaim.

In 2000, *Crouching Tiger, Hidden Dragon*, an elaborate and chivalric martial arts drama, was awarded an Oscar for Best Foreign Language Film, which proved that Lee's innovative filmmaking style had mass audience appeal. In 2005, Lee directed *Brokeback Mountain*, a movie about the love between two homosexual cowboys. The movie garnered eight Academy Award nominations, winning three, including one for Best Director. In doing so, Lee became not only the first Asian but also the first non-Caucasian to ever receive the Best Director Oscar.

The Girls Club

Traditionally, the film industry has been very male-oriented. Females are commonly associated with the role of producer, but still constitute only a small percentage of directors. Even independently made films are surprisingly male-oriented when it comes to directors. But some women have taken the big leap and have been very successful.

How many women have won the Academy Award for Best Director?
No female to date has won this award. Three women have been nominated: Lina Wertmüller for *Seven Beauties* in 1976, Jane Campion for *The Piano* in 1993, and Sofia Coppola for *Lost in Translation* in 2003.

Notable female filmmakers include Penny Marshall (*Big, Awakenings, A League of Their Own, Riding in Cars with Boys*), Barbra Streisand (*Yentl, The Prince of Tides, The Mirror Has Two Faces*), Jodie Foster (*Little Man Tate, Nell, Waking the Dead*), and Kathryn Bigelow (*Blue Steel, Point Break, K-19: The Widowmaker*).

Appendix A

Glossary

above-the-line costs:
Fees for things like script cost, producer, director, and cast salaries that are negotiated prior to production and won't alter during the course of the production.

adaptations:
Screenplays that are written from an existing piece of literature, including books, articles, and short stories.

agent:
A licensed individual who represents someone in the entertainment industry.

ambient noise:
Continuous sounds common to our everyday environment (e.g., humming refrigerators, chirping birds, traffic).

analog tape:
The tape used for recording sound on a film production. Digital audiotape (DAT) is a smaller analog tape that is also used.

animal handler:
Also known as animal wrangler, these individuals are in charge of any animals used on a film set.

antagonist:
The opposing character to your protagonist, usually a villain.

art director:
The individual responsible for seeing that the production designer's vision is carried out.

assistant camera operator:
An individual who assists the camera operator by setting up the camera, maintaining proper lens focus, and changing lenses for various effects.

assistant director (AD):
The individual who monitors the balance between filming and the production schedule. Often aided by first, second, and third assistant directors.

associate producer:
An individual who performs certain tasks, depending on the production, delegated by the producer or production manager.

automated dialogue replacement (ADR):
See redubbing.

back light:
Lighting placed behind a subject and aimed toward its front in order to generate depth and emphasis.

backstory:
The history of a character that allows an audience to better understand that character.

barneys:
Also called blimps. Specialized camera covers used to muffle camera noise.

below-the-line costs:
Costs covering virtually every item a production will require in regard to crew, set production, equipment rentals, location fees, props, office space, and so on.

best boy:
An individual who serves as first assistant to the gaffer, and is in charge of additional electrical crew members and all of the electrical equipment.

blue screens:
A monochromatic background (not necessarily blue) used in filming so that images can be easily replaced behind an actor during a scene.

boom operator:
A member of the sound crew who operates the boom microphone.

bounce light:
A method of pointing light at something on-set and allowing the light to "bounce" back onto the subject.

breakdown sheets:
Individual pages with header space for filling in the scene number, script page, set or location, daytime or nighttime shoot, exterior or interior shots, and scene synopses.

budget top sheet:
Also called top sheet. The first sheet of a filmmaker's final budget estimate.

callback:
An invitation from a casting director or director to an actor to return for a second audition.

camera operators:
An individual, sometimes the cinematographer, who operates the camera during filming.

casting director (CD):
The individual who finds and auditions potential cast members.

character development:
The process of creating a character's background, physicality, appearance, and personality.

cinematographer:
Also called the director of photography or DP. The individual responsible for bringing a director's vision to fruition.

clapper:
Also called a loader or second assistant camera-man. An individual who loads film into the camera, operates the clapper slate for each film take, and keeps records of the scenes and shots.

closing credits:
A list that scrolls at the end of a film showing the names of everyone involved in the production.

composer:
An individual who creates the musical score that relates directly to the conceptual element of a film.

compositing:
Bringing together layers of imagery to complete a full image.

comprehensive liability insurance:
Protection against claims of property damage or personal injury when filming on public property.

computer graphics imagery (CGI):
Creation of visual effects involving three-dimensional (3-D) computer graphics that are created entirely in the "virtual" world using specialized 3-D software.

contingencies:
Unexpected cost overages that are typically unavoidable during the course of filming.

co-producer:
Title used when two or more producers split the job of producer.

costume supervisor:
See wardrobe supervisor.

coverage:
A script summary created by a script reader that lists comments and opinions about the script and its writer.

dailies:
Also called rushes. Unedited film footage that a director and film editor view after a day's shooting schedule has ended.

diffusion filter:
Used to reduce harshness and hard lines to create a soft, dream-like quality.

digital editor:
An individual who provides digital enhancement by electronically editing digital images.

digital image technician (DIT):
An individual who works with a digital camera in regard to image manipulation, continuity, color correction, and quality control.

directional microphone:
A microphone that picks up sounds from a limited area.

director:
The individual who provides the vision of a film, directs the actors, and oversees production.

director of photography (DP):
See cinematographer.

dolly grip:
The individual who operates the camera dolly.

double:
An actor who stands in for the "official" actor while lighting is being set up. She may appear in the final cut of a film where the actor would be unrecognizable. (See stand-in.)

entertainment attorney:
An attorney who specializes in entertainment law, often hired to prepare and negotiate contractual arrangements.

errors and omissions insurance:
Insurance for protection against civil actions brought against a production for plagiarism, unauthorized use of branded items or locations, and defamation of character.

executive producer:
Typically an individual focused on the financial and business dealings of a film.

extras:
Hired individuals or volunteers who appear in the background of certain scenes.

fill light:
A nondirectional, softer light, often placed in a position opposite the key light in relation to the camera.

film editor:
An individual who follows the script to assemble the filmed footage into logical sequences that tell a story.

film score:
The background music of any film.

film speed:
A film's emulsion and its sensitivity to light exposure.

flat reflector:
Reflector used in broad light that produces a diffuse beam.

focal length:
The length, in millimeters, by which camera lenses are identified.

focus group:
The audience that attends a test screening of a film and comments on it.

foley artist:
An individual who creates sound effects that enhance key visual scenes and that are added to the soundtrack during film and sound editing.

Foley, Jack:
Innovator of many of the sound-effect techniques used in films. Foley artists are named for him.

footcandles (fc):
A measure of intensity of light being given off by a particular source.

four walling:
Renting theaters to screen your own film.

gaffer:
The chief lighting technician who works directly with the cinematographer to create the proper lighting for each scene.

genre:
A distinctive style or film format.

gofer:
Another name for a production assistant.

gross returns:
All of the income a film generates (see net returns).

hero's journey:
A typical storyline where a hero and his or her journey is central to the plot.

Hot Head camera:
A camera that is controlled remotely, like those that would be mounted on the front of a speeding car.

image package:
Also known as identity package. Part of a production package given to financiers and producers. It includes business cards, letterheads, and envelopes.

independent film:
Also called an indie. A film funded and produced outside the auspices of a studio.

key grip:
The individual in charge of the crew who moves lighting gear, camera equipment, and all other production equipment.

key light:
The primary source of light when lighting a set. It mimics the motivating light in both intensity and direction.

Lavalier:
A fingertip-sized microphone that can be clipped to an actor's clothes or taped to the skin.

leadman:
Individual in charge of the swing gang.

linear editing:
Film cut into long strips divided by scene and take, and then glued or taped back together to create a film in logical sequence.

lining a script:
Color-coding screenplay elements to represent a single category of the screenplay (e.g., sets, locations, wardrobe).

loader:
See clapper.

location:
An existing place for filming, distinct from a constructed set. Locations are differentiated as "close," meaning within thirty miles of the home base of production, and "distant," which are any farther than thirty miles.

location manager:
The individual who works with property owners, companies, or authorities to secure permits, negotiate fees, and coordinate location availability and shooting dates.

location scout:
An individual who searches for filming locations and deals with fees, permits, and all related paperwork.

logline:
A one-sentence synopsis of a script.

looping:
See redubbing.

makeup artist:
The individual responsible for an actor's makeup and prosthetic devices.

manager:
An artist's representative. Similar to an agent, but a manager receives a higher percentage as a fee and focuses more on career strategies and getting her clients work.

master use license:
A license from the owner of the rights to a specific recording, usually a record producer, permitting its use.

miscellaneous equipment insurance:
Insurance for damage to camera equipment, lighting and sound gear, and related equipment that the production owns, rents, or borrows.

music supervisor:
The individual who oversees and works with the sound editors, mixer, and composer.

natural density filter:
Used when shooting outdoor scenes with too much natural light.

needle drops:
Pre-existing songs, often well-known or currently popular music, that is "dropped" into a film to highlight a story point or character moment.

net returns:
All the funds that are left after the distributor deducts its share and expenses and other profits from the total gross.

nonlinear editing:
Digital editing systems that allows users to access any given frame, scene, or groups of scenes. Film can be edited in any sequence.

omnidirectional microphone:
A microphone that picks up sound in a nearly 360-degree sphere.

one-sheet:
A single page listing the logline and short summary of your script.

open-face housing:
The structure of a lighting instrument in which a light bulb is placed in front of a reflector.

opening credits:
The titles that run at the beginning of a film.

option deal:
A small amount of money given to a writer in exchange for exclusive rights to the script for a specified length of time.

overcranking:
The process of increasing the camera speed so that more frames pass by the lens each second, resulting in slow-motion playback on screen.

parabolic reflector:
A reflector that surrounds a bulb to create a highly directional, highly intense beam of light.

peak program meter (PPM):
A meter on a sound recorder used to measure peak signal levels.

per diem pay:
An agreed-upon daily amount paid to cast and crew for each day they are required to be away from their homes.

pitch:
A sales pitch used to promote your film to potential investors and producers.

plot points:
Apex moments in your script that signal a shift from one act to another.

polarizing filters:
Used on camera lenses to selectively remove excess light.

producer:
The individual in charge of the overall production of a film.

production assistants (PAs)
Also known as gofers. Individuals who perform all types of tasks ranging from traffic control to office work to food service.

production designer:
The individual who creates the overall visual appearance of a film including sets, props, makeup, and wardrobe.

production manager:
The individual hired to keep the shooting schedule on track and the film on budget.

production package:
A business plan that includes a cover letter, script synopsis, budget breakdown, and resume, presented to prospective financiers or producers.

production strip boards:
An oversize panel that utilizes vertical slots for holding individual strips of production information taken from corresponding breakdown sheets.

prop:
Any object an actor will touch, pick up, or interact with.

property damage insurance:
Protection against damage to rented or leased properties used for filming.

prop master:
Also known as property master. The individual in charge of prop acquisitions, prop maintenance, and the distribution of props to the film production as needed.

protagonist:
The main character of your screenplay, usually the hero.

proximate pyrotechnics:
Professionally done non-fireworks-type effects that can be done onstage, in front of the camera (e.g., smoke, flames, flashes, and explosions).

publicist:
Also known as publicity director. An individual hired to generate publicity for a film.

radio microphone:
A small radio transmitter with its own frequency. It can fit in an actor's pocket or be clipped to their clothing.

raw film stock:
Unshot motion picture film.

THE EVERYTHING FILMMAKING BOOK

rear screen projection:
Previously shot footage that is projected from behind onto an opaque screen with a high transmission factor.

recordist:
An audio engineer who records dialogue and all other necessary sounds during film production.

redubbing:
Also known as looping or automated dialogue replacement (ADR). The process of recording or replacing voices during editing, long after a film is done.

resume reel:
Several of your best film clips together on a DVD, Web site, or VHS video tape.

room tone:
Background ambiance unique to a specific room or location.

rushes:
See dailies.

Screen Actors Guild (SAG):
The union that represents many of Hollywood's actors and entertainment professionals.

screen test:
An audition by an actor that is filmed or video recorded for later reference.

script reader:
An individual who is paid to read scripts by an agency or production company.

script supervisor:
The individual who monitors the script and filming in regard to continuity.

script synopsis:
A single page that describes a film so that anyone can easily understand it.

set decorator:
The individual who designs and oversees the setting up and maintenance of the appearance of sets. Most often the department head in charge of a team of set dressers.

set designer:
An individual who creates working drawings and blueprints for set construction. Works closely with the production designer.

set dresser:
The individual responsible for setting up and maintaining the appearance of sets.

shot list:
A list of every single shot that will be made from each camera position in every scene.

skylight filter:
Used to counteract or eliminate haze.

solarization:
A blinding white effect created by purposely overexposing film.

sound designer:
The individual responsible for the overall soundtrack of a film.

274

sound editor:
An audio engineer who synchronizes the audio recordings of the film production to the screen images in the postproduction editing process by using a mixing board.

soundstage:
A building used for filming that provides the best possible acoustic atmosphere.

special effects:
Effects done on-set that can include smoke, fire, fog, and fake blood. Commonly called practical effects.

spec script:
An original screenplay that was written or a script that was written for an existing sitcom or drama. In either case, the writer was never paid to write it.

squibs:
Exploding bullet hits.

standard screenplay format:
The industry-wide universal format for a screenplay: double-spaced twelve-point Courier typeface with margins set at one and one-half inches on the left and right.

stand-in:
An individual who fills in for an actor during lighting and scene setups. Is rarely on-set when shooting begins.

Steadicam:
A camera rig with an inflexible harness worn by an operator with a mounting arm attached to the camera.

step deal:
When a producer and writer agree to develop a project together, but do so in "steps."

still photographer:
The individual who maintains a photographic record of significant production scenes that are often used for publicity purposes.

stock music:
Music controlled and copyrighted by libraries that sell the use of that music for predetermined rights and fees.

stop motion animation:
A painstaking method of filmmaking in which miniatures are positioned and then photographed one frame at a time before being moved.

storyboard:
Drawings rendered by a storyboard artist that portray each scene and all its elements as written in a script.

storyline:
The consistent aspect of your story that holds the entire story together.

stunt coordinator:
Individual who plans and helps execute the physical stunts for a film production.

stunt doubles:
Stunt performers who take the place of specific actors in a film production during potentially dangerous scenes.

stunt performers:
Specialized athletes and actors who perform stunts for a film.

subtext:
The underlying content of the screenplay.

swing gang:
The crew that assembles and disassembles sets. Members, called swings, are overseen by a leadman.

synchronization license:
A license issued by the copyright owner of music to permit the synchronizing of their music to the visual image of a film.

synopsis:
A condensed version of your script used as a tool for selling your story.

system noise:
Sound that results from the imperfections in sound-recording equipment.

telephoto lens:
A camera lens that moves past unwanted foreground images, focusing on background imagery, and shortening the distances between them.

test screening:
A showing of a film prior to its being released. Generally shown to a focus group audience.

three-act structure:
The beginning, middle, and end of your script. Commonly referred to as acts one, two, and three.

top sheet:
See budget top sheet.

transportation manager:
Also known as transportation captain, this individual coordinates all of a production's transportation requirements and oversees all drivers.

treatment:
An outline of a script.

undercranking:
A process that slows film through the camera so the resulting action is accelerated.

visual effect:
A trick of the eye that forces the audience to see only what they are supposed to see.

volume unit (VU) meter
Used in sound recording. A meter that measures signal amplitude as an approximate average.

wardrobe supervisor:
Also called costume supervisor. An individual in charge of the wardrobe department who oversees a staff of costume designers. Works closely with the art director.

wide-angle lens:
A camera lens used to capture broad areas of imagery from left to right in camera perspective, while increasing the difference between objects in the foreground and background.

Appendix B

Recommended Reading

Armer, Alan A. *Writing the Screenplay: TV and Film*. Wadsworth Publishing Company, Belmont, California, 1988.

Ascher, Steven, Edward Pincus. *The Filmmaker's Handbook: A Comprehensive Guide for the Digital Age*. Plume, New York, 1984.

Ballou, Glen M. *Handbook for Sound Engineers* (third edition). Focal Press, Jordan Hill, Oxford, England, 2005.

Bayer, William. *Breaking Through, Selling Out, Dropping Dead and Other Notes on Filmmaking* (revised and updated edition). Limelight Editions, New York, 2004.

Becker, Josh. *The Complete Guide to Low-Budget Feature Filmmaking*. Point Blank Press, Rockville, Maryland, 2006.

Begleiter, Marcie. *From Word to Image: Storyboarding and the Filmmaking Process*. Michael Weise Productions, Studio City, California, 2001.

Bernstein, Steven. *Film Production* (second edition). Focal Press, Oxford, England, 1994.

Bogdanovich, Peter. *Who the Devil Made It: Conversations with Legendary Film Directors*. Ballantine Books, New York, 1997.

Carr, Jay. Editor. *The A List: The National Society of Film Critics' 101 Essential Films*. Da Capo Press, Cambridge, Massachusetts, 2002.

Cook, David A. *A History of Narrative Film, Second Edition*. W.W. Norton & Company, Inc., New York, London, 1991.

Cooper, Donna. *Writing Great Screenplays for Film and TV*. Macmillan, Inc., New York, 1997.

Dannenbaum, Jed, Carroll Hodge, Doe Mayer. *Creative Filmmaking from the Inside Out*. Fireside, New York, 2003.

Goldman, William. *Adventures in the Screen Trade*. Warner Books, New York, 1983.

Griffin, Nancy, Kim Masters. *Hit & Run*. Simon & Schuster, New York, 1996.

Halperin, Michael, Ph.D. *Writing Great Characters: The Psychology of Character Development in Screenplays*. Lone Eagle Publishing Co., Los Angeles, 1996.

Hauge, Michael. *Writing Screenplays that Sell*. HarperPerennial, New York, 1988.

Kronschnabl, Ana, Tomas Rawlings. *Plug In Turn On: A Guide to Internet Filmmaking*. Marion Boyars Publishers Ltd., London, 2004.

Landau, Camille, Tiare White. *What They Don't Teach You at Film School.* Hyperion, New York, 2000.

Merritt, Greg. *Film Production: The Complete Uncensored Guide to Independent Filmmaking.* Lone Eagle Publishing Co., Los Angeles, 1998.

Obst, Lynda. *Hello, He Lied and Other Truths from the Hollywood Trenches.* Little, Brown and Company, New York, 1996.

O'Donnell, Pierce, Dennis McDougal. *Fatal Subtraction: How Hollywood Really Does Business.* Dove Books, West Hollywood, California, 1996.

Ohanian, Thomas A., Michael E. Phillips. *Digital Filmmaking: The Changing Art and Craft of Making Motion Pictures.* Focal Press, Boston, Massachusetts, 1996.

Rahmel, Dan. *Nuts and Bolts Filmmaking: Practical Techniques for the Guerilla Filmmaker.* Focal Press, Burlington, Massachusetts, 2004.

Rea, Peter W., David K. Irving. *Producing and Directing the Short Film and Video* (second edition). Focal Press, Boston, Massachusetts, 2001.

Robertson, Patrick. *Guinness Film Facts and Feats.* Guinness Books, New York, 1985.

Schmidt, Rick. *Feature Filmmaking at Used-Car Prices.* Penguin Books, New York, 1988.

Seger, Linda, Edward J. Whetmore. *From Script to Screen: The Collaborative Art of Filmmaking.*

Lone Eagle Publishing Company, Los Angeles, California, 2004.

Simonelli, Rocco, Roy Frumkes. *Shoot Me: Independent Filmmaking from Creative Concept to Rousing Release.* Allworth Press, New York, 2002.

Walker, John, Editor. *Halliwell's Who's Who in the Movies* (fifteenth edition). HarperCollins, New York, 2003.

Wolff Jurgen, Kerry Cox. *Successful Script Writing.* Writer's Digest Books, Cincinnati, Ohio, 1988.

Yoneda, Kathy Fong. *The Script-Selling Game: A Hollywood Insider's Look at Getting Your Script Sold and Produced.* Michael Weise Productions, Studio City, California, 2002.

Appendix C

Film Schools

Chapman University
Dodge College of Film and Media Arts
One University Drive
Orange, CA 92866
714-997-6765
✐*www.chapman.edu*

Columbia College Hollywood
18618 Oxnard St.
Tarzana, CA 91356-1411
818-345-8414
✐*www.columbiacollege.edu*

Columbia University
2960 Broadway
New York, NY 10027-6902
212-854-2134
✐*www.columbia.edu*

Emerson College
Department of Visual and Media Arts
120 Boylston St.
Boston, MA 02116-4624
617-824-8500
✐*www.emerson.edu*

Florida State University
School of Motion Picture, Television,
and Recording Arts
Tallahassee, FL 32306
850-644-7728
✐*www.fsu.edu*

New York University
Tisch School of Arts
721 Broadway, 8th Floor
New York, NY 10013
212-889-1900
✐*www.tisch.nyu.edu*

San Francisco State University
1600 Holloway Ave.
San Francisco, CA 94132
415-338-1629
✐*www.cinema.sfsu.edu*

Syracuse University
School of Film and Media Arts
900 South Crouse Ave.
Syracuse, NY 13244
315-443-2769
✐*www.syr.edu*

University of California Los Angeles
Department of Film, Television
and Digital Media
Los Angeles, CA 90095
310-825-3101
✐*www.ucla.edu*

University of Southern California
University Park Campus
School of Cinema and Television
Los Angeles, CA 90089
213-740-8358
✐*www.usc.edu*

Appendix D

Who's Who of Directors

Woody Allen

Match Point (2005), Sweet and Lowdown (1999), Mighty Aphrodite (1995), Crimes and Misdemeanors (1989), Hannah and Her Sisters (1986), Zelig (1983), Manhattan (1979), Annie Hall (1977), Sleeper (1973), Everything You Always Wanted to Know about Sex (1972), Bananas (1971)

Robert Aldrich

The Frisco Kid (1979), The Longest Yard (1974), The Dirty Dozen (1967), The Flight of the Phoenix (1965), Hush . . . Hush, Sweet Charlotte (1964), The Last Days of Sodom and Gomorrah (1962), What Ever Happened to Baby Jane? (1962), Vera Cruz (1954)

Robert Altman

Gosford Park (2001), Cookie's Fortune (1999), Prêt-à-Porter (1994), Short Cuts (1993), The Player (1992), Vincent & Theo (1990), Come Back to the Five and Dime, Jimmy Dean (1982), Popeye (1980), M*A*S*H (1970)

Dorothy Arzner

First Comes Courage (1943), Dance, Girl, Dance (1940), The Bride Wore Red (1937), Nana (1934), Christopher Strong (1933), Merrily We Go to Hell (1932), Working Girls (1931), The Wild Party (1929), Get Your Man (1927)

Ingmar Bergman

Fanny and Alexander (1983), Autumn Sonata (1978), The Magic Flute (1975), Scenes from a Marriage (1973), Through a Glass Darkly (1962), Winter Light (1962), The Magician (1958), The Seventh Seal (1957), Smiles of a Summer Night (1955)

Busby Berkeley

Take Me Out to the Ballgame (1949), Cinderella Jones (1946), The Gang's All Here (1943), For Me and My Gal (1942), Babes on Broadway (1941), Strike Up the Band (1940), Babes in Arms (1939), Hollywood Hotel (1937), Bright Lights (1935)

Bernardo Bertolucci

The Dreamers (2003), Besieged (1998), Stealing Beauty (1996), Little Buddha (1993), The Sheltering Sky (1990), The Last Emperor (1987), Last Tango in Paris (1972), The Conformist (1970)

Katherine Bigelow

K-19: The Widowmaker (2002), Strange Days (1995), Point Break (1991), Blue Steel (1990), Near Dark (1987), The Loveless (1982)

Frank Borzage

The Big Fisherman (1959), Moonrise (1948), The Spanish Main (1945), Strange Cargo (1940), The Shining Hour (1938), Green Light (1937), Desire (1936), Flirtation Walk (1934), A Farewell to Arms (1932)

Mel Brooks

Dracula: Dead and Loving It (1995), Robin Hood: Men in Tights (1993), Life Stinks (1991), Spaceballs (1987), History of the World, Part I (1981), High Anxiety (1977), Silent Movie (1976), Young Frankenstein (1974), Blazing Saddles (1974), The Producers (1968)

Clarence Brown

Angels in the Outfield (1951), The Yearling (1946), The White Cliffs of Dover (1944), National Velvet (1944), Anna Karenina (1935), Ah Wilderness! (1935), Sadie McKee (1934), Anna Christie (1930), The Last of the Mohicans (1920)

Tim Burton

The Corpse Bride (2005), Charlie and the Chocolate Factory (2005), Big Fish (2003), Planet of the Apes (2001), Sleepy Hollow (1999), Mars Attacks! (1996), Ed Wood (1994), Batman Returns (1992), Edward Scissorhands (1990), Batman (1989), Beetlejuice (1988), Pee-wee's Big Adventure (1985)

James Cameron

Aliens of the Deep (2005), Ghosts of the Abyss (2003), Titanic (1997), True Lies (1994), Terminator 2: Judgment Day (1991), The Abyss (1989), Aliens (1986), The Terminator (1984)

Frank Capra

Pocketful of Miracles (1961), Here Comes the Groom (1951), It's a Wonderful Life (1946), Arsenic and Old Lace (1944), Meet John Doe (1941), Mr. Smith Goes to Washington (1939), You Can't Take It with You (1938), Lost Horizon (1937), Mr. Deeds Goes to Town (1936), It Happened One Night (1934)

John Carpenter

Escape from L.A. (1996), Village of the Damned (1995), Big Trouble in Little China (1986), Starman (1984), Christine (1983), The Thing (1982), Escape from New York (1981), The Fog (1980), Halloween (1978), The Eyes of Laura Mars (1978), Assault on Precinct 13 (1976)

John Cassavetes

Big Trouble (1985), Love Streams (1984), Gloria (1980), Opening Night (1977), The Killing of a Chinese Bookie (1976), A Woman under the Influence (1974), Husbands (1970), Faces (1968), Shadows (1961)

Charlie Chaplin

A Countess from Hong Kong (1967), A King in New York (1957), Limelight (1952), The Great Dictator (1940), Modern Times (1936), The Gold Rush (1925), A Dog's Life (1918), Easy

Street (1917), The Immigrant (1917), The Tramp (1915)

Joel and Ethan Coen

The Ladykillers (2004), O Brother, Where Art Thou? (2000), The Big Lebowski (1998), Fargo (1996), The Hudsucker Proxy (1994), Barton Fink (1991), Miller's Crossing (1990), Raising Arizona (1987), Blood Simple (1984)

Chris Columbus

Rent (2005), Harry Potter and the Chamber of Secrets (2002), Harry Potter and the Sorcerer's Stone (2001), Stepmom (1998), Nine Months (1995), Mrs. Doubtfire (1993), Home Alone 2: Lost in New York (1992), Home Alone (1990), Adventures in Babysitting (1987)

Martha Coolidge

Out to Sea (1997), Three Wishes (1995), Angie (1994), Lost in Yonkers (1993), Rambling Rose (1991), Real Genius (1985), Joy of Sex (1984), Valley Girl (1983)

Francis Ford Coppola

The Rainmaker (1997), Bram Stoker's Dracula (1992), The Godfather Part III (1990), Peggy Sue Got Married (1986), The Cotton Club (1984), Apocalypse Now (1979), The Conversation (1974), The Godfather Part II (1974), The Godfather (1972)

Sofia Coppola

Lost in Translation (2003), The Virgin Suicides (1999)

Roger Corman

Frankenstein Unbound (1990), Bloody Mama (1970), The Tomb of Ligeia (1965), The Terror (1963), The Raven (1963), The Pit and the Pendulum (1961), The Wasp Woman (1960), The Little Shop of Horrors (1960), House of Usher (1960), Machine Gun Kelly (1958), Not of This Earth (1957)

Wes Craven

Cursed (2005), Scream 3 (2000), Scream 2 (1997), Scream (1996), The People under the Stairs (1991), The Serpent and the Rainbow (1988), A Nightmare on Elm Street (1984), Deadly Blessing (1981), The Hills Have Eyes (1978), The Last House on the Left (1972)

George Cukor

Rich and Famous (1981), My Fair Lady (1964), Let's Make Love (1960), Les Girls (1957), A Star Is Born (1954), Pat and Mike (1952), Adam's Rib (1949), Gaslight (1944), The Philadelphia Story (1940), The Prisoner of Zenda (1937), Romeo and Juliet (1936), Camille (1936), David Copperfield (1935), Little Women (1933)

Michael Curtiz

The Comancheros (1961), We're No Angels (1955), White Christmas (1954), The Egyptian (1954), Life with Father (1947), Mildred Pierce (1945), Casablanca (1942), Yankee Doodle Dandy (1942), Angels with Dirty Faces (1938), The Adventures of Robin Hood (1938), The Charge of the Light Brigade (1936)

Cecil B. DeMille

The Ten Commandments (1956), The Greatest Show on Earth (1952), Samson and Delilah (1949), Reap the Wild Wind (1942), The Buccaneer (1938), Cleopatra (1934), The King of Kings (1927), The Ten Commandments (1923), Forbidden Fruit (1921)

Jonathan Demme

The Manchurian Candidate (2004), Beloved (1998), Philadelphia (1993), The Silence of the Lambs (1991), Swimming to Cambodia (1987), Something Wild (1986), Swing Shift (1984), Stop Making Sense (1984), Crazy Mama (1975), Caged Heat (1974)

Brian De Palma

Femme Fatale (2002), Mission to Mars (2000), Mission: Impossible (1996), Carlito's Way (1993), Raising Cain (1992), The Bonfire of the Vanities (1990), Casualties of War (1989), The Untouchables (1987), Body Double (1984), Scarface (1983), Dressed to Kill (1980), Carrie (1976)

Stanley Donen

Blame It on Rio (1984), Arabesque (1966), Charade (1963), Grass Is Greener (1960), Damn Yankees! (1958), The Pajama Game (1957), Funny Face (1957), Seven Brides for Seven Brothers (1954), Singing in the Rain (1952)

Clint Eastwood

Million Dollar Baby (2004), Mystic River (2003), Midnight in the Garden of Good and Evil (1997), The Bridges of Madison County (1995), *Unforgiven (1992), Bird (1988), Pale Rider (1985), The Outlaw Josey Wales (1976), High Plains Drifter (1972), Play Misty for Me (1971)*

Federico Fellini

Amarcord (1974), Fellini's Roma (1972), Juliet of the Spirits (1965), 8 ½ (1963), La Dolce Vita (1960), Nights of Cabiria (1957), Il Bidone (1955), La Strada (1954), I Vitelloni (1953), The White Sheik (1952), Paisan (1946), Open City (1945)

Victor Fleming

Joan of Arc (1948), A Guy Named Joe (1943), Tortilla Flat (1942), Dr. Jekyll and Mr. Hyde (1941), The Wizard of Oz (1939), Gone with the Wind (1939), Captains Courageous (1937), Treasure Island (1934), The Virginian (1929)

John Ford

Cheyenne Autumn (1964), Donovan's Reef (1963), The Man Who Shot Liberty Valance (1962), The Wings of Eagles (1957), The Searchers (1956), Mister Roberts (1955), Mogambo (1953), The Quiet Man (1952), How Green Was My Valley (1941), The Grapes of Wrath (1940), Stagecoach (1939)

Terry Gilliam

The Brothers Grimm (2004), Fear and Loathing in Las Vegas (1998), 12 Monkeys (1995), The Fisher King (1991), The Adventures of Baron Munchausen (1988), Brazil (1985), Monty Python and the Holy Grail (1975), And Now for Something Completely Different (1971)

Jean-Luc Godard

Notre Musique (2004), In Praise of Love (2001), Hail Mary (1985), Passion (1982), Every Man for Himself (1980), Two or Three Things I Know about Her (1966), Pierrot le fou (1965), Alphaville (1965), Band of Outsiders (1964), Breathless (1959)

D. W. Griffith

One Million B.C. (1940), Abraham Lincoln (1930), Isn't Life Wonderful (1924), America (1924), Orphans of the Storm (1922), Way Down East (1920), Hearts of the World (1918), Intolerance (1916), The Birth of a Nation (1915)

Randa Haines

Dance with Me (1998), Wrestling Ernest Hemingway (1993), The Doctor (1991), Children of a Lesser God (1986)

Howard Hawks

Rio Lobo (1970), El Dorado (1967), Hatari! (1962), Rio Bravo (1959), Land of the Pharaohs (1955), Gentlemen Prefer Blondes (1953), I Was a Male War Bride (1949), Red River (1948), The Big Sleep (1946), To Have and Have Not (1944), His Girl Friday (1940), Bringing Up Baby (1938), Barbary Coast (1935)

Alfred Hitchcock

Family Plot (1976), Frenzy (1972), Torn Curtain (1966), Marnie (1964), The Birds (1963), Psycho (1960), North by Northwest (1959), Vertigo (1958), To Catch a Thief (1955), Rear Window (1954), Strangers on a Train (1951), Rope (1948), Spellbound (1945), Rebecca (1940), The Thirty-Nine Steps (1935), The Man Who Knew Too Much (1934), The Lodger (1926)

Ron Howard

The Da Vinci Code (2006), Cinderella Man (2005), The Missing (2003), A Beautiful Mind (2001), Dr. Seuss' How the Grinch Stole Christmas (2000), Ransom (1996), Apollo 13 (1995), Far and Away (1992), Backdraft (1991), Willow (1988), Cocoon (1985), Splash (1984), Night Shift (1982)

John Huston

The Dead (1987), Prizzi's Honor (1985), The Man Who Would Be King (1975), The Misfits (1961), Heaven Knows, Mr. Allison (1957), A Farewell to Arms (1957), Moby Dick (1956), Moulin Rouge (1952), The African Queen (1951), The Treasure of the Sierra Madre (1948), Key Largo (1948), The Maltese Falcon (1941)

Peter Jackson

King Kong (2005), The Lord of the Rings: The Return of the King (2003), The Lord of the Rings: The Two Towers (2002), The Lord of the Rings: The Fellowship of the Ring (2001), The Frighteners (1996), Heavenly Creatures (1994), Bad Taste (1987)

Lawrence Kasdan

Dreamcatcher (2003), French Kiss (1995), Wyatt Earp (1994), Grand Canyon (1991), I Love You to Death (1990), The Accidental Tourist (1988), Silverado (1985), The Big Chill (1983), Body Heat (1981)

Elia Kazan

The Last Tycoon (1976), Splendor in the Grass (1961), East of Eden (1955), On the Waterfront (1954), A Streetcar Named Desire (1951), Gentleman's Agreement (1947), A Tree Grows in Brooklyn (1945)

Buster Keaton

Spite Marriage (1929), The General (1927), Go West (1925), The Navigator (1924), The Balloonatic (1923), The Three Ages (1923), The Boat (1921), The Playhouse (1921), One Week (1920)

Henry King

The Old Man and the Sea (1958), The Sun Also Rises (1957), Love Is a Many-Splendored Thing (1955), The Snows of Kilimanjaro (1952), David and Bathsheba (1951), Twelve O'Clock High (1949), Jesse James (1939), Stella Dallas (1925)

Stanley Kramer

Bless the Beasts & Children (1971), Guess Who's Coming to Dinner (1967), Ship of Fools (1965), It's a Mad, Mad, Mad, Mad World (1963), Judgment at Nuremberg (1961), Inherit the Wind (1960), On the Beach (1959), The Defiant Ones (1958)

Stanley Kubrick

Eyes Wide Shut (1999), Full Metal Jacket (1987), The Shining (1980), Barry Lyndon (1975), A Clockwork Orange (1971), 2001: A Space Odyssey (1968), Dr. Strangelove or: How I Learned to Stop Worrying and Love the Bomb (1964), Lolita (1962), Spartacus (1960)

Akira Kurosawa

Ran (1985), Dersu Uzala (1975), Sanjuro (1962), Yojimbo (1961), The Hidden Fortress (1958), Throne of Blood (1957), Seven Samurai (1954), Ikiru (1952), Rashomon (1950)

Fritz Lang

While the City Sleeps (1956), Beyond a Reasonable Doubt (1956), The Big Heat (1953), Cloak and Dagger (1946), The Woman in the Window (1945), The Return of Frank James (1940), You Only Live Once (1937), Metropolis (1927)

David Lean

A Passage to India (1984), Doctor Zhivago (1965), Lawrence of Arabia (1962), The Bridge on the River Kwai (1957), Summertime (1955), Oliver Twist (1948), Great Expectations (1946), Brief Encounter (1946), Blithe Spirit (1945)

Mimi Leder

Pay It Forward (2000), Deep Impact (1998), The Peacemaker (1997)

Ang Lee

Brokeback Mountain (2005), Hulk (2003), Crouching Tiger, Hidden Dragon (2000,) The Ice Storm (1997), Sense and Sensibility (1995), Eat Drink Man Woman (1994)

Spike Lee

She Hate Me (2004), Summer of Sam (1999), He Got Game (1998), Clockers (1995), Crooklyn (1994), Malcolm X (1992), Jungle Fever

(1991), Mo' Better Blues (1990), Do the Right Thing (1989), School Daze (1988), She's Gotta Have It (1986)

Sergio Leone

Once upon a Time in America (1984), A Fistful of Dynamite (1971), Once upon a Time in the West (1969), The Good, the Bad and the Ugly (1966), For a Few Dollars More (1965), A Fistful of Dollars (1964)

Barry Levinson

Envy (2004), Bandits (2001), Liberty Heights (1999), Bugsy (1991), Avalon (1990), Rain Man (1988), Tin Men (1987), Good Morning, Vietnam (1987), Diner (1982)

Jerry Lewis

The Family Jewels (1965), The Nutty Professor (1963), The Ladies' Man (1961), The Bellboy (1960)

Ernst Lubitsch

Cluny Brown (1946), Heaven Can Wait (1943), Ninotchka (1939), Angel (1937), The Merry Widow (1934), Trouble in Paradise (1932), If I Had a Million (1932), The Love Parade (1929)

George Lucas

Star Wars: Episode III—Revenge of the Sith (2005), Star Wars: Episode II—Attack of the Clones (2002), Star Wars: Episode I—The Phantom Menace (1999), Star Wars (1977), American Graffiti (1973), THX-1138 (1971), Herbie (1966)

Sydney Lumet

Gloria (1999), Running on Empty (1988), The Morning After (1986), The Verdict (1982), Equus (1977), Network (1976), Dog Day Afternoon (1975), Murder on the Orient Express (1974), Serpico (1973), Long Day's Journey into Night (1962), 12 Angry Men (1957)

David Lynch

Mulholland Drive (2001), Lost Highway (1997), Twin Peaks: Fire Walk with Me (1992), Wild at Heart (1990), Blue Velvet (1986), Dune (1984), Elephant Man (1980), Eraserhead (1977)

Louis Malle

Vanya on 42nd Street (1994), Damage (1992), Au Revoir, Les Enfants (1987), Alamo Bay (1985), My Dinner with Andre (1981), Atlantic City (1980), Pretty Baby (1978), The Thief of Paris (1967)

Rouben Mamoulian

Silk Stockings (1957), Summer Holiday (1948), Blood and Sand (1941), The Mark of Zorro (1940), The Gay Desperado (1936), Queen Christina (1933), Dr. Jekyll and Mr. Hyde (1932)

Joseph L. Mankiewicz

Sleuth (1972), Cleopatra (1963), Guys and Dolls (1955), The Barefoot Contessa (1954), Julius Caesar (1953), All about Eve (1950), A Letter to Three Wives (1949), The Ghost and Mrs. Muir (1947), Dragonwyck (1946)

Michael Mann

Miami Vice (2006), Collateral (2004), Ali (2001), The Insider (1999), Heat (1995), The Last of the Mohicans (1992), Manhunter (1986), The Keep (1983)

Penny Marshall

Riding in Cars with Boys (2001), The Preacher's Wife (1996), Renaissance Man (1994), A League of Their Own (1992), Awakenings (1990), Big (1988), Jumpin' Jack Flash (1986)

Leo McCarey

Rally 'Round the Flag, Boys! (1958), An Affair to Remember (1957), The Bells of St. Mary's (1945), Going My Way (1944), Once upon a Honeymoon (1942), Love Affair (1939), Duck Soup (1933)

Lewis Milestone

Mutiny on the Bounty (1962), Ocean's Eleven (1960), Pork Chop Hill (1959), Halls of Montezuma (1950), The Red Pony (1949), A Walk in the Sun (1945), Of Mice and Men (1939), All Quiet on the Western Front (1930)

Anthony Minghella

Cold Mountain (2003), The Talented Mr. Ripley (1999), The English Patient (1996), Mr. Wonderful (1993), Truly, Madly, Deeply (1991)

Vincente Minelli

On a Clear Day You Can See Forever (1970), Gigi (1958), Tea and Sympathy (1956), Brigadoon (1954), Father's Little Dividend (1951), An American in Paris (1951), The Father of the Bride (1950), Madame Bovary (1949), Ziegfeld Follies (1946), Meet Me in St. Louis (1944)

F. W. Murnau

Tabu (1931), City Girl (Our Daily Bread) (1930), Sunrise (1927), Faust (1926), Tartuff (1926), The Last Laugh (1924), Nosferatu, the Vampire (1922)

Mike Nichols

The Birdcage (1996), Wolf (1994), Postcards from the Edge (1990), Biloxi Blues (1988), Working Girl (1988), Silkwood (1983), The Day of the Dolphin (1973), Catch-22 (1970), The Graduate (1967), Who's Afraid of Virginia Woolf? (1966)

Sam Peckinpah

The Osterman Weekend (1983), Convoy (1978), Cross of Iron (1977), Bring Me the Head of Alfredo Garcia (1974), Straw Dogs (1971), The Wild Bunch (1969), Major Dundee (1965), Ride the High Country (1962)

Arthur Penn

Inside (1996), Penn and Teller Get Killed/Dead Funny (1989), Dead of Winter (1987), Four Friends (1981), Little Big Man (1970), Bonnie and Clyde (1967), The Chase (1966), The Miracle Worker (1962)

Roman Polanski

The Pianist (2002), The Ninth Gate (1999), Death and the Maiden (1994), Frantic (1988), Pirates (1986), Tess (1979), The Tenant (1976), Chinatown (1974), Macbeth (1971), Rosemary's Baby (1968), Repulsion (1965)

Sydney Pollack

Random Hearts (1999), The Firm (1993), Out of Africa (1985), Tootsie (1982), Absence of Malice (1981), The Electric Horseman (1979), Three Days of the Condor (1975), The Way We Were (1973), Jeremiah Johnson (1972), They Shoot Horses, Don't They? (1969), Castle Keep (1969)

Otto Preminger

Tell Me that You Love Me, Junie Moon (1970), Bunny Lake Is Missing (1965), Exodus (1960), Porgy and Bess (1959), Anatomy of a Murder (1959), The Man with the Golden Arm (1955), Carmen Jones (1954), Laura (1944)

Sam Raimi

Spider-Man (2002), A Simple Plan (1998), The Quick and the Dead (1995), Army of Darkness (1993), Darkman (1990), Evil Dead II (1987), Crimewave (1985), The Evil Dead (1982)

Nicholas Ray

King of Kings (1961), Bigger than Life (1956), Rebel Without a Cause (1955), Johnny Guitar (1954), Flying Leathernecks (1951), On Dangerous Ground (1951), In a Lonely Place (1950)

Rob Reiner

Ghosts of Mississippi (1996), A Few Good Men (1992), Misery (1990), When Harry Met Sally . . . (1989), The Princess Bride (1987), Stand by Me (1986), This Is Spinal Tap (1984)

Ken Russell

Mindbender (1995), Whore (1991), Salome's Last Dance (1988), The Lair of the White Worm (1988), Gothic (1986), Crimes of Passion (1984), Altered States (1980), Tommy (1975)

John Schlesinger

The Next Best Thing (2000), Cold Comfort Farm (1995), Pacific Heights (1990), The Believers (1987), The Falcon and the Snowman (1985), Marathon Man (1976), The Day of the Locust (1975), Sunday Bloody Sunday (1971), Midnight Cowboy (1969), Far from the Madding Crowd (1967)

Martin Scorsese

The Aviator (2004), Gangs of New York (2002), Casino (1995), The Age of Innocence (1993), Cape Fear (1991), GoodFellas (1990), The Last Temptation of Christ (1988), Raging Bull (1980), Taxi Driver (1976), Alice Doesn't Live Here Anymore (1974), Mean Streets (1973)

Ridley Scott

Black Hawk Down (2001), Hannibal (2001), Gladiator (2000), G.I. Jane (1997), Thelma & Louise (1991), Black Rain (1989), Someone to Watch Over Me (1987), Legend (1985), Blade Runner (1982), Alien (1979), The Duellists (1977)

Tony Scott

Spy Game (2001), Enemy of the State (1998), Crimson Tide (1995), True Romance (1993), The Last Boy Scout (1991), Revenge (1990), Days of Thunder (1990), Beverly Hills Cop II (1987), Top Gun (1986), The Hunger (1983)

M. Night Shyamalan

The Village (2004), Signs (2002), Unbreakable (2000), The Sixth Sense (1999), Wide Awake (1998), Praying with Anger (1992)

Don Siegel

Escape from Alcatraz (1979), Telefon (1977), The Shootist (1976), Charley Varrick (1973), Dirty Harry (1971), Two Mules for Sister Sara (1969), Coogan's Bluff (1968), Baby Face Nelson (1957), Invasion of the Body Snatchers (1956)

Steven Soderbergh

Ocean's Twelve (2004), Ocean's Eleven (2001), Erin Brockovich (2000), Traffic (2000), Out of Sight (1998), Kafka (1991), sex, lies and video-tape (1989)

Steven Spielberg

Munich (2005), War of the Worlds (2005), Minority Report (2002), Saving Private Ryan (1998), Amistad (1997), Schindler's List (1993), Jurassic Park (1993), Always (1989), The Color Purple (1985), Poltergeist (1982), E. T. the Extra-Terrestrial (1982), Raiders of the Lost Ark (1981), Close Encounters of the Third Kind (1977), Jaws (1975), Duel (1971)

George Stevens

The Greatest Story Ever Told (1965), The Diary of Anne Frank (1959), Giant (1956), Shane (1953), A Place in the Sun (1951), I Remember Mama (1948), Woman of the Year (1942), The Talk of the Town (1942), Gunga Din (1939)

Oliver Stone

Alexander (2004), Nixon (1995), Natural Born Killers (1994), Heaven and Earth (1993), JFK (1991), The Doors (1991), Born on the Fourth of July (1989), Wall Street (1987), Salvador (1986), Platoon (1986), The Hand (1981)

Barbra Streisand

The Mirror Has Two Faces (1996), The Prince of Tides (1991), Yentl (1983)

Preston Sturges

The Beautiful Blonde from Bashful Bend (1949), Unfaithfully Yours (1948), The Miracle of Morgan's Creek (1944), Hail the Conquering Hero (1944), The Lady Eve (1941), Christmas in July (1940), The Great McGinty (1940)

Quentin Tarantino

Kill Bill, Vol. II (2004), Kill Bill, Vol. I (2003), Jackie Brown (1997), Pulp Fiction (1994), Reservoir Dogs (1992)

Francois Truffaut

Confidentially Yours (1983), The Woman Next Door (1981), The Man Who Loved Women (1977), The Story of Adele H (1975), Day for Night (1973), The Bride Wore Black (1968), Fahrenheit 451 (1967), Jules et Jim (1962)

King Vidor

Solomon and Sheba (1959), War and Peace (1956), Ruby Gentry (1952), The Fountainhead (1949), Duel in the Sun (1946), Northwest Passage (1940), Comrade X (1940), Stella Dallas (1937), The Champ (1931)

Josef von Sternberg

Jet Pilot (1957), The Shanghai Gesture (1941), The Devil Is a Woman (1935), The Scarlet Empress (1934), Shanghai Express (1932), The Blue Angel (1930)

Raoul Walsh

The Naked and the Dead (1958), Battle Cry (1955), Along the Great Divide (1951), Captain Horatio Hornblower (1951), Objective, Burma! (1945), Gentleman Jim (1942), They Died with Their Boots On (1941), High Sierra (1941), Sadie Thompson (1928)

Peter Weir

Master and Commander: The Far Side of the World (2003), The Truman Show (1998), Green Card (1990), Dead Poets Society (1989), The Mosquito Coast (1986), Witness (1985), The Year of Living Dangerously (1982), Gallipoli (1981)

Orson Welles

F for Fake (1975), The Trial (1962), Touch of Evil (1958), Mr. Arkadin (1955), Othello (1952), Macbeth (1948), The Lady from Shanghai (1948), The Stranger (1946), The Magnificent Ambersons (1942), Citizen Kane (1941)

William A. Wellman

Track of the Cat (1954), The High and the Mighty (1954), Island in the Sky (1953), The Story of G.I. Joe (1945), The Ox-Bow Incident (1943), Roxie Hart (1942), Beau Geste (1939), A Star Is Born (1937), The Call of the Wild (1935)

Billy Wilder

Buddy Buddy (1981), The Private Life of Sherlock Holmes (1970), Irma la Douce (1963), The Apartment (1960), Some Like It Hot (1959), The Spirit of St. Louis (1957), Love in the Afternoon (1957), The Seven Year Itch (1955), Sabrina (1954), Stalag 17 (1953), Sunset Boulevard (1950), Double Indemnity (1944)

Robert Wise

Star Trek: The Motion Picture (1979), The Andromeda Strain (1971), The Sound of Music (1965), The Haunting (1963), West Side Story (1961), Run Silent, Run Deep (1958), The Day the Earth Stood Still (1951), The Body Snatcher (1945), The Curse of the Cat People (1944)

Sam Wood

The Stratton Story (1949), For Whom the Bell Tolls (1943), The Pride of the Yankees (1942), The Devil and Miss Jones (1941), Our Town (1940), Goodbye, Mr. Chips (1939), A Day at the Races (1937), A Night at the Opera (1935)

William Wyler

Funny Girl (1968), Ben-Hur (1959), The Desperate Hours (1955), Roman Holiday (1953), The Best Years of Our Lives (1946), Mrs. Miniver (1942), The Little Foxes (1941), The Westerner (1940), Wuthering Heights (1939), Jezebel (1938)

Robert Zemeckis

The Polar Express (2004), Cast Away (2000), Contact (1997), Forrest Gump (1994), Death Becomes Her (1992), Who Framed Roger

Rabbit (1988), Back to the Future (1985), Romancing the Stone (1984), I Wanna Hold Your Hand (1978)

Fred Zinnemann

Five Days One Summer (1982), Julia (1977), The Day of the Jackal (1973), A Man for All Seasons (1966), The Sundowners (1960), Oklahoma! (1955), From Here to Eternity (1953), The Member of the Wedding (1952), High Noon (1952)

Appendix E

Contact Information

Networks and Major Cable Channels

ABC
500 S. Buena Vista St.
Burbank, CA 91521
818-460-7777
www.abc.com

CBS
7800 Beverly Blvd.
Los Angeles, CA 90036-2188
323-575-2345
www.cbs.com

CW
4000 Warner Blvd.
Burbank, CA 91522
818-977-2500
www.cwtv.com

FOX
10201 W. Pico Blvd.
Los Angeles, CA 90035
310-369-1000
www.fox.com

HBO
1100 Avenue of the Americas
New York, NY 10036
212-512-1000
www.hbo.com

NBC
3000 W. Alameda Ave.
Burbank, CA 91523-0001
818-840-4444
www.nbc.com

PBS
1320 Braddock Place
Alexandria, VA 22314-1698
703-739-5000
www.pbs.org

Showtime
1633 Broadway
New York, NY 10019
212-708-1600
www.sho.com

International Film and Television Distribution Companies

American Public Television
✎www.aptonline.org

Atlas Worldwide
✎www.atlasworldwide.net/home

BBC
✎www.bbc.co.uk

BBC Films
✎www.bbc.co.uk/bbcfilms

Bravo Network
✎www.bravotv.com

Buena Vista
✎http://disney.go.com or www.bvitv.com

Carsey-Werner Distribution
✎www.carseywerner.com

Dimension Films
✎www.weinsteinco.com

DirecTV
✎www.directv.com

Discovery Networks
✎www.discovery.com

The Walt Disney Company
✎www.Disney.com

DreamWorks SKG
✎www.dreamworks.com

Film Music and Entertainment
✎www.fame.uk.com

First Look Studios
✎www.firstlookmedia.com

Focus Features
✎www.focusfeatures.com

Fox Broadcasting Company
✎www.fox.com

FremantleMedia North America
✎www.fremantlemedia.com

Granada International
✎www.int.granadamedia.com

Hallmark Entertainment Network
✎www.hallmarkchannel.com

HBO
✎www.hbo.com

Icon Entertainment International
✎www.iconmovies.net

IFC Films
✍*www.ifcfilms.com*

IMAX
✍*www.imax.com*

New Line Cinema
✍*www.newline.com*

Nickelodeon
✍*www.nick.com*

Paramount
✍*www.paramount.com*

PBS
✍*www.pbs.org*

Showtime
✍*www.sho.com*

Sony Pictures
✍*www.sonypictures.com*

Universal Pictures International
✍*www.universalstudios.com*

The Weinstein Company
✍*www.weinsteinco.com*

Additional Contact Information

American Film Institute (AFI)
2021 North Western Ave.
Los Angeles, CA 90027
323-856-7600
✍*www.AFI.com*

Directors Guild of America (DGA)
7920 Sunset Blvd.
Los Angeles, CA 90046-3347
310-289-2000
✍*www.dga.org*

Screen Actors Guild (SAG), Hollywood
5757 Wilshire Blvd.
Los Angeles, CA 90036-3600
323-954-1600
✍*www.sag.org*

Screen Actors Guild (SAG), New York
360 Madison Ave., 12th Floor
New York, NY 10017
212-944-1030
✍*www.sag.org*

The Sundance Institute
8539 Wilshire Blvd., 3rd Floor
Beverly Hills, CA 90211
310-360-1969
✍*www.sundance.org*

Writers Guild of America, East
555 West 57th St., Suite 1230
New York, NY 10019
212-767-7800
✍*www.wgaeast.org*

Writers Guild of America, West
7000 West Third St.
Los Angeles, CA 90048
323-951-4000
800-548-4532
✍*www.wga.org*

Index

THE EVERYTHING SERIES!

BUSINESS & PERSONAL FINANCE

Everything® Accounting Book
Everything® Budgeting Book
Everything® Business Planning Book
Everything® Coaching and Mentoring Book
Everything® Fundraising Book
Everything® Get Out of Debt Book
Everything® Grant Writing Book
Everything® Home-Based Business Book, 2nd Ed.
Everything® Homebuying Book, 2nd Ed.
Everything® Homeselling Book, 2nd Ed.
Everything® Investing Book, 2nd Ed.
Everything® Landlording Book
Everything® Leadership Book
Everything® Managing People Book, 2nd Ed.
Everything® Negotiating Book
Everything® Online Auctions Book
Everything® Online Business Book
Everything® Personal Finance Book
Everything® Personal Finance in Your 20s and 30s Book
Everything® Project Management Book
Everything® Real Estate Investing Book
Everything® Robert's Rules Book, $7.95
Everything® Selling Book
Everything® Start Your Own Business Book, 2nd Ed.
Everything® Wills & Estate Planning Book

COOKING

Everything® Barbecue Cookbook
Everything® Bartender's Book, $9.95
Everything® Chinese Cookbook
Everything® Classic Recipes Book
Everything® Cocktail Parties and Drinks Book
Everything® College Cookbook
Everything® Cooking for Baby and Toddler Book
Everything® Cooking for Two Cookbook
Everything® Diabetes Cookbook
Everything® Easy Gourmet Cookbook
Everything® Fondue Cookbook
Everything® Fondue Party Book
Everything® Gluten-Free Cookbook
Everything® Glycemic Index Cookbook
Everything® Grilling Cookbook

Everything® Healthy Meals in Minutes Cookbook
Everything® Holiday Cookbook
Everything® Indian Cookbook
Everything® Italian Cookbook
Everything® Low-Carb Cookbook
Everything® Low-Fat High-Flavor Cookbook
Everything® Low-Salt Cookbook
Everything® Meals for a Month Cookbook
Everything® Mediterranean Cookbook
Everything® Mexican Cookbook
Everything® One-Pot Cookbook
Everything® Quick and Easy 30-Minute, 5-Ingredient Cookbook
Everything® Quick Meals Cookbook
Everything® Slow Cooker Cookbook
Everything® Slow Cooking for a Crowd Cookbook
Everything® Soup Cookbook
Everything® Tex-Mex Cookbook
Everything® Thai Cookbook
Everything® Vegetarian Cookbook
Everything® Wild Game Cookbook
Everything® Wine Book, 2nd Ed.

GAMES

Everything® 15-Minute Sudoku Book, $9.95
Everything® 30-Minute Sudoku Book, $9.95
Everything® Blackjack Strategy Book
Everything® Brain Strain Book, $9.95
Everything® Bridge Book
Everything® Card Games Book
Everything® Card Tricks Book, $9.95
Everything® Casino Gambling Book, 2nd Ed.
Everything® Chess Basics Book
Everything® Craps Strategy Book
Everything® Crossword and Puzzle Book
Everything® Crossword Challenge Book
Everything® Cryptograms Book, $9.95
Everything® Easy Crosswords Book
Everything® Easy Kakuro Book, $9.95
Everything® Games Book, 2nd Ed.
Everything® Giant Sudoku Book, $9.95
Everything® Kakuro Challenge Book, $9.95
Everything® Large-Print Crossword Challenge Book
Everything® Large-Print Crosswords Book
Everything® Lateral Thinking Puzzles Book, $9.95
Everything® Mazes Book

Everything® Pencil Puzzles Book, $9.95
Everything® Poker Strategy Book
Everything® Pool & Billiards Book
Everything® Test Your IQ Book, $9.95
Everything® Texas Hold 'Em Book, $9.95
Everything® Travel Crosswords Book, $9.95
Everything® Word Games Challenge Book
Everything® Word Search Book

HEALTH

Everything® Alzheimer's Book
Everything® Diabetes Book
Everything® Health Guide to Adult Bipolar Disorder
Everything® Health Guide to Controlling Anxiety
Everything® Health Guide to Fibromyalgia
Everything® Health Guide to Thyroid Disease
Everything® Hypnosis Book
Everything® Low Cholesterol Book
Everything® Massage Book
Everything® Menopause Book
Everything® Nutrition Book
Everything® Reflexology Book
Everything® Stress Management Book

HISTORY

Everything® American Government Book
Everything® American History Book
Everything® Civil War Book
Everything® Freemasons Book
Everything® Irish History & Heritage Book
Everything® Middle East Book

HOBBIES

Everything® Candlemaking Book
Everything® Cartooning Book
Everything® Coin Collecting Book
Everything® Drawing Book
Everything® Family Tree Book, 2nd Ed.
Everything® Knitting Book
Everything® Knots Book
Everything® Photography Book
Everything® Quilting Book
Everything® Scrapbooking Book
Everything® Sewing Book
Everything® Woodworking Book

HOME IMPROVEMENT

Bolded titles are new additions to the series.
All Everything® books are priced at $12.95 or $14.95, unless otherwise stated. Prices subject to change without notice.

Everything® Feng Shui Book
Everything® Feng Shui Decluttering Book, $9.95
Everything® Fix-It Book
Everything® Home Decorating Book
Everything® Home Storage Solutions Book
Everything® Homebuilding Book
Everything® Lawn Care Book
Everything® Organize Your Home Book

KIDS' BOOKS

All titles are $7.95

Everything® Kids' Animal Puzzle & Activity Book
Everything® Kids' Baseball Book, 4th Ed.
Everything® Kids' Bible Trivia Book
Everything® Kids' Bugs Book
Everything® Kids' Cars and Trucks Puzzle
& Activity Book
Everything® Kids' Christmas Puzzle
& Activity Book
Everything® Kids' Cookbook
Everything® Kids' Crazy Puzzles Book
Everything® Kids' Dinosaurs Book
Everything® Kids' First Spanish Puzzle and
Activity Book
Everything® Kids' Gross Hidden Pictures Book
Everything® Kids' Gross Jokes Book
Everything® Kids' Gross Mazes Book
Everything® Kids' Gross Puzzle and
Activity Book
Everything® Kids' Halloween Puzzle
& Activity Book
Everything® Kids' Hidden Pictures Book
Everything® Kids' Horses Book
Everything® Kids' Joke Book
Everything® Kids' Knock Knock Book
Everything® Kids' Learning Spanish Book
Everything® Kids' Math Puzzles Book
Everything® Kids' Mazes Book
Everything® Kids' Money Book
Everything® Kids' Nature Book
Everything® Kids' Pirates Puzzle and Activity
Book
Everything® Kids' Princess Puzzle and Activity
Book
Everything® Kids' Puzzle Book
Everything® Kids' Riddles & Brain Teasers Book
Everything® Kids' Science Experiments Book
Everything® Kids' Sharks Book
Everything® Kids' Soccer Book
Everything® Kids' Travel Activity Book

KIDS' STORY BOOKS

Everything® Fairy Tales Book

LANGUAGE

Everything® Conversational Chinese Book with

CD, $19.95
Everything® Conversational Japanese Book
with CD, $19.95
Everything® French Grammar Book
Everything® French Phrase Book, $9.95
Everything® French Verb Book, $9.95
Everything® German Practice Book with CD,
$19.95
Everything® Inglés Book
Everything® Learning French Book
Everything® Learning German Book
Everything® Learning Italian Book
Everything® Learning Latin Book
Everything® Learning Spanish Book
Everything® Russian Practice Book with CD,
$19.95
Everything® Sign Language Book
Everything® Spanish Grammar Book
Everything® Spanish Phrase Book, $9.95
Everything® Spanish Practice Book
with CD, $19.95
Everything® Spanish Verb Book, $9.95

MUSIC

Everything® Drums Book with CD, $19.95
Everything® Guitar Book
Everything® Guitar Chords Book with CD,
$19.95
Everything® Home Recording Book
Everything® Music Theory Book with CD,
$19.95
Everything® Reading Music Book with CD,
$19.95
Everything® Rock & Blues Guitar Book
(with CD), $19.95
Everything® Songwriting Book

NEW AGE

Everything® Astrology Book, 2nd Ed.
Everything® Birthday Personology Book
Everything® Dreams Book, 2nd Ed.
Everything® Love Signs Book, $9.95
Everything® Numerology Book
Everything® Paganism Book
Everything® Palmistry Book
Everything® Psychic Book
Everything® Reiki Book
Everything® Sex Signs Book, $9.95
Everything® Tarot Book, 2nd Ed.
Everything® Wicca and Witchcraft Book

PARENTING

Everything® Baby Names Book, 2nd Ed.
Everything® Baby Shower Book
Everything® Baby's First Food Book
Everything® Baby's First Year Book
Everything® Birthing Book
Everything® Breastfeeding Book
Everything® Father-to-Be Book
Everything® Father's First Year Book
Everything® Get Ready for Baby Book
Everything® Get Your Baby to Sleep Book, $9.95
Everything® Getting Pregnant Book
Everything® Guide to Raising a
One-Year-Old
Everything® Guide to Raising a
Two-Year-Old
Everything® Homeschooling Book
Everything® Mother's First Year Book
Everything® Parent's Guide to Children
and Divorce
Everything® Parent's Guide to Children
with ADD/ADHD
Everything® Parent's Guide to Children
with Asperger's Syndrome
Everything® Parent's Guide to Children
with Autism
Everything® Parent's Guide to Children with
Bipolar Disorder
Everything® Parent's Guide to Children
with Dyslexia
Everything® Parent's Guide to Positive Discipline
Everything® Parent's Guide to Raising a
Successful Child
Everything® Parent's Guide to Raising Boys
Everything® Parent's Guide to Raising Siblings
Everything® Parent's Guide to Sensory
Integration Disorder
Everything® Parent's Guide to Tantrums
Everything® Parent's Guide to the Overweight
Child
Everything® Parent's Guide to the Strong-Willed
Child
Everything® Parenting a Teenager Book
Everything® Potty Training Book, $9.95
Everything® Pregnancy Book, 2nd Ed.
Everything® Pregnancy Fitness Book
Everything® Pregnancy Nutrition Book
Everything® Pregnancy Organizer, 2nd Ed.,
$16.95
Everything® Toddler Activities Book
Everything® Toddler Book
Everything® Tween Book
Everything® Twins, Triplets, and More Book

PETS

Everything® Aquarium Book
Everything® Boxer Book
Everything® Cat Book, 2nd Ed.
Everything® Chihuahua Book
Everything® Dachshund Book
Everything® Dog Book
Everything® Dog Health Book
Everything® Dog Owner's Organizer, $16.95
Everything® Dog Training and Tricks Book
Everything® German Shepherd Book
Everything® Golden Retriever Book
Everything® Horse Book
Everything® Horse Care Book
Everything® Horseback Riding Book
Everything® Labrador Retriever Book
Everything® Poodle Book
Everything® Pug Book
Everything® Puppy Book
Everything® Rottweiler Book
Everything® Small Dogs Book
Everything® Tropical Fish Book
Everything® Yorkshire Terrier Book

REFERENCE

Everything® Blogging Book
Everything® Build Your Vocabulary Book
Everything® Car Care Book
Everything® Classical Mythology Book
Everything® Da Vinci Book
Everything® Divorce Book
Everything® Einstein Book
Everything® Etiquette Book, 2nd Ed.
Everything® Inventions and Patents Book
Everything® Mafia Book
Everything® Philosophy Book
Everything® Psychology Book
Everything® Shakespeare Book

RELIGION

Everything® Angels Book
Everything® Bible Book
Everything® Buddhism Book
Everything® Catholicism Book
Everything® Christianity Book
Everything® History of the Bible Book
Everything® Jesus Book
Everything® Jewish History & Heritage Book
Everything® Judaism Book
Everything® Kabbalah Book
Everything® Koran Book
Everything® Mary Book
Everything® Mary Magdalene Book

Everything® Prayer Book
Everything® Saints Book
Everything® Torah Book
Everything® Understanding Islam Book
Everything® World's Religions Book
Everything® Zen Book

SCHOOL & CAREERS

Everything® Alternative Careers Book
Everything® Career Tests Book
Everything® College Major Test Book
Everything® College Survival Book, 2nd Ed.
Everything® Cover Letter Book, 2nd Ed.
Everything® Filmmaking Book
Everything® Get-a-Job Book
Everything® Guide to Being a Paralegal
Everything® Guide to Being a Real Estate Agent
Everything® Guide to Being a Sales Rep
Everything® Guide to Careers in Health Care
Everything® Guide to Careers in Law Enforcement
Everything® Guide to Government Jobs
Everything® Guide to Starting and Running a Restaurant
Everything® Job Interview Book
Everything® New Nurse Book
Everything® New Teacher Book
Everything® Paying for College Book
Everything® Practice Interview Book
Everything® Resume Book, 2nd Ed.
Everything® Study Book

SELF-HELP

Everything® Dating Book, 2nd Ed.
Everything® Great Sex Book
Everything® Kama Sutra Book
Everything® Self-Esteem Book

SPORTS & FITNESS

Everything® Easy Fitness Book
Everything® Fishing Book
Everything® Golf Instruction Book
Everything® Pilates Book
Everything® Running Book
Everything® Weight Training Book
Everything® Yoga Book

TRAVEL

Everything® Family Guide to Cruise Vacations
Everything® Family Guide to Hawaii
Everything® Family Guide to Las Vegas, 2nd Ed.

Everything® Family Guide to Mexico
Everything® Family Guide to New York City, 2nd Ed.
Everything® Family Guide to RV Travel & Campgrounds
Everything® Family Guide to the Caribbean
Everything® Family Guide to the Walt Disney World Resort®, Universal Studios®, and Greater Orlando, 4th Ed.
Everything® Family Guide to Timeshares
Everything® Family Guide to Washington D.C., 2nd Ed.
Everything® Guide to New England

WEDDINGS

Everything® Bachelorette Party Book, $9.95
Everything® Bridesmaid Book, $9.95
Everything® Destination Wedding Book
Everything® Elopement Book, $9.95
Everything® Father of the Bride Book, $9.95
Everything® Groom Book, $9.95
Everything® Mother of the Bride Book, $9.95
Everything® Outdoor Wedding Book
Everything® Wedding Book, 3rd Ed.
Everything® Wedding Checklist, $9.95
Everything® Wedding Etiquette Book, $9.95
Everything® Wedding Organizer, 2nd Ed., $16.95
Everything® Wedding Shower Book, $9.95
Everything® Wedding Vows Book, $9.95
Everything® Wedding Workout Book
Everything® Weddings on a Budget Book, $9.95

WRITING

Everything® Creative Writing Book
Everything® Get Published Book, 2nd Ed.
Everything® Grammar and Style Book
Everything® Guide to Writing a Book Proposal
Everything® Guide to Writing a Novel
Everything® Guide to Writing Children's Books
Everything® Guide to Writing Research Papers
Everything® Screenwriting Book
Everything® Writing Poetry Book
Everything® Writing Well Book